The Computer Book

by the same author
COPPOLA

The Godfather™ Book

PETER COWIE

faber and faber

LONDON · BOSTON

First published in 1997
by Faber and Faber Limited
3 Queen Square London WC1N 3AU

Typeset by Faber and Faber Ltd
Printed in England by Butler and Tanner Ltd,
Frome

A CIP record for this book
is available from the British Library

ISBN 0-571-19011-1

10 9 8 7 6 5 4 3 2 1

Françoise,
the remarkable wife who has lived with this
book through countless weekends and bleary
dawns,

and Tom Luddy,
whose inspiring friendship first brought me
close to Francis Coppola and the spirit of
American Zoetrope.

Contents

Foreword

On an almost balmy night in San Francisco, searchlights arc and wheel above the crowds outside the Castro Theatre. It is 20 March 1997, twenty-five years to the week since the première of *The Godfather*. One by one the stars alight from the anonymity of their limousines: Al Pacino, Robert Duvall, James Caan . . . Francis Coppola, sober in a double-breasted suit, his beard freshly trimmed, poses with friends and colleagues as the flash-bulbs pop.

Inside the cinema, a Wurlitzer organ plays themes from Nino Rota's bewitching score. Then some 1,400 people hear the Mayor of San Francisco, Willie L. Brown, describe Coppola as 'our first citizen of theatre, motion picture, and, really, the arts'.

The director mounts the stage, waits for the applause to subside, and gives but a fleeting address. Modest in this moment of acclaim, he thanks Mario Puzo, who cannot attend for health reasons. Then Coppola introduces the film's producer, Al Ruddy, and hastens back to his seat in the audience.

Ruddy, silver-haired now like so many *Godfather* veterans, quips that 'a few of the people who made this movie may be in jail, but I think most of them are here tonight'. Faces made familiar by the film rise to take a bow: Al Martino, Gianni Russo, Alex Rocco, Talia Shire, then Bobby Duvall ('the proto-typical consigliere', says Ruddy), Jimmy Caan, and finally Al Pacino – 'the pre-eminent actor in film and in the theatre'.

For Pacino, the roars become insistent. He tries to sit down, then recognizes the futility of resistance and rises a second time, and again, and again, hands clasped at last above

Reunion at 25: Alex Rocco, James Caan, Al Pacino, Gianni Russo and Robert Duvall outside the Castro Theatre on 20 March 1997. (Photo courtesy of Audrey Shehyn/Reuters/Archive Photos, © Archive Photos, 1997.)

his head in happy harmony with his stardom.

Some sit unacknowledged, yet content: Robert Evans and Peter Bart, the Paramount executives responsible for *The Godfather*; Sherry Lansing and Jonathan Dolgen, their present-day inheritors at the studio; production designer Dean Tavoularis, casting wizard Fred Roos, associate producer Gray Frederickson . . .

As the film unfurls, the audience embraces it with a fervour that must surprise even the most cynical of industry observers. A production that hardly anybody at Paramount Pictures had liked during shooting is now enshrined in legend. Its soundtrack restored and enhanced by Coppola's old friend Walter Murch, the picture tonight looks more and more like the greatest Hollywood achievement of the postwar era. In the dizzy exultation of the crowd's response, *The Godfather* becomes unmistakably, irrevocably, myth. Coppola savours the electric sizzle of this occasion, when he can do no wrong and the audience would gladly grant him a hundred million dollars for any project he desired.

At a party afterwards at Bimbo's 365 Club in North Beach, five hundred guests feed from an elegant Italian buffet, and half-listen to the rhythm 'n' blues classics pounded out by the Big Bad Voodoo Daddy band. Individuals great and small wend to the family table to pay homage to Coppola and express delight: 'Godfather . . .'.

Coppola looks relaxed, perhaps startled by the passion of everyone's enthusiasm. 'Yeah, it was very good, very good,' he says of the screening with a kind of detached grace. He remains frustrated by his memories of the film, his battles with the studio, and even the wealth that box-office success bestowed upon him. 'In some ways it did ruin me,' he says in an interview in the *New Yorker* recently. 'It just made my whole career go this way instead of the way I really wanted it to go, which was into doing original work as a writer-director. It just inflamed so many other desires.' *The Godfather Part II* may have excelled the original film in terms of sustained sorcery and intelligence, but tonight the populist skills of Hollywood have been in glori-

ous evidence once again. 'It's simply the best movie Paramount ever made,' purrs studio president Jonathan Dolgen, Chairman of Viacom Entertainment Group.

Round midnight, Paramount musters its guests for the limo ride to the airport and the corporate jet that will whisk them back to L.A. Old colleagues, reunited by this brief historic circumstance, embrace and then vanish into the night.

Tom Luddy, who has worked with Francis Coppola for almost two decades, darts among the guests exclaiming: 'In years to come there'll be those who can declare, "I was there! I was there!"'

After all, twenty-five is young. Who among these stars and players will survive to the fiftieth anniversary? For sure the film and its sequels, wrought as they were with such passion and high drama – as this book seeks to show . . .

Prologue

A ten-second limousine ride north of Wilshire Boulevard stands a rather brash, Art Deco style building on the corner of North Cañon Drive and Clifton Way, in the consumer heart of Beverly Hills. On either side of the pillared entrance, bulbous Oriental faces are sculpted into the walls, beaming a derisory smile at all and sundry. Inside, a single staircase swirls up to the first floor. The executive suite downstairs now houses the production offices of the Zanuck Company, but more than twenty-five years ago this two-storey structure, 202 North Cañon, belonged to Paramount Pictures.

Here, on 29 September 1970, four men sat behind a table in the most sumptuous office in the building. The Hollywood press corps in those days did not comprise significant numbers, but the trade magazines and the

Mario Puzo, Francis Ford Coppola, Robert Evans and Al Ruddy at the press conference announcing the production of *The Godfather*. (Photo courtesy of the Ruddy Morgan Organization.)

local newspapers were represented.

Three of the four men seated at the table would become multi-millionaires as a result of that afternoon's announcement. The fourth, Robert Evans, seemed to dominate them by virtue not just of a superior sun-tan, but also of well-dressed charisma and enthusiasm. Bob Evans's full title boomed with satisfaction: Senior Vice-president in Charge of Worldwide Production, Paramount Pictures. Now he could announce that the studio would be making a screen version of Mario Puzo's *The Godfather*. 'It will be our big picture of 1971,' declared Evans. The film would commence shooting after the first of the year, with a release at Christmas 1971.

Evans introduced the talented individuals on either flank. Mario Puzo, the plump and easy-going author of the novel, a man who by his own admission had reached the age of forty-five 'owing $20,000 to friends, bookmakers and assorted Shylocks'. A chance meeting with an old friend then working at Putnam's, the New York publishing house, had led to his researching and writing *The Godfather*. Now, with one million hardcover copies sold and Fawcett paying $410,000 for paperback rights, Puzo could afford to return to the tables at Reno and Las Vegas.

To Evans's left sat Al Ruddy, a lanky thirty-six-year-old Canadian, whose skill at undershooting his budget on such films as *Making It* and *Little Fauss and Big Halsey* had earned him the task of producing *The Godfather*. Ahead of him lay months of contentious casting and a series of precarious negotiations with the East Coast Mafia. His reward would be a prodigious $7\frac{1}{2}$ per cent of the net receipts of the film.

The fourth man, his bespectacled face emblazoned with a full, black beard, struck the press as out of place. Francis Ford Coppola, despite his ample girth, appeared more at ease in a safari jacket than Evans did in a white silk suit. At thirty-one years of age, Coppola had made four feature films and written a host of scripts (*Patton*, already released, was to win him an Academy Award the following spring for best original screenplay). None of his four pictures had earned much money and as of that afternoon in 1970, Coppola's company, American Zoetrope, owed some $300,000 to Warner Bros.

Coppola's parents, however, were first-generation Italian-Americans, and Francis had grown up enveloped in the same family values as those adumbrated by Puzo in his novels. Numerous 'hot' directors had turned down the *Godfather* project, and Coppola had been suggested by Peter Bart, Bob Evans's number two at the studio, as having the right pedigree for the job. Given that Paramount wanted to produce *The Godfather* as a $2 million gangster movie with no frills, the risk inherent in Coppola's appointment seemed modest.

Journalists pressed Evans on the issue of casting. Rumour suggested that Anthony Quinn or Ernest Borgnine might play the ageing Don Corleone, with Frank Sinatra as singer–actor Johnny Fontane and Robert Redford as Michael, the Don's wilful yet mature young son. Bob Evans fended off such speculation with the suave bonhomie for which he was known and secretly admired in Hollywood: casting would be announced in the weeks to come, and that was an end of it. Few of the journalists who filed out of 202 North Cañon Drive that day could have realized that they had just attended the birth announcement of one of the most popular films of the century, the first in a trilogy that would earn more than a billion dollars around the world and an achievement that in critics' and audience polls would consistently rank in the top half-dozen motion pictures ever made.

Part One

1 Acquisition

As the 1960s bled to a close in Vietnam, Hollywood found itself in an identity crisis. For the first time since the Second World War, American cinema could not prevail as it wished. Throughout that turbulent decade, 'the foreign film' had acquired mystical status in cocktail chatter from Sydney to Manhattan. The French New Wave, the Italian triumvirate of Antonioni, Fellini and Visconti, Czechs and Poles, Swedes and Spaniards – all had supplanted Hollywood as the source of intelligent and inventive movies.

The Sound of Music had displaced *Gone With the Wind* as the all-time box-office champion in 1965, but during the late 1960s few films came even close to its box-office rentals of more than $70 million. A respectable hit such as *Bob & Carol & Ted & Alice* earned some $14 million in its opening engagements, and even *Airport* and *Butch Cassidy and the Sundance Kid* brought in only $46 million in domestic rentals (the money the studios receive from movie theatres).

The identity crisis coloured countless executive meetings on the cusp of the 1970s. The major studios were in the process of decamping to Los Angeles. Warner Bros had shifted its home-office operations from New York to Burbank. Only Paramount, Columbia and United Artists remained in Manhattan, along with such minor, transient players as Avco Embassy and Allied Artists. Besides, few of the studios controlled their own destiny. Warner's belonged to the Kinney Corporation, a garage conglomerate, Universal had been absorbed by MCA, and

Paramount had become a minor division in the behemoth known as Gulf + Western – or 'Engulf and Devour' as Mel Brooks would term it.

Paramount had been ailing throughout the 1960s, until a studio executive named Martin Davis had the thought of approaching Gulf + Western. Agricultural and building products, financial services, wire, paper, confectionery, sugar, zinc – all were grist to the G + W mill. By 1970, Gulf + Western enjoyed a capitalization value of $6 billion and profits of a shade under $50 million a year. Its undisputed boss was Charles G. Bluhdorn; dubbed 'the mad Austrian' by *Life* magazine, he boasted an explosive temperament as well as a guttural accent. 'He was vulgar to his core and had terrible taste in everything,' recalls Peter Bart. 'Always barking, always yelling. He'd fly into these rages. For some reason he wanted to do musicals like *Paint My Wagon* and epics like *The Adventurers*.'

But Bluhdorn took great pride in Paramount Pictures. The studio may have constituted only 5 per cent of his empire, but it attracted 95 per cent of the publicity. He had the courage to appoint former matinee idol Robert Evans head of production out on the West Coast. In an ironic profile, *Life* lamented the choice: 'Robert Evans is an outrage, he has no more right to be where he is than a burglar. He has no credentials, none of the requirements for membership.' The article exposed Evans's lack of experience as a producer, and the awesome responsibility he now wielded (some twenty-five films each year, with a combined budget of around $100 mil-

lion). 'He is entirely too good-looking, too rich and too lucky, and too damned charming, the playboy peacock of Paramount. Who the hell does he think he is?'

Evans had been introduced to Peter Bart by Abby Mann, the screenwriter of *Judgment at Nuremberg*. Bart was a journalist at the *New York Times*. He and Evans liked each other immediately, and Bart joined Paramount in 1967. Together they acquired new material and packaged future film projects for the studio, a role that received an official accolade in August 1970, when Bart became Vice-president of Creative Affairs at Paramount.

'There's never been a better partnership between two people than Peter and I,' maintains Evans. 'The reason? We were opposites. he was Mr Inside, I was Mr Outside. He could read six books in one weekend and I could read one book in six days. So we didn't overlap in any way. When I was in London, I'd phone Peter every night from the Connaught Hotel and ask him about this and that property, did you ever read this or that book?'

'Charlie Bluhdorn believed in Bob Evans,' recalls Bart. 'He believed that he had the instincts to be another Zanuck. Bob had modelled himself after a combination of Mike Todd and Darryl Zanuck.'

Paramount's slate for 1970 featured all too many clinkers: *Norwood, Tell Me That You Love Me, Junie Moon, On a Clear Day You Can See Forever, Darling Lili* and *Paint Your Wagon*. *Catch 22* and *The Out of Towners* performed better, but the only jewel in the crown proved to be Evans's own, much beloved project, *Love Story*, starring his wife, Ali MacGraw.

Yet the team had youth on its side. Stanley Jaffe, President of Paramount Pictures, was just thirty years of age, Frank Yablans, Vice-president for Domestic Sales, was thirty-three, Peter Bart a mere thirty-seven and Bob Evans, by his own admission, the 'old man of the team' at forty.

The Godfather would change the fortunes of Paramount and of Hollywood. It heralded the rise of a new generation of directors (Coppola, Scorsese, Spielberg, Lucas, De Palma) capable of becoming auteurs in their own backyard, and bringing creative lustre back to Hollywood. They hoisted their names above the title, in the tradition of Capra and Hitchcock. 'The new Coppola' would soon sound as significant as 'the new Bergman'. For a spell, the studios were in culture shock, unable to cope with the new approach to music, cinematography, casting and storyline.

The rights to *The Godfather* reached Paramount by circuitous means. Today, when dozens of executives are copied on every inter-office memorandum, tracing a deal is much easier than it was thirty years ago.

In 1965 Mario Puzo published his second novel, *The Fortunate Pilgrim*. *The Dark Arena*, his first, had painted a searing portrait of the post-war years, as an Italian-American returns to Germany to pursue a love affair. With prescience, the *San Francisco Chronicle* remarked, 'The author is able, honest and intelligent. He will write more novels, and good ones. You may be sure of that.' *The Fortunate Pilgrim* retreated in time, to the Great Depression and its impact on the Italian citizens of Manhattan. Its pivotal figure is a woman, Lucia Santa, a proud and unforgiving mother who survives the loss of both son and husband. Not for her an affectionate link with the Naples or Sicily of yore. In a stern and eloquent passage, Puzo concedes that 'Natives of the south, Sicily, Naples, the Abruzzi, these Italians on Tenth Avenue [. . .] had never loved their country of birth, it meant nothing to them. For centuries its government had been the most bitter enemy of their fathers and their fathers' fathers before them.'

Both novels received excellent reviews – and sold in miserable numbers. Together they netted Puzo a paltry $6,500. 'Then I met a guy who worked at Putnam's. I gave him a copy of *The Fortunate Pilgrim*, and he arranged for me to meet the Putnam people. I sat around and told them Mafia stories. They were obviously impressed and gave me a $5,000 advance to write *The Godfather*.

'My final $1,500 depended on my delivering a completed manuscript, and I wanted to take my family to Europe, so that's what made me finish it.' Puzo gambled his money away in European casinos and returned to the United States owing some $8,000 on his credit cards. Then his agent, Candida Donadio, phoned to say that Putnam's had just rejected an offer of $375,000 for the paperback rights to *The Godfather*. Ralph Daigh at Fawcett eventually paid $410,000 for those rights and recovered his investment many times over. 'I was downtown in New York when I found out all of this,' recalls

Puzo. 'I rounded up my wife and kids. My wife had been dozing off. I said, "I have an announcement to make. We do not have to worry about money any more." So what happened? My kids went to play and my wife made supper and went to bed. [. . .] As a writer, all I could think was, "Gee, I finally fooled everyone." Writers can feel like charlatans.'

The late George Wieser acted as a valuable tipster for the studios during the late 1960s. A gadfly, he served in a minor capacity at *Library Journal*, which had access to all books prior to publication. Wieser had leaked to Bob Evans the potential of *The Detective*, which became a vehicle for Frank Sinatra in 1968. Even before the galleys of *The Godfather* reached *Library Journal*, Wieser was on the phone to his contacts at Paramount, including the late Barry Beckerman (who proved an enthusiastic advocate for the project) and, of course, Bob Evans – saying they should look at the material. 'Maybe Wieser had just heard about it and not even seen it at that juncture,' says Peter Bart.

Evans called Bart and they agreed that they should option the book. Bart wrote to Norman Flicker, then head of business affairs at Paramount, ordering him to do just that. His memo was copied to nobody. 'In those days,' remembers Bart, 'the studio was so small that if you called a meeting and one person came, it was considered extraordinary.' Gray Frederickson, Ruddy's colleague who would become Associate Producer on *The Godfather*, concurs. 'Nowadays, there are fifteen or twenty vice-presidents at each studio, and everybody waits for everybody else to green-light a project. Nobody wants to make a decision. In those days, Paramount production was run by just two people, Bob Evans and Peter Bart, and they had a couple of readers and that was that.'

The acquisition was not a sudden coup. Puzo had written only a hundred pages when his agent informed him that a bidding war had started between Paramount and Universal. Hecht-Hill-Lancaster wanted to buy the rights also, and Bob Evans recalls being 'one day away from Burt Lancaster buying *The Godfather*, and Burt wanted to play the Don.'

'I had just changed agents,' says Puzo, 'but William Morris had the authority to represent me on movie rights. The deal they cut [with Paramount] was terrible, $12,000 option against $85,000 with "escalators" *if* they exercised the option.' Puzo wanted the money and told William Morris to proceed with the deal. Peter Bart reminisces about the impact of the acquisition: 'Charlie Bluhdorn came charging into my office, and Bob Evans came in at the tail-end of the conversation, and he was screaming because Bob and I bought two properties. *The Godfather* was called *Mafia*, while *True Grit* was 120 pages long, and Bluhdorn measured things by acreage, so he thought it was absurd to pay $300,000 for a total of 180 pages.'

In fact, Evans and Bart had glimpsed but sixty pages when they decided to buy the property in March of 1967. It included some of the juiciest scenes in the novel, such as Woltz's discovery of the stallion's head in his bedclothes and the murder of Luca Brasi. 'It wasn't great writing,' says Bart, 'but he had so many fascinating ideas, it was riveting stuff.' In his memoirs, Evans would boast of helping Puzo when the novelist came to him with some 'rumpled pages' one afternoon in the spring of 1968 [*sic*]. 'Thinkin' of writin' an inside story on the boys, the Organization – part real, part fiction,' Puzo told him. 'Callin'

it *Mafia*. Name's never been used,' he laughed. 'Kefauver Committee branded it. You got yourself an original. Could be good.'

'I never saw or heard of Evans or Bart until I got to Hollywood,' claims Puzo. 'I dealt with Barry Beckerman.'

In fact, the first Paramount personality to

Producer Al Ruddy in 1971.

meet Puzo face to face was Al Ruddy, who had been appointed to the project by Bart because he was 'a good, bright young producer, the best man for the job'. Ruddy lived over a delicatessen and his mother slept in another bed in the same room so he could save on his studio per diem allowance. 'When I told him we wanted to produce *The Godfather*,' smiles Bart, 'he asked me if I had a copy so he could read it. "I'd rather you go out and buy one," I said. "Oh, you're sure you don't have one around?" boomed Ruddy.' Summoned to meet Charlie Bluhdorn, Ruddy had to say what he would do with *The Godfather* if he were confirmed as producer. 'Make an ice-blue, terrifying movie about people you love,' snapped Ruddy. The Gulf + Western boss liked that, and confirmed Evans's and Bart's choice.

Ruddy flew to New York to persuade Puzo, who lived on Long Island and relished the privacy of his Bayshore residence, to collaborate on the screenplay. 'I explained that it would be difficult for him to cut out so much of the book (reducing it from some 600 pages to around 150), but Mario replied, "I don't ever have to see this book again in order to do a screenplay from it".'

Puzo still clung to his ideals as a novelist and refused Ruddy's first offer. After calling the Coast, Ruddy agreed to include a percentage of the picture's profits. He and his wife met Puzo for lunch at the Plaza Hotel in Manhattan. Puzo liked the producer's relaxed, New York charm, and became fascinated when his wife 'produced from her handbag a miniature live poodle who let out a yip and had the handbag zipped over his head again

before the enraged maître d' spotted where the sound came from [. . .] At the end of the lunch I was enchanted by them and the poodle, and I agreed to write the script.' This deal had an altogether more lucrative ring to it. Puzo would receive $100,000 against 2 ½ per cent of the profits, along with $500 a week for expenses.

When he settled into the indulgent luxury of the Beverly Hills Hotel, however, Puzo found that his entire weekly allowance quickly evaporated. He dashed off the first draft of the screenplay in the summer of 1970, working on the third floor of a 'barracklike building' on Paramount's Marathon Street lot, and ambling down the stairs to Ruddy's more spacious quarters on the ground floor, where he could confer with the producer on points in the screenplay. By coincidence, in July of 1970, Gulf + Western sold a 50 per cent stake in the Paramount studio lot to Società Generale Immobiliare, the real estate and construction conglomerate owned in part by the Vatican. A disguised version of the same company would emerge as a crucial element in *The Godfather Part III* some twenty years later.

Puzo wrote later of his impressions of the studio executives. '[Bob] Evans was unpretentious and usually said or seemed to say exactly what he thought. He said it the way children tell truths, with a curious innocence that made the harshest criticism or disagreement inoffensive.' And he noted that Peter Bart 'liked to think things out before voicing an opinion, and he hadn't yet picked up the California trick of being charming while he was thinking.'

One evening, Puzo dined with Al Ruddy at Chasen's restaurant. When 'some unfortunate mutual acquaintance' persuaded Puzo to approach Frank Sinatra's table, the singer screamed abuse at him, accusing Puzo of being a 'stool-pigeon and a fink for the FBI'. He threatened to break Puzo's legs, at which the novelist lost his own temper and had to be restrained. John Wayne, seated near by, offered to punch Puzo too if help were needed. Sinatra's fury stemmed from his suspicion that Johnny Fontane had been based on his own career and personality. How ironic that Sinatra should have embraced Coppola at a club in Los Angeles not long afterwards, saying, 'Francis, I'd play the Godfather for you. I wouldn't do it for those guys at Paramount, but I'd do it for you.' Almost two decades later, Sinatra was offered the chance to play Don Altobello in *Part III*.

Al Ruddy adhered to the studio's mandate to produce *The Godfather* on a modest budget. 'The studio was on shaky ground,' he recalls. 'Films like *Darling Lili, Paint Your Wagon* and *Catch 22* had gone way over budget, and Paramount had lost $70 million that year. I'd produced *Little Fauss and Big Halsey* for just $2,300,000, and had persuaded Robert Redford to honour an old pledge, right after he came off *Butch Cassidy*. So the studio saw me as a producer who could bring a film in on a modest budget.' He abandoned any thought of shooting the film in New York, where the novel was set. 'It costs more to film in New York,' he told *Daily Variety*, 'for what you could easily spend and never see on the screen. One reason is that the International Alliance of Theatrical Stage Employees and the Teamsters are much tougher to deal with in New York than they are in other cities.' Ruddy began considering such cities as Cleveland, Kansas City, or Cincinnati. 'In Cleveland there's a section of Murray Hill extremely similar to the original locale in Puzo's book.' Privately, Bob Evans had pegged the budget at $2 million, wary of repeating the disaster of *The Brotherhood*, a Mafia picture produced by Paramount only eighteen months earlier. In public, Ruddy could talk of 'a $3,000,000 film. It could just as easily run into $4,000,000 if we get to the bottom line and see we need the money.'

Soon the studio began searching for a director.

At first the headhunting fell to Al Ruddy and his associate, Gray Frederickson. Arthur Penn, the talk of the town after *Bonnie and Clyde* and *Little Big Man*, said his schedule was full. Peter Yates (*Bullitt*), and Costa-Gavras (*Z*) declined the offer. Sidney J. Furie, the Canadian who had made *The Ipcress File*, and recently *Big Fauss and Little Halsey* for Ruddy and Frederickson, divided the friends. 'Ruddy really wanted him,' said Frederickson, 'but I fought him all the way.' Three elder statesmen in Hollywood, Otto Preminger, Richard Brooks and Elia Kazan, received offers from Paramount and said no. Fred Zinnemann and Franklin Schaffner also turned down *The Godfather*, on the grounds that it was too kind to the Mafia. The youngest contender was Larry Peerce, thirty-five at the time and hot off *Goodbye Columbus*, which had made a star of Bob Evans's inamorata, Ali MacGraw. 'Sam

Peckinpah wanted to do it,' recalls Bart, 'but Bob and I wouldn't let him. In his vision of the film the body count would have been astonishing.'

Then Peter Bart thought of approaching Francis Ford Coppola. Bart by this time had immersed himself in the project. He had assigned Al Ruddy as producer, and he had been poring over the screenplay with Puzo during the summer. 'I had met Francis when I was preparing an article for the *New York Times* about young directors who were doing nudie pictures (he was working at UCLA), and I met him again when he was hanging around town as a rewrite man. Francis was thin, self-deprecating, ferociously ambitious, delightful company.' Jeff Berg, an early friend of Bart's in Hollywood, and Coppola's agent, told the Paramount executive of Zoetrope's indebtedness to Warner's.

So Peter Bart tracked Francis Coppola down at the home of George Lucas in Mill Valley, reminded him of his perilous economic situation – and suggested that he should direct *The Godfather*. Francis at first demurred. 'I did not immediately see myself directing this book, which seemed to me to be rather Irwin Shaw in tone (the whole subplot about the woman with the enlarged vagina).' But the novel continued to dominate the bestseller lists, in the United States and in Europe, and little by little Coppola became more sympathetic to the project. Quite by chance, he met his own father, the composer Carmine Coppola, at Burbank Airport. 'I was at Paramount all day yesterday,' he told Carmine, 'and they want me to direct this hunk of trash. I don't want to do it. I want to do art

films.' His father encouraged him to make some money from *The Godfather*, and then use it to do the kind of movies he really relished. George Lucas, a friend as well as a protégé, agreed, pointing out that if Francis did not accept the Paramount offer, he might lose all he had struggled to build up at Zoetrope. On further reflection, Coppola told Bart that he would make the picture on one condition – that it would not be a film about organized gangsterism, but rather a family chronicle: a metaphor for capitalism in America.

Bart enlisted Al Ruddy to his cause. 'You should meet this guy Francis Coppola,' he told Ruddy one morning. 'He's a good writer and a good director, and you'd like him.' Ruddy flew to the Bay area, and did indeed like Francis. 'Then I had to bring him back to Los Angeles for a meeting with Bob Evans and Stanley Jaffe [at the studio]. Well, we sat outside for a good twenty minutes in the car, and I fed him the lines that I thought he ought to say and so persuade them to hire him. But once we were inside, Francis showed what a brilliant salesman he was. He could have sold me the Brooklyn Bridge that day!'

Although Coppola was a mere thirty-one years old and could boast of no consistent track record in Hollywood, his pedigree appealed to Bob Evans. 'There hadn't been one successful Mafia picture,' declared Evans, 'and I worked out why. They were usually written by Jews, directed by Jews and acted by Jews. There's a thin line between a Jew and a Sicilian. And that thin line makes the difference.' Evans wanted to smell the spaghetti on the screen. '[Coppola] knew the way these men in *The Godfather* ate their food, kissed each other, talked. He knew the grit' (even though, one might add, Francis was no relation to one of Vito Genovese's lieutenants, 'Trigger Mike' Coppola).

After a late-night negotiating session at Paramount, Coppola agreed to direct *The Godfather* for $125,000 and 6 per cent of the gross rentals. 'Paramount cheated me out of a point,' he smiles wryly. 'They said, "You can do it two ways. Number one, for $125,000 and 10 per cent, or number two, for $175,000 and 6 per cent of the net. I replied, I'll do it for $125,000 and 7 per cent. But Frank Yablans said, okay, we've drafted only 6 per cent in this document but don't worry, you'll get 7 per cent." I never did!'

Coppola let the studio know that he wanted to make the film in period, and in New York. He raised eyebrows when he mentioned Marlon Brando as a potential Don Corleone, but nobody believed he would seriously pursue the idea, and Francis set sail blithely for Europe, where he attended the Sorrento Film Festival with his family. 'We took the *Michelangelo* or one of those Italian boats to Italy,' says his wife, Eleanor, 'and I remember him with the book on board, and maybe he was breaking it down and starting to deal with it. I recall other people on the deck reading it because it was a bestseller.'

On 29 September 1970 *Daily Variety* announced that Coppola would direct the film. Behind the scenes, arguments were already raging over the possibility that Marlon Brando might play the Don. On 10 August Puzo had completed the first full draft of his screenplay. He mailed a copy to Brando and the actor promptly read both script and

novel. But, with an ironic sense of his recent appalling record at the box office, Brando told Puzo that no studio would take the film if he were to star in it. 'Wait until the studio assigns a director,' he advised Puzo.

Anthony Quinn, in a 1996 appearance on the *Larry King Live* show, remembered visiting Brando in his home, trying to interest him in playing opposite him in a new film about Pancho Villa. 'You couldn't even get $50,000 for me now, Tony,' replied the actor, 'but what's that other script you're holding?' It was *The Godfather*, which Paramount had sent to Quinn, in the hope that he would agree to play the Don.

Soon afterwards, Coppola phoned Mario Puzo and said that he felt Brando was perfect for the part. 'It's odd, but one day in early 1970 two things happened on the same day,' muses Coppola. 'Al Ruddy and Peter Bart knocked at the door of my house on Webster in San Francisco, on a matter unrelated to *The Godfather* (I don't think Ruddy had even been assigned to the production at that point) – and then Marlon Brando called to say that he could not agree to my request to play the Harry Caul part in *The Conversation*.

'So when I read *The Godfather*, I thought of Brando, but Paramount hated the idea. The fact that he had appeared in [Gillo Pontecorvo's flop] *Burn!* meant in their eyes that he would prove a negative factor, that he'd keep people *away* from the film.' No less a Solon than Dino de Laurentiis had warned Gulf + Western chief Charlie Bluhdorn: 'If Brando plays the Don, forget opening the film in Italy. They'll laugh him off the screen.' Bluhdorn, like everyone else who read the trades, knew of the problems and delays involving Brando on *Mutiny on the Bounty*. Brando was then forty-seven years old. 'To Evans,' he wrote in his autobiography, 'I looked too young to play Don Corleone, who aged in the story from his late forties to his early seventies.' Evans leaned towards casting Carlo Ponti, the husband of Sophia Loren, who had plenty of experience as a producer but none as an actor. If not, then there was always Ernest Borgnine, a 1955 Oscar-winner for *Marty* and a gap-toothed thug in numerous films since.

Virtually the entire Paramount hierarchy regarded the casting of Brando as a time bomb. Stanley Jaffe, whizz-kid President of Paramount Pictures, and his protégé-cum-acolyte, Frank Yablans, led the opposition. Yablans was the son of an immigrant taxi-driver. He voted against Brando because he'd seen him in 'a piece of shit' and said no one would go to watch a picture with Brando in it. Bluhdorn also did not relish the prospect of seeing Brando as the Don, and even Bob Evans concurred when Jaffe pounded the table at a studio meeting and shouted at Coppola, 'So long as I am President of Paramount Pictures, you will absolutely not have Brando!' Prophetic words, because the furore over Brando's eventual casting brought about Jaffe's resignation, and by late July 1971 he had quit the studio.

Coppola persisted, however, and Paramount sought to buy time by imposing three conditions on Brando's taking the part. One, he would have to post a bond, so that the studio could be reimbursed for any delays provoked by the actor's failing to keep to schedule. Two, he would work for a per diem and expenses only, and maybe a percentage of the film's rentals. Three (and this, thought the studio, would kill off Brando's lingering enthusiasm), he would have to take a screen test.

Dean Tavoularis, the production designer who would become an essential member of Coppola's creative team, flew with him across the States soon after they had met and agreed to work together on *The Godfather*. 'On the plane Francis said to me, "When I get back to L.A. I'd like to meet with Brando . . ." He didn't know that I'd become friends with Brando on Terry Southern's *Candy*, the film in Rome I'd been working on. He used to come over for dinner. The French actor–director Christian Marquand was a friend of mine, so I called Christian and told him Coppola would like to meet Brando. So we went to Chianti (a very good Italian restaurant on Melrose), Marlon, Christian, Francis and myself.'

Coppola approached the screen test with apprehension. He flew down from San Francisco, purchased some prosciutto, cheese and Italian cigars, and then drove up to Brando's home, with its all-white decor and carpets, on Mulholland Drive. 'I took a talented Japanese documentary photographer, Hiro Narita, with me,' says Coppola, 'and we did the whole thing very discreetly, on videotape. Brando emerged, and didn't say much. He had his hair in a sort of blond pony-tail, and when he saw the prosciutto and cheese he began to nibble at it, and then he ran some boot polish through his hair, slicking it back. He put some tissue paper in his mouth, and I admired the way he even wrinkled the tips of his shirt collar to get into character. He came up with the idea of talking huskily because the Don had been wounded in the throat, and when his phone rang he answered it in this Italian-style grumpy voice.' Brando remembers that before the test took place, he 'put on some make-up, stuffed Kleenex in [his] cheeks, and worked out the characterization first in front of a mirror, then on a television monitor.' Coppola had described his old Italian uncle's thin moustache, and so Brando quickly pencilled one in on his upper lip. Shadows had also been added beneath Brando's eyes, to make him look older.

Hiro Narita set up a single light for his 16-mm camera, as Coppola wanted to be as discreet as possible. 'We just watched for fifteen to twenty minutes while this man slowly underwent a transformation,' recalls Narita. 'Then he turned to us and said, "Okay, I'm ready." He had not figured out the voice for Don Corleone, so the test was really like a pantomime.' Brando permitted just one roll of film to be exposed, then he called a halt and Coppola and his team departed.

When Coppola ran Brando's test for the Paramount executives, they all changed their minds, most notably Charlie Bluhdorn. Tavoularis remembers being in an office on the thirty-third floor of the Gulf + Western Building in New York, and watching the test on a monitor with Coppola and others. Suddenly Bluhdorn could be seen staring curiously from the corridor. 'That's incredible! Who's dat man? Who's dat man? Dat

Marlon Brando as he was off-set during the making of *The Godfather.*

man's the Godfather. Gotta get him!' He did not realize that he was watching Marlon Brando. The actor agreed to work for a $50,000 fee, plus $10,000 a week expenses 'during his contracted six weeks on the shoot'. He would also receive a percentage of the film's profits – 1 per cent of the gross after the first $10 million, climbing to a maximum 5 per cent for a $60 million gross. But according to Bob Evans, he sold his percentage points back to the studio not long afterwards, for a flat fee of $100,000. That cost him a likely $11 million, and, says Evans, Brando 'fired his lawyer, his agent, and everyone else close to him' as the grosses soared.

About a month prior to shooting Brando was told that he looked too heavy for the part.

'So I went on a diet,' recalled Brando, 'but I lost too much weight and had to put twenty pounds back on before the picture could start.'

2 Casting and Writing

'The Godfather became like the biggest home movie in history'
– Francis Ford Coppola

Everyone involved with *The Godfather*, even Mario Puzo himself, made the mistake of underestimating the novel. Many of the initial problems that plagued the production stemmed from the disdain with which the raw material was viewed. Paramount regarded the book as mere pulp fiction, to be transformed into a routine gangster movie on a modest budget, rather similar to *The FBI* series on TV.

For Puzo, his new novel marked a deliberate descent from the literary uplands he had essayed with *The Dark Arena* and, in particular, *The Fortunate Pilgrim*. He read an interview in which Coppola explained that he was directing *The Godfather* so that he could get the capital to make pictures he really wanted to make. 'What depressed me,' said Puzo, 'was that he was smart enough to do this at the age of thirty-two, when it took me forty-five years to figure out I had to write *The Godfather* so that I could do the other books I really wanted to do.' The outbursts of violence, often savage in their cynicism, that punctuate *The Godfather* cannot be located in Puzo's earlier work.

Once Coppola had overcome his initial repugnance for the book, however, he began to see the story 'as that of a king, almost Greek – a king with three sons. That's why I cut out all the subplots in Las Vegas and so on. I never felt that Italian-Americans were being portrayed exclusively as gangsters by Mario.' The novel contains a grandeur of characterization that elevates it far beyond the domain of Harold Robbins or, indeed, Irwin Shaw. The central personality of Don Vito Corleone has an indispensable place in the lives of those around him – not just his immediate family, but characters such as Bonasera (the undertaker), Enzo (the baker) and Johnny Fontane (the singer). Through the Don, the key themes of the novel emerge: family values, the importance of political influence, absolute fealty (alias 'friendship') to the Godfather, who never utters a threat ('He always used logic that proved to be irresistible'). Mercy flows only from the Family, 'more loyal and more to be trusted than society'. Puzo describes the assembled Dons thus: 'They were those rarities, men who had refused to accept the rule of civilized society, men who refused the dominion of other men.' Coppola concedes that *The Godfather* projects an idealized image of the Mafia in the public consciousness. 'People love to read about an organization that's really going to take care of us,' he has said. 'When the courts fail you and the whole American system fails you, you can go to Don Corleone and get justice.'

Not that Puzo approves of the Mafia per se. In the eyes of the Organization, he writes, 'Merit meant nothing. Talent meant nothing. Work meant nothing. The Mafia Godfather gave you your profession as a gift.' He blames the United States for having permitted the resurrection of the Mafia after the Second World War: 'American military government officials believed that anyone imprisoned by the Fascist regime was a democrat, and many of these *mafiosi* were appointed as mayors of villages or interpreters to the military government.' This good fortune, writes Puzo, enabled the Mafia to recover and to establish itself as more formidable than ever before.

Coppola's film renders the *caporegimes* in more engaging tones than Puzo's original. In the novel, Clemenza has little charm: 'Though he was very fat, his face had none of the usual stout man's benignity.' Tessio is described as 'ferret-faced'. Neri, the Don's bodyguard, practises his craft with 'vicious brutality'. Even Connie Corleone 'was not quite a pretty girl, thin and nervous and certain to become shrewish later in life'. Tom Hagen, the *consigliere* (counsellor) played with such kindliness by Robert Duvall, is 'a tall crew-cut man, very slender, very ordinary-looking.' Paulie, the button-man (or family thug) alleged to have betrayed the Don, cuts a pathetic figure on screen, while in the novel he is nothing better than a vicious thug.

The popular crooner Vic Damone had been offered the part of Johnny Fontane and might indeed have been shocked when he found the character truncated to just eight pages of screenplay. An entire section of the novel charts Johnny's fortunes in Hollywood, including his relationship with his estranged wife, Ginny; his trying to make a one-night stand with a budding actress; his being set up by Tom Hagen as a movie producer for the Don; his winning of the Academy Award for Best Actor and the orgiastic celebrations that follow; and his friendship with Nino Valenti, a close friend of the Family who joins Johnny out west, becomes a movie star and drinks himself to death. Some of this material, reworked, features in Puzo's 1996 novel, *The Last Don*.

The original novel moves back and forth in time and place to an epic degree. Had Coppola been given unlimited resources in

1971, he might never have felt the need to embark on a sequel. So much of the structure of *The Godfather Part II* already exists in Puzo's novel. Book III (out of nine) begins with the childhood of Don Vito, for example, a sequence that Coppola would place at the very forefront of *Part II*. Puzo charts Vito Corleone's rise 'from a quite ordinary, somewhat ruthless businessman to a great Don in the world of criminal enterprise', helping to smuggle in bootleg liquor from Canada (a habit referred to *en passant* by Hyman Roth in a speech in *The Godfather Part II*). The role of Genco Abbandando, the Don's youthful partner and his first *consigliere*, carries some weight during these years, but Abbandando would appear only fleetingly – on his deathbed – in the television omnibus version of *The Godfather*.

A good friend of Mario Puzo's, Peter Maas, had assembled *The Valachi Papers*, and Puzo's publisher, G. P. Putnam's Sons, had released it in 1968. Joseph Valachi had written some 300,000 words in jail, exposing the Cosa Nostra as umbilically tied to the Sicilian Mafia. When the Justice Department suppressed this manuscript, Maas simply 'interviewed' Valachi in prison, and published the results. Puzo enjoyed access to Maas's papers during the research period he needed to write *The Godfather*. 'But,' he maintains, 'the characters in fiction need to hold more interest than real-life personalities. My characters are more like the original Sicilian Mafia guys – they were more honourable and came from a more unified social structure.'

Still, Valachi's own lavish wedding at Palm Gardens, off Broadway, in 1932, may have served as a model for the opening sequence of *The Godfather*. Two bands played and 'envelopes' were sent by everyone as gifts for the bride. In another parallel with the book, Francesco Castiglia (better known as Frank Costello) was shot in an apartment-house lobby and rushed to the nearby Roosevelt Hospital, where he survived in the manner of Don Vito Corleone. In the same year of 1957, Frank (Don Cheech) Scalice was gunned down, again like Don Vito, while purchasing fruit in front of a Bronx store. Also in 1957, one of New York's most dreaded mobsters, Albert Anastasia, was shot while relaxing under hot towels at his barber's shop – an assassination not unlike that of Moe Greene in the film.

Avoiding a war between the Families preoccupies Don Vito Corleone. In real life, the five Families (Bonanno, Gambino, Genovese, Colombo and Lucchese) have refrained from all-out conflict since the 1930s and the so-called Castellamarese war. It has been pointed out that the small number of Families in the United States has helped to keep the internecine peace. Palermo alone boasts eighteen Families, and hundreds of murders have resulted from the two all-out battles that have occurred in Sicily since the 1930s.

Puzo and Coppola lay emphasis on what Leopoldo Franchetti, writing in 1876, termed 'l'industria della violenza'. The Mafia has effectively *privatized* the administration of justice. Don Corleone remains an entrepreneur all his life, buying and selling commodities. Occasionally, like his Sicilian forebears, he would play the Robin Hood, robbing the rich to help the poor. But most of the time he deals in olive oil and other imports, drawing the line (as Sollozzo discovers in the film) at drugs. After all, in its nineteenth-century infancy, the Mafia consisted of 'market brokers, barbers, shepherds, bakers, millers, pasta makers, coachmen and carters'.

Puzo asserts that he selected the name 'Corleone' for his Family 'because [he] thought it didn't sound *too* Italian.' Don Vito may have been a synthesis of two Mafia chieftains, Vito Genovese and olive-oil magnate Joseph Profaci, but on the whole he remains a creature of fiction. His birthplace, Corleone, lies about 40 km south of Palermo in the western interior of Sicily. Homicide was rampant there during the 1950s. The grubby little town has spawned several famous *mafiosi*: Carmelo Lo Bue, Luciano Liggio and, of course, Bagarella. Liggio 'made his bones' in 1958 when, in his early thirties, he murdered Dr Michele Navarra and restored the power of the Corleone Family. Two generations later, a daughter of Corleone, Antonina Bagarella, flouted the traditional *omertà* and pleaded on behalf of her four children in the pages of *La Repubblica* : 'Our life is hell. My children are innocent [. . .] Their only fault is to have been born of a father named Riina and a mother named Bagarella: a generic sin that no catharsis can wash away.' Another member of the Corleone clan is Francesco Di Carlo, under investigation for the alleged murder of Vatican banker Roberto Calvi in 1982 (see Chapter 11).

During the winter of 1970–71, Francis Coppola worked to assemble a loyal team of technicians, and also to hone the screenplay in tandem with Mario Puzo.

Some of the colleagues he recruited for *The Godfather* – Gray Frederickson, Fred Roos, Dean Tavoularis, even cinematographer Gordon Willis – would become friends and allies for a generation and more. Gray Frederickson, a specialist in scouting locations and solving logistical problems, worked alongside Al Ruddy. Prior to that he had spent seven years in Italy, working with some twenty directors, including Sergio Leone. 'This was the period when an Italian producer would fly a unit to location in Las Vegas or wherever, then return to the studios in Italy and shoot there, passing the picture off as American.' Frederickson then took a job on *The Good, The Bad and The Ugly*, and spent a lengthy spell in Spain, becoming friendly with Clint Eastwood and going into business for him for a while. Gray had first seen Francis Coppola outside a movie theatre in Los Angeles during the late 1960s, wearing a yellow corduroy suit. 'I'd seen *You're a Big Boy Now*, and liked it, so I went across and chatted to him,' says Frederickson.

During those years in Italy, Frederickson had encountered Dean Tavoularis, an art director who became noted in Hollywood for his design on *Bonnie and Clyde* and *Zabriskie Point*. 'Gray called me in New York and said he was going to be making the film with Al Ruddy, and Francis Ford Coppola was going to direct it. He said, "Why don't you go over and see him at the St. Regis Hotel?"' Tavoularis bought a copy of *The Godfather* and devoured it at a single sitting. When he met Coppola at the St. Regis he 'liked everything he said because, instead of a predictably cast gangster movie, he said he wanted to shoot it in New York. I said I wouldn't want to use the Paramount back lot either. The studio preferred to use the back lot either at Paramount or Universal, so they could make it a contemporary story and save on expense.'

If Frederickson would prove indispensable as a location scout (especially in Sicily) on all three *Godfather* films, then his friend Fred Roos exercised an equally crucial role. A casting director who had passed through film school at UCLA just prior to Coppola, Roos had chosen actors for such offbeat, egghead films as *Five Easy Pieces, The King of Marvin Gardens, Petulia* and *Zabriskie Point.* 'During the late 1960s Francis used to call me up on the phone and sort of schmooze with me about actors. I'd never met him. Conversations that didn't lead to anything in particular – have you seen this or that person on screen, etc. We'd just talk, and that was it.

'Then one day he called and said, "I've got this movie, you know, *The Godfather*, it's a bestseller. Do you want to cast it for me?" I said yes, and he told me, "Come on over to Paramount and make your deal with Al Ruddy, and let's go to work."'

A casting director had already been hired by the studio, but Coppola insisted on using Roos. The casting process continued for month after month, with tests run in Los Angeles, New York and even Italy (where Louis Digiaimo aided Roos). Despite their squabbles, Coppola and Evans agreed on one key point: that where possible Italian-Americans should play Italian-Americans in the film. Even those Italian-American actors without an agent succeeded in reaching Roos for at least an interview, if not a test.

A good example of this is the part of the Corleones' chief executioner Luca Brasi. Coppola wanted Timothy Carey to play the role, and he tested well. But Ruddy had difficulty negotiating with him and his agent. Two days later, and without warning, the 320-pound Lenny Montana was standing on the set. 'I introduced him to Francis,' says Ruddy, 'and Francis loved him.' Few would argue that Lenny Montana, a former heavyweight wrestler, was not absolutely perfect for the part of the ox-like Brasi.

Gianni Russo, who played Connie's hus-

Lenny Montana as Luca Brasi.

band, Carlo, had no previous acting experience (other than emceeing in a Las Vegas night-club) and was accused in *Time* of consorting with the Mob, but always denied it. For a meeting with Al Ruddy he arrived in a classic Bentley, driven by a mini-skirted Japanese girl chauffeur. Ruddy could not take him seriously, but four months later Russo popped up in New York and demanded a screen test. Asked to attack a secretary who volunteered to stand in for 'Carlo's wife', Russo said: 'I did a lot of the scene in Italian and I started beating the broad up – literally beating the shit out of her. At one point she went flying over a coffee table and Evans almost had an orgasm and yelled "cut". Then they said I had the part.' The real casualty of this violent display was not Stanley Jaffe's secretary, but Jack Ryan, passed over for the role of Carlo, for which he had tested magnificently. 'Ryan was so stunning,' wrote Puzo, 'that I sought him out to tell him how great he played the part.'

The casting worksheets for *The Godfather* amount to a roll-call of almost every significant European or American actor and actress of the era. Had Brando refused to play the Don, Roos might have turned to George C. Scott, Raf Vallone, Adolfo Celi, Jean Gabin, Richard Conte, Vittorio De Sica, John Huston, Paul Scofield or even Victor Mature. Laurence Olivier was a starred 'possible', but he was ailing at the time.

Robert Duvall, fresh from an acclaimed role (as Major Frank Burns) in *M*A*S*H*, earned the part of Tom Hagen, but Roy Thinnes, Barry Primus, Robert Vaughn and Richard Mulligan headed Roos's list – as well

Robert Duvall as Tom Hagen.

as intriguing possibilities such as Keir Dullea, Dean Stockwell and Jack Nicholson (whom Roos knew from his work with Bob Rafelson). John Cassavetes and Peter Falk both approached Coppola about taking the role.

Robert De Niro tested well for Sonny, and Roos had him in mind to play Enzo the baker. He was actually cast as one of the Family's button-men (Paulie), but suddenly De Niro gained the lead in *The Gang That Couldn't Shoot Straight*, so he was released, 'which was lucky,' smiles Roos, 'because if he had played the button-man he could never have been the Don in *Part II*.'

The part of Fredo seemed difficult to cast.

Sal Mineo, Martin Sheen and Paul Mantee might have been tested had Roos not discovered John Cazale. 'Richard Dreyfuss was a friend of mine,' recalls Roos. 'I'd known him since he was a teenager, and I'd cast him in the upcoming *American Graffiti*. He invited me to see him on stage in *Line*, a new play by Israel Horovitz. Richard was terrific and all that, but there was this guy John Cazale and it was like, there's Fredo, end of story. I went to Francis and said I saw Fredo last night, he's it, we don't have to look any longer.' Cazale flew to the Coast for an interview, and Coppola agreed immediately with Roos's selection.

Roos compiled a list of Italian-American actors, alongside pure Italians, who could conceivably appear in *The Godfather*. There were literally hundreds, from Vittorio

Richard Castellano as Clemenza.

Abe Vigoda as Tessio.

John Marley as Jack Woltz.

Salvatore Corsitto as Bonasera.

Al Lettieri as Sollozzo.

Gassman to Ugo Tognazzi, from Harry Guardino to Vincent Gardenia. Morgana King, a Sicilian-American jazz singer, won the role of Mama Corleone in a putative competition with Alida Valli, Giulietta Masina, Irene Pappas and Silvana Mangano.

Diane Keaton would become a memorable Kay Adams, but Roos also considered other actresses embodying the requisite WASP innocence and resolve, including Michelle Phillips, Jennifer Salt, Susan Blakely, Joanna Shimkus, Geneviève Bujold, Blythe Danner and Jill Clayburgh – none of whom had reached the peak of her popularity in 1971.

The only example of family nepotism seemed to be the casting of Talia Shire, Francis's sister, as Connie. The director at first forbade her from auditioning for the role. Before she was offered a contract, Coppola agonized over his choice, and his mother remembers his screaming: 'Tally's too pretty for the part. [. . .] A guy who's going to marry into a Mafia family has to have a fat little dumpy Italian girl with an ugly face.' Shire's performance struck audiences and critics alike as most persuasive, however, and in *Part II* and *Part III* her role would increase in stature and presence. For fun, Coppola encouraged his parents to come to the set during shooting, father Carmine playing the piano during the scene when the Corleone soldiers 'go to the mattresses', mother Italia cast as a switchboard operator in an office scene virtually eliminated at editing stage, and both of them appearing as diners in Louie's restaurant in the Bronx, where Michael shoots Sollozzo and McCluskey.

✳

In these early months, by far the most protracted struggle between Coppola and the studio concerned the casting of Michael Corleone. Bob Evans recommended several popular actors of the time, among them Robert (*Sundance Kid*) Redford, Ryan (*Love Story*) O'Neal and a young Tommy Lee Jones. Roos also tested innumerable aspirants, including David Carradine, Dean Stockwell, Martin Sheen, James Caan and Robert De Niro. The studio kept telling Coppola that none of these actors fitted the character of Michael or, indeed, Sonny.

Coppola had encountered Pacino while preparing a screenplay that never saw the light of day. 'When I read the novel I saw his face in the role of Michael, I kept seeing his features.' He could discern in the thirty-year-old New Yorker the potential for menace that Puzo ascribes to the youngest son of the family in *The Godfather*: 'Michael was not tall or heavily built but his presence seemed to radiate danger.' Puzo refers to Michael's 'cold stare', to an 'anger that came off him like cold smoke off ice'. This attribute ultimately outweighed any need for Pacino to demonstrate an Ivy League classiness.

Pacino had enrolled in the Actors Studio in 1966. Two years later he won an Obie Award for his performance in the off-Broadway production *The Indian Wants the Bronx*. In 1969 he gained a Tony Award for *Does a Tiger Wear a Necktie?*, and the following year made his début on screen in *The Panic in Needle Park*, which was selected for the Cannes Film Festival. Pacino had always figured at the very top of Roos's casting worksheets. 'The studio didn't want him,' explains Roos. 'They

Diane Keaton as Kay Adams.

Al Pacino as Michael.

thought he was a shrimp, funny-looking, not attractive.' Roos and Coppola found an ally in Robert Duvall, cast as Tom Hagen. Duvall had seen Pacino perform on Broadway, and agreed that he would be 'terrific' as Michael.

Coppola insisted on testing Pacino over and over again, smuggling him in to play opposite different partners, and even unfurling a screen test that Pacino had done for some Italian film. 'It was his tenacity that got me in there,' agrees Pacino. When George Lucas's wife, Marcia, edited the various tests together, she told Coppola: 'Cast Pacino, because he addresses you with his eyes.' Stanley Jaffe grew bored as he sat in the screening room and watched one unknown actor after another strut his stuff. 'You guys really wanta know?' he exploded at one point. 'I think you got the worst bunch of lampshades I've ever seen!'

Al Ruddy claims some credit for the eventual decision to sign Pacino. 'I was with Bluhdorn one night and I said to him, "Charlie, sooner or later there's going to be a compromise on Michael. So why not take Al Pacino, he's perfect for the role, and everyone'll be happy." So Charlie agreed, and I called Francis in Paris with the news.'

So finally Evans had to relent. Coppola could have Pacino as Michael if James Caan could be Sonny in place of New York actor Carmen Caridi. Caan had starred in a few films such as Howard Hawks's *Red Line 7000* and *El Dorado* (opposite John Wayne); he came from a German-Jewish background, whereas Sonny in the book was described as an Italian bull, 'tall for a first-generation American of Italian parentage, almost six feet,

and his crop of bushy, curly hair made him look even taller'. Still, Caan at least was an actor Coppola liked; he had sustained the lead in the young director's previous picture, *The Rain People*, and he brought to the role a cocksure charisma that only a budding star could do. The unfortunate Caridi had already thrown a party for his family and friends, announcing that he had won the part of Sonny.

'I'm not even Italian,' admitted Caan, 'but I went to Brooklyn for several weeks and hung around with Italian guys, picking up their language and mannerisms. One guy always talked to everybody like you were across the room from him – even when he was sitting beside you. I used him as a model.' Caan would go home to dinner with his parents in the midst of shooting the film and say, 'Hey, ma, pass the fucking salt. Holy Jesus, what did I say? I'm sorry!'

Gordon Willis, the cinematographer, had been working in a commercials house when he met Aram Avakian, who asked him to light *The End of the Road*. When, at Coppola's suggestion, Willis received an approach from producer Al Ruddy, he did not like the project. But somehow a deal materialized, and Willis came aboard *The Godfather*. Although he and Francis would have furious arguments on and off set, Willis contributed the distinctive 'Kodachromey' look to the film and its sequels. The prowess of his work for Woody Allen gave Willis an exalted place among Hollywood cinematographers, and he did not join Coppola on any of his films apart from *The Godfather* trilogy. His operator on the original *Godfather*, Michael Chapman, later

James Caan as Sonny.

became a director of photography in his own right.

Meanwhile, the screenplay occupied a major portion of most days for Coppola. He would spend the morning whenever possible in the Caffè Trieste in San Francisco's North Beach, scribbling away at revisions. Puzo already felt respect for Francis, and accepted his suggestion that the two men work separately on the script. 'He rewrote one half and I rewrote the other,' recalled Puzo. 'Then we traded and rewrote each other's.'

Puzo's first draft, completed 10 August 1970, commences with shots of Michael and Kay driving off to the wedding and a cut to Sollozzo talking with Barzini, Tattaglia and then McCluskey. The final credit crawl would come up over a scene of Kay in church, lighting candles for the soul of Michael Corleone, although the last decisive scene shows Kay's realization of the truth as she sees Clemenza kissing 'Don' Michael's hand. This draft ran to 151 pages (as compared with about 120 pages for most two-hour films).

Puzo then added a new opening, involving an affectionate scene between Michael and Kay, followed by a courtroom sequence describing the case of Bonasera's assaulted daughter (the original novel's overture).

A 'Second Draft', signed by both Puzo and Coppola, was dated 1 March 1971 and ran to 173 pages. On 29 March there was a 'Third Draft,' also signed by both writers, although it had in fact been completed on 16 March. This version retains the final shot of Kay lighting thirty candles in a church. It also still includes the reunion scene between Michael

and Kay in a hotel room, chatting in bed after the outlaw's return from Sicily, preceded by a brief reunion with his father, in which Michael declares without preamble, 'I want to be your son.' In the actual film, the bedroom scene vanishes, replaced by an abrupt and sinister encounter outside Kay's school in (presumably) New Hampshire. 'It was done long after the rest of the picture had wrapped,' says Coppola today, 'when we discovered we needed a scene of that kind.'

In the Paramount offices on North Cañon Drive, studio executives also devoted hours to commentary on the emerging screenplay. Peter Bart sent a lengthy memo to Coppola (copied to Puzo, Ruddy and Bob Evans) on 19 January. Expressed in cordial if lethally precise language, the memo covered major themes and minor details alike.

'I think that everyone has worked so hard to include all the best plot elements of the novel,' wrote Bart, 'that the texture of the characters has suffered. Basically, we have too much dialogue relating to plot and to strategy and too little relating to character.' He complained that Michael seems 'strangely lacking in dimension. In the novel, one felt an inner conflict implicit in his personality [. . .] It was this inner ambivalence which created a sense of jeopardy for Michael since one really didn't know whether he would become the Godfather or whether he would successfully bring off the murder of McCluskey. Michael regarded himself as a math professor and not as a gangster.' There had to be some way, he continued, of restoring the ambivalence, and hence the vulnerability, in Michael's personality.

Bart urged the shedding of certain ballast

from the screenplay, such as 'six pages' from the wedding sequence, the scene of Hagen on the plane flying out to see Woltz in California and the character of Dr Taza in the Sicilian episode. Coppola seems to have acted on these recommendations, although he resisted Bart's objections to one now-famous line of dialogue: 'What does Michael mean,' asks Bart, 'when he says "That's my family, Kay, not me"? Doesn't he have an instinctive pride in his family?'

Reflecting the studio's anxiety that *The Godfather* might attract an 'R' rating from the MPAA – which it did – Bart finds Sonny's dialogue 'unnecessarily crude', and also points out that 'The word "balls" came into widespread use only in the last several years. Would the Godfather use such an expression in the 1940s?'

In the most telling of all his remarks, Bart asks, 'Is it ever really clear why Michael dumps Hagen?' This was something that Puzo and Coppola never satisfactorily resolved, and Duvall's sympathetic performance makes it all the more difficult to comprehend, even in *Part II*.

On 5 March, less than a month before the commencement of principal photography, Bob Evans sent a brisk memo to Coppola that indicated far less concern than Bart's for a restrictive rating: 'Feel that the character of Sonny is not nearly as flamboyant and exciting as the book. The sexuality that everyone remembers is totally missing in the script. I think the size of his cock and the horse's head are the two most remembered scenes from the book and the former is so lacking that I think we would be criticized for not doing more with Sonny.'

3 Coppola's Bible

'If the audience does not jump out of their seat on this one, you have failed' – Francis Coppola

On a flight from Los Angeles to Las Vegas that spring, Gray Frederickson sat next to Coppola. 'He showed me a huge spiral notebook in which he'd pasted pages from the book,' recalls Frederickson. '"This is what the movie should be," he said.' This massive tome, biblical in proportions, served as Coppola's vade-mecum throughout the making of *The Godfather*, and he did not circulate it among studio executives. It meant more to him than any formal version of the script. He began by cutting up a copy of the novel, and pasting pages down on each left-hand folio (except for pages he intended to omit from the screenplay, which were pasted in sequence with a bold, black marker pen line drawn across them). On the right-hand page he typed his detailed observations on each 'scene': what it involved, what should be avoided, what should be concentrated upon and how he would achieve this.

Coppola saw the film as a drama in five acts and fifty scenes, running to close on three hours. Act 1 would take audiences up to the end of the big meeting between Don Corleone and Sollozzo. Act 2 up to and including the murder of Sollozzo in the restaurant. Act 3 up to and including the gathering of the Dons. Act 4 up to and including the murder of Apollonia. Act 5 to the finale. He deleted certain characters from the start: Dr Jules Segal, the physician boyfriend of Lucy Mancini in Las Vegas; Felix Bocchicchio, 'who takes [the] rap for Michael Corleone in [the] Sollozzo and Police Captain McCluskey killing'; and the parents of Kay Adams.

Scene 1 – the wedding – would last sixteen

Go really big in this scene! Its one of the few opportunities to do so — it immediately says that this Big Book has been made into A BIG Movie, which in fact later on will look less so. the sheer enormity of the party also speaks of the Don's wealth, influence, and respect.

BOOK I · 19

"No, they're not," he said. "They're waiting to see my father in private. They have favors to ask." And indeed it was easy to see that all four men constantly followed the Don with their eyes.

As Don Corleone stood greeting guests, a black Chevrolet sedan came to a stop on the far side of the paved mall. Two men in the front seat pulled notebooks from their jackets and, with no attempt at concealment, jotted down license numbers of the other cars parked around the mall. Sonny turned to his father and said, "Those guys over there must be cops."

Don Corleone shrugged. "I don't own the street. They can do what they please."

Sonny's heavy Cupid face grew red with anger. "Those lousy bastards, they don't respect anything." He left the steps of the house and walked across the mall to where the black sedan was parked. He thrust his face angrily close to the face of the driver, who did not flinch but flapped open his wallet to show a green identification card. Sonny stepped back without saying a word. He spat so that the spittle hit the back door of the sedan and walked away. He was hoping the driver would get out of the sedan and come after him, on the mall, but nothing happened. When he reached the steps he said to his father, "Those guys are FBI men. They're taking down all the license numbers. Snotty bastards."

Don Corleone knew who they were. His closest and most intimate friends had been advised to attend the wedding in automobiles not their own. And though he disapproved of his son's foolish display of anger, the tantrum served a purpose. It would convince the interlopers that their presence was unexpected and unprepared for. So Don Corleone himself was not angry. He had long ago learned that society imposes insults that must be borne, comforted by the knowledge that in this world there comes a time when the most humble of men, if he keeps his eyes open, can take his revenge on the most powerful. It was this knowledge that prevented the Don from losing the humility all his friends admired in him.

But now in the garden behind the house, a four-piece band began to play. All the guests had arrived. Don Corleone put the intruders out of his mind and led his two sons to the wedding feast.

There were, now, hundreds of guests in the huge garden, some dancing on the wooden platform bedecked with flowers, others sitting at long tables piled high with spicy food and gallon jugs of

Sonny is a hot head.

Immediately the Don's character is juxtaposed with Sonny's

. FBI — Action. perhaps devise of juxaposing license numbers with Guests, etc as M. Tells Kay about them.

Hundreds of guests NICE

So really big in this scene

Extract from Coppola's 'bible', showing his comments on a page from Mario Puzo's novel. (Reproduced by courtesy of Francis Coppola.)

minutes and thirty seconds. In the finished film it runs more than twenty-six minutes. Coppola sketches the circumstances: 'My first concern is a sense of the times. The last Saturday in August 1945. The Japanese have just surrendered. The guests are relieved and anxious to enjoy themselves on what is probably the first big affair since the end of the war. Their sons are safe.'

Seeking as he does throughout this handbook to transcend mere detail, he notes that 'The first thing that interested me when I read [the novel] was the many levels going on at once . . .' For Coppola, the essential focus of this first scene is certainly on the Don. 'In all the business scenes in the Don's study, one must always see the party going on either through the windows or however; and during the singing and family and children and dancing and flirting, there must be evidence of the business tacitly present. Each is fused with the other: Family and Business; and this continues throughout the film.' He also reminds himself to check the *Oxford Companion to Music* to verify if Bonasera's story about the attack on his daughter is similar to the plot of *Rigoletto* . . . He notes some 'textures' to be included in the scene: 'fat, older man dancing with a ten-year-old girl in confirmation dress. Her little shoes on his big ones . . . Guest in an inappropriate tux, uncomfortable, adjusting it so he'll look just right'.

Coppola wanted to shoot the scene in which Tom Hagen flies to Hollywood on 'a real Constellation, with lots of vibration to suggest propeller-driven, and air-stream from ventilators playing with cigarette smoke'. In the overture to this scene, he wanted to fea-

ture one of Puzo's favourite lines: 'Remember, Tom, a lawyer with his briefcase can steal more than a hundred men with guns.' The line never appeared in the final film, nor even in *Part II* or *Part III*, much to Puzo's chagrin. ('But since then, my son and my nephew have become lawyers,' says Puzo wryly, 'so . . .')

There follows another detached 'aside', of the kind rarely found in screenplays: 'In a sense, this is an educational film. After seeing it, one should come out "knowing" lots of things about the Mafia, etc., terms, procedures, rationales, secrets. Not unlike *Airport*, in the sense that you are giving some "real workings" of something exotic.'

Scenes 4, 5 and 8 involved the movie mogul Jack Woltz, modelled on Harry Cohn, the late head of Columbia Pictures. 'Woltz must be plausible,' writes Coppola. 'As Hitchcock said, good villains make good movies. He is bigger than life, but we believe him, and see that he has other areas to him [. . .] The Don, like Italian men of this background and age, has let himself get old physically and sexually, whereas Woltz, a New World Jew, is lean and hard and young, and sexually anxious, and screwed up.'

The thirty-second-long Scene 8, in Woltz's bedroom, would be the first explosion of violence in *The Godfather*. Coppola reminded himself of the danger of falling short: 'If the audience does not jump out of their seat on this one, you have failed. Too much in the Corman horror film tradition would also be a big mistake.' To achieve the horror, he likes the idea of Woltz 'waking, and eventually feeling something wet. Then feel the wetness, and seeing it is blood, and he (and we) thinking it is his, then he quickly sits up, already in a level of terror from the blood on his hand, and sees the severed gory head of Khartoum. His scream should be enormous, and continuous for a long, long, hysterical time.'

Puzo's invention renders this scene beautifully in his novel, but he places the stallion's head at the foot of the bed, not inside the sheets. 'The shock of what he saw made him physically ill. It seemed as if a great sledgehammer had struck him on the chest, his heartbeat jumped erratically and he became nauseous. His vomit spluttered on the thick flair rug [. . .] Woltz was struck by a purely animal terror and out of that terror he screamed for his servants . . .'

Scene 9 brings Don Vito and Sollozzo together for the first and last time. Coppola: 'This scene should play like a poker game between the Cincinnati Kid [Steve McQueen] and the old man [Edward G. Robinson], with a couple of million dollars on the table.'

The second Act begins with Michael and Kay in the snow-covered streets of Manhattan. 'One of the first Christmases after the War,' writes Coppola. 'Store windows showing the "new Dior look".' He notes *Miracle on 34th Street* as a bench-mark.

Scene 13 describes the Don's shooting, and Coppola reminds himself of Hitchcock as an influence. The Don 'sees the men, and he makes the move: suddenly, and with a sprightliness we would never have imagined him capable of.' In the aftermath (Scene 14) Sonny takes over in the Family mall, 'rather like Alexander Haig at the White House [during the Reagan administration] ("I'm in charge here").' But he's 'someone competent, clicking into gear'. Sonny 'becomes the main character from here until his death. The more so, the better the shock when he is killed à la *Psycho*.'

Throughout the handbook, Coppola types out caveats for himself as a director. For example, in Scene 15 (between Sollozzo and Hagen), he writes: 'There is a lot of people reacting to bad news in this film, i.e. that someone they love is in danger or already dead. This is tough. Think about it. AND BE PREPARED, FRANCIS.'

He already estimates that Scene 17 – the murder of Paulie Gatto – will occupy two days of shooting. 'When Clemenza takes the leak it might be terrific if we stay on Clemenza and don't see the killing, but hear it while he actually takes the leak.' In the novel, Clemenza returns to the car after relieving himself, and then gives the order for Rocco to shoot the traitor.

The following sequence, Scene 18, lingers in most people's minds as a terrifying expression of Mafia violence, involving as it does the use of the garrotte in the murder of Luca Brasi. Coppola notes to himself: 'Find out what really happens when someone is strangled. Does the face actually turn colour? If so, it would be great if Brasi's face actually turned purple-black right in front of us.' This may have been written around the time when Coppola sent a memo (dated 22 January 1971) to his colleagues in the pre-production team: 'I hope to have very stunning and original effects WITHOUT the need of merely going further in blood and guts than has ever been done before. Sometimes a striking and

'It would be great if Brasi's face actually turned purple-black right in front of us.'

original detail, such as a shattered eyeglass or a bullet hole through the hand can be much more unsettling and moving, than a ton of innards and blood.' A. D. Flowers, the veteran special-effects maestro, would help Coppola to realize this palpable quality of violence.

The director's sound knowledge of world cinema peppers this 'ur-treatment' with useful references. In Scene 21, set in the hospital where the Don lies wounded, Coppola refers to Michael's conversation with him as being 'one-way', like the scene where Jack Nicholson talks to his paralysed father out in the fields in *Five Easy Pieces*. It's a scene 'in the best Hitchcock tradition', and then there is 'the almost dream-like view of the incidents after Michael is hit in the jaw [by McCluskey]'. In Scene 23, back in the Mall, Coppola wants to 'shoot like Bergman . . . Starting on one character, keeping other dialogue off-screen then move to the next, all round the circle.'

Act 3 belongs to Sonny Corleone. Throughout Scenes 29 to 33, Coppola enhances his character with little asides: 'Sonny's concern over his sister's well-being. Sonny's extreme vulnerability [when away from the Mall]'. When the would-be Don beats up his brother-in-law, 'We must really think that Sonny's going to kill Carlo [. . .] [It shows us how] exposed and close Sonny is to his own death.'

It was Coppola's idea that Connie should receive a phone call from some girl, to trigger her fury with Carlo, and then make a call to Mama Corleone in the kitchen, which in turn provokes Sonny to drive off in a rage. The murder at the tollbooths strikes Coppola as 'incredible overkill, as in [*Viva*] *Zapata*, they just riddle him, they can't afford that he survive'.

Scene 35 was estimated at a full ten minutes by Coppola, analysing as it does the political and psychological ramifications of Sollozzo's and McCluskey's death at the hands of Michael, followed by the assassination of Sonny. The Dons gather in a bank boardroom to discuss the crisis. 'One must feel the subtext in the room,' observes Coppola. 'Power and influence shifting, and being manipulated, quite underneath what is being said.'

Although as late as the summer of 1971 Paramount would still be asking Mario Puzo if shooting on location in Sicily was essential to the film's credibility, Coppola and his closest associates were prepared to go to the wire on the issue. In his handbook, the director notes that what needed to flow most of all from the opening Sicilian sequence (Scene 36) was 'a feeling of Sicily's rituals and roots'. Michael's broken jaw distorts his face, which Coppola describes as 'a visual symbol of his state (Dorian Gray)'.

When Michael finds himself confronted by the ravishing young Apollonia, he must sense 'a different kind of love from what he felt for Kay. THE DESIRE TO POSSESS'. He recommends using a sixteen-year-old, in the Stefania Sandrelli mould.

Scene 38 would demand four days of shooting, and would comprise Michael's Sunday call on Apollonia's family, the courtship and the wedding. 'I like the feeling that all of this – the courtship, the marriage – is the same as it might have been a thousand years ago.'

Coppola had already decided to eliminate dialogue from the wedding scene, confident that music could serve his purpose better.

News of Sonny's death filters through to Sicily and, in Scenes 39 and 40, 'places it in time; and, in a sense, puts Michael into the dilemma of needing to return. [. . .] I think [people will] be excited to know we're getting back to the main story.'

As the fifth and final Act begins, Coppola allows himself a quote from the novel that embodies the very core of the story: '[The Don's] ultimate aim is to enter that society with a certain power since society doesn't really protect its members who do not have their own individual power. In the meantime, he operates on a code of ethics he considers far superior to the legal structures of society.'

Scene 44 posed one of the most daunting hurdles for Coppola and Puzo. 'I'd like the scene with Mike and the Don,' wrote Francis, 'to really resolve their character dialectic. This is necessary, that they really have a good moment together, even if it's only something physical, where the family really accepts him as his son.' Only the skills of Robert Towne, an old friend from the time when Francis was directing his first feature film, *Dementia 13*, would free this scene from its marble block (see Chapter 5).

In Scene 46, the Don succumbs in his garden. 'This scene should be evocative of Sicily,' stresses Coppola, '– a sense of the Don's roots; a primeval feeling, almost on the verge of a fantasy.' He achieves exactly this mood in the film.

For Scene 47, the Don's funeral, Francis wanted to consult a newsreel film of Michael Luciano's funeral in Naples. It should be a truly 'royal' occasion. 'Don't stint with extras,' he warns himself. 'This is the counterpart to the opening of the film.'

Recognizing that the baptism and Michael's 'big move' against his enemies would require some seven days of shooting, Coppola notes: 'This sequence must be very carefully designed and planned. It must take away the audience's breath in its fury.' Mario Puzo recalls that 'When I got to the end [of the screenplay] I couldn't solve the difficulty of how to deal with the christening, and all the murders that Michael had ordered. "So why don't we combine them?" said Francis, and I clapped my hands and felt embarrassed that I hadn't thought of that perfect solution.'

Scene 49 would become the final scene of the film, in which Kay challenges Michael to admit he gave the order to kill her brother-in-law, Carlo, and then from the kitchen witnesses Clemenza's kissing of Michael's hand in fealty. 'After Kay asks if it is all true,' maintains Coppola, 'there must be a very telling moment between Kay and Michael. *They must really make eye contact*, she is really asking him. And then, coolly and convincingly – he lies.'

Scene 50 portrayed Kay in church, lighting candles as the credits roll up. It should not, writes Coppola, 'be a religious thing. And it's really not. It's clutching at straws or recognition of evil.'

This momentous document demonstrates that *The Godfather*, although a magnificent product of the Hollywood studio system, depends for its intensity, its richness of characterization, and its wealth of incident, on the vision of one man – Francis Ford Coppola. The finished film adheres in spirit as well as detail to the outline adumbrated by him in his handbook. Its authenticity is attested to by colleagues, and it resides in the American Zoetrope Research Library in Rutherford, Coppola's home in the Napa Valley. If ever proof were needed that auteurist theory – and practice – was alive and well in North America in 1971, this hefty volume provides it.

4 Coming to Terms with the Mafia

In February 1971 Bob Evans declared in an interview that he wanted 'to cut directors down to size', and to be involved in all the major aspects of production. Despite this, Francis Coppola pressed ahead with his own agenda, commuting from his offices at 827 Folsom Street, San Francisco, to the Paramount production building at 202 North Cañon Drive in Beverly Hills.

Casting continued apace and Francis kept a special eye on Marlon Brando, who was away in England filming *The Nightcomers* for producer Jay Kanter and director Michael Winner. A postal strike in the UK made communications difficult. Francis wrote to Brando telling him that he hoped to be in Britain on or about 15 February. Brando wrote a reply by hand on azure paper from the University Arms in Cambridge, saying he was anxious about the need to *prepare*, but that he looked forward to working with Francis. Back came the response from the West Coast assuring him that there would be some two weeks for preparation.

Coppola travelled to Europe to visit Brando. 'We had given Marlon tapes of Valachi and those guys testifying,' recalls Fred Roos, who also came to England. 'Well, as we walked into the house where he was staying, we heard this voice talking like Genovese or one of those Mafia chieftains. Marlon was in the tub, practising his voice and his speech, after studying the tapes we'd sent him.'

Back home, Coppola worked on Al Ruddy to raise the budget for *The Godfather*. The studio still considered it unreasonably expensive to shoot on real streets in New York, let alone Sicily, but by the sheer force of his will, and his selling skills in the front office, Coppola managed to persuade Paramount to inch ever upwards, to a ceiling of $6 million (the final cost was $6.2 million). Although Coppola dealt with executives at the level of Bob Evans, Peter Bart and Al Ruddy, the real judgements fell to Charlie Bluhdorn, Chairman of Gulf + Western. Bluhdorn flew to the West Coast on frequent occasions, but more often than not, crucial decisions concerning *The Godfather* were made in the corporate headquarters on Columbus Circle in Manhattan. There, Bluhdorn had erected a slender, elegant skyscraper. An architectural fault caused it to sway in high winds and private screenings often had to be abandoned during a storm. Peter Bart remembers accompanying Coppola in an elevator to Bluhdorn's suite on the 33rd floor, 'for yet another of those horrendous meetings', when significant scratching could be heard as the car scraped against one side or the other. 'It's Charlie's breath,' laughed Coppola, 'creating sparks for us!'

Stanley Jaffe, humiliated by Bluhdorn's anointing of Brando as the Don, quit as president of Paramount that spring, although he soldiered on until August, grooming his successor Frank Yablans, who, when asked if any of his family had been in show business, admitted, 'My father was a cab-driver, and they're all comics.'

Dean Tavoularis had allied with Coppola in pressing the studio for the money to shoot in New York. He pointed out that buildings on the studio back lot reached only three storeys. He demanded at least five, and so Evans agreed to let Ruddy have a further $1

million for shooting in New York.

In early March, Coppola and his family moved into a two-bedroom apartment in Manhattan, his two sons sleeping in one room, and he and his wife Eleanor in the other. 'I was seven months pregnant,' says Eleanor, 'and we had to get a place in New York, and we really tried to save money because we had all these debts. I took an apartment that belonged to our brother-in-law, David Shire, sort of his bachelor pad. It was like a total nightmare, in this tiny apartment with two kids, and me pregnant. The kids got chicken-pox, and the apartment needed repainting. It was living hell. And it seemed like Francis was going to get fired, so we didn't want to sign some lease for some fancy apartment.'

A further complication arose when Al Pacino was signed to make *The Gang That Couldn't Shoot Straight* for MGM. Exasperated, and furious that his own prevarication over Pacino had brought about this situation, Bob Evans asked Sidney Korshak, his friend and mentor, to call billionaire Kirk Kerkorian to solve the situation. Kerkorian, not for the last time the owner of MGM, saw to it instantly that Pacino would be available to shoot *The Godfather*.

Not that Pacino became rich overnight. The budget ceiling of $6 million meant, according to Evans, that no actor could be paid more than $35,000 (probably around $175,000 in today's money). James Caan also received $35,000, and Robert Duvall's fee amounted to $36,000. Diane Keaton earned only $6,000 for her role in the first *Godfather*, while Talia Shire's contract brought her a

Richard Castellano (at left), the highest-paid actor on *The Godfather*.

mere $1,500. Initially, Pacino had the longest contract (sixteen weeks), and Brando one of the shortest, at just six weeks (14 April–21 May), although Gianni Russo as Carlo upstaged them all by being on call for seventeen weeks – at $1,000 a week. The highest-paid actor on *The Godfather* was none other than Richard Castellano who had impressed the industry with his performance in *Lovers and Other Strangers*. For the role of Clemenza, involving twelve weeks' work, he received $50,000. On the day the cameras began turning (23 March 1971), Coppola himself was due $35,000 from the studio against his $125,000 fee.

That final month of pre-production, however, acquired nightmarish overtones for everyone involved with *The Godfather*.

While Mario Puzo himself suffered no harassment from the Mafia, he warned Coppola that he might be approached by its members, 'because in a way they're fans too, and they want to be your friend and hang out, and it's not a good idea because sooner or later they'll feel close enough to you to ask you to do something.' His advice to Coppola was to be friendly and pleasant to such individuals, while refraining from any kind of social contact. Otherwise he would be sucked into their world, which, of course, was their intention.

Bob Evans's son was born that spring, and one day he received a personal call: ' "Get out of fuckin' town, or your kid won't be alive." I said, "I'm not the producer, try Al Ruddy." And this voice said, "When you wanna kill something, you go for the head." '

On 20 March 1971 the studio's fears materialized when a ponderous letter (leaked to the press) arrived from one P. Vincent Landi, 'Grand Venerable of the Grand Lodge of the State of New York, Order Sons of Italy in America':

At the request of the Grand Council of the Grand Lodge of the State of New York, Order Sons of Italy in America, representing ninety-eight lodges throughout the State of New York, I am communicating with you to express our opinion concerning the novel known as 'The Godfather', and the possible production of the motion picture based on the said novel.

A reading of 'The Godfather', by Mario Puzo, leaves one with a sickening feeling that a great deal of effort and labour to eliminate a false image concerning Americans of Italian descent and also an ethnic connotation to organized crime has been wasted.

In our opinion, the book is a cruel hoax, and unfairly stigmatizes all Americans of Italian descent [. . .]

The letter proposed that instead there could be 'constructive and intelligent movies' made from the lives of Enrico Fermi, the great scientist; Mother Cabrini; Gianinni [sic]; Colonel Ceslona, a hero of the Civil War; Garibaldi,

the great Italian who unified Italy; William Paca, a signer of the Declaration of Independence; Guglielmo Marconi; and many, many others. (Coppola later took his revenge by having G. D. Spradlin pronounce a very similarly worded protest at the Senate hearings in *The Godfather Part II*.)

The Grand Venerable then outlined the 'suggestions' that the Gabriele d'Annunzio Lodge had adopted by unanimous vote:

(1) Economic boycott of the picture;
(2) Petitions of protest from all of our lodges;
(3) Regional meetings of protest;
(4) The filing of a complaint with the Human Rights Commission;
(5) No cooperation should be granted the producers of this picture by any governmental authority;
(6) A communication of protest to the producers of the motion picture.

The letter landed on the desk of numerous elected officials in national government. Almost at once, Paramount felt the pressure in small, niggling ways. Gray Frederickson recalls, for example, that the crew had started construction in a location on Long Island when suddenly the homeowners stopped them, 'and I think that was from pressure from the Italian [-American] League'.

Executives now recalled that during the autumn of 1970, the League had staged a huge rally in Madison Square Garden, starring Frank Sinatra. The gathering raised some $600,000 for the express purpose of stopping the filming of *The Godfather*.

Al Ruddy received a score of abusive phone calls, and decided to keep a .45 automatic in his desk drawer. 'I didn't know whether the calls were coming from the Mafia or not. But they threatened my life. It was disconcerting. I told the local police, and they also informed me that I was being followed by unknown persons.' Each night Ruddy and four of his colleagues at Paramount would switch cars to throw their tails off the scent. One morning Ruddy's secretary awoke to find that the side windows of her car had been blown out by a shotgun blast.

Despite this ominous atmosphere, Ruddy adopted a calm, rational aproach to the problem. Through intermediaries, he made contact with one of the heads of the 'five Families', Joseph Colombo Sr, who was gunned down by rivals in Columbus Circle three months later – just yards from the Gulf + Western corporate skyscraper, and only a few blocks away from the St Regis Hotel, where Coppola was filming *The Godfather* at the time.

The initial parleys took place with Colombo's son, Anthony, at midtown restaurants such as La Scala on West 54th Street. Ruddy, always an enthusiastic man and now confident of striking a deal, agreed to see the Mafia boss at the Park Sheraton Hotel.

To his chagrin, he found himself confronted by an angry assembly of some 600 delegates of the Italian-American Civil Rights League. 'I couldn't care less if [the studio] gave us $2 million,' intoned Joe Colombo. 'No one can buy the right to defame Italian-Americans.' Ruddy responded by saying that the film would concern individuals and would not denigrate or stereotype any one group. Suddenly he realized that the delegates wanted to feature in the picture, and when he began pointing out certain members of the audience at random, indicating that they might be bit players or extras, the crowd broke into cheering. By the time he left that evening, Ruddy was the proud and relieved bearer of a lapel pin designating him a Captain in the League.

'I explained to Joe Colombo that no one had seen the script,' recalls Ruddy, 'but that if he came along to my office the next day I would gladly show him a copy. So he duly arrived with a couple of his guys. Now the script was over 150 pages long, and neither Colombo nor his companions seemed inclined to settle down and read it from cover to cover. "All right," said Colombo. "I trust you, I believe what you're telling us."'

Ruddy immediately issued assurances that 'in place of the words "Mafia" and "Cosa Nostra", the crime syndicate will be referred to in the film as "the five Families" and other non-Italian phrases.' As the term 'Mafia' and 'Cosa Nostra' never figured in the original screenplay, Ruddy appears to have bought off his opponents for the price of a charity première, proceeds for which would be earmarked for a hospital owned by the Italian-American Civil Rights League. Such derogatory terms as 'greaseball' and 'gombah' would not be mentioned in the film, he promised. But they were, in fact. By the time *Part II* came to be shot, any threat of disruption from the Mafia had evaporated, and Coppola and Puzo were able to refer to the 'Cosa Nostra' (literally, 'Our World', implying traditions and values) and the 'Black Hand' (a euphemism for gangsters or racketeers up to the Prohibition era).

'Yet even after I made the deal,' Ruddy said in 1972, 'some League members wanted us to drop Italian surnames and use names like Smith and Jones and Johnson.'

The day after Ruddy's declaration, the *New York Times* ran a front-page article claiming that the Mafia was muscling in at Gulf + Western. The major TV networks repeated the story, and G + W stock lurched on the stock exchange. Charlie Bluhdorn broke into one of his hysterical fits. Summoning Ruddy to his office, he accused him of 'ruining my company'.

'Charlie,' retorted the younger man, 'I'm not in the business of protecting the price of your stock. My job is to make this movie. Now if you want me to quit I'll do so, I've got my points, and I'm the producer of the film.' Bluhdorn fired him without a moment's hesitation. 'I was so pissed off that I took some of his expensive cigars as I left the office,' remembers Ruddy. 'Bob Evans called me from the Bahamas the next day: "Not only did you insult Bluhdorn, but you stole some of his cigars too!"'

Soon afterwards the Gulf + Western honcho calmed down and reinstated Ruddy. 'But one more line in the press,' Bluhdorn warned Ruddy as he reinstated him as producer, 'and I'll kill you!'

Not all Italian-Americans sided with the League. New York State Senator John J. Marchi, Republican of Staten Island, attacked the League's efforts to expunge the terms 'Mafia' and 'Cosa Nostra'. He wrote to Ruddy: 'Apparently you are a ready market for the league's preposterous theory that we can exorcize devils by reading them out of the English language.'

In the wake of this brouhaha, Paramount disavowed the idea of a charity première. Joe Colombo, accepting that Ruddy had acted in good faith, called him and said, 'You've tried to do everything you could, and we're going to support you.' Ruddy managed to arrange a secret screening for Colombo and his pals just prior to the film's release. 'They *loved* the picture,' recalls Ruddy. Even so, the Italian-American League protested at not receiving the $100,000 that the New York première raised for the New York Boys' Club. This was due, the League felt, because it had 'helped' Ruddy and Paramount to obtain locations in Sheepshead Bay and on Staten Island.

At least the production could now proceed without undue hindrance. Having the co-operation of what Ruddy diplomatically termed 'Syndicate men' avoided problems during the shoot in New York. 'There would have been pickets, breakdowns, labour problems, cut cables, all kinds of things. I don't think anyone would have been physically hurt. But the picture simply could not have been made without their approval,' said the producer.

On 29 March 1971 *The Godfather* launched into principal photography, although a second unit had been out one day the previous week to take advantage of falling snow in Manhattan. Dean Tavoularis had worked overtime to prepare the sets. De Soto taxis of 1941 to 1950 vintage had to be found for the Mott Street scenes. Best & Co.'s store in Manhattan needed re-dressing, circa 1946, for the sake of authenticity. Studio work took place on a cramped, tiny stage at the

Artificial snow for the first day's shooting on *The Godfather*.

Filmways Studio way up on 127th Street. 'It was a very seedy area,' recalls Tavoularis, 'and the studio no longer exists.'

Building the Don's 'den' offered a challenge to Tavoularis. 'Here was this place,' he says, 'which was beyond just a room, but a symbolic thing, kind of sticky pink, with sticky flowers and dark panelling. Kind of like a church. When you come out of a church you feel a bit more alive.'

'The main idea,' according to the designer, 'was that they would have this shuttered light and the party would be going on outside and you could hear it via the soundtrack and that on one side was the wedding, which was in bright sunlight, and then inside people would be coming to the Don and asking for favours.'

By way of a rehearsal, Coppola had invited the cast to enjoy an Italian meal in a private room at Patsy's restaurant in New York. 'Brando sat at the head of the table,' the director recalls, 'and there was Al Pacino and Bobby Duvall and Jimmy Caan; and my sister Talia served the pasta. I was not sitting at that table, but gradually it lightened up, and they got to know each other. It was like playing at a family, a kind of sensual opportunity for them to relate to each other.' Next day they did a reading of the screenplay.

'I remember the first time Brando came on the film,' laughs Al Ruddy today. 'Duvall and Caan and Pacino were horsing around and

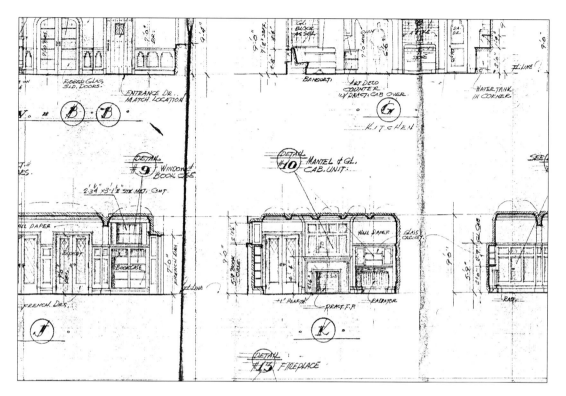

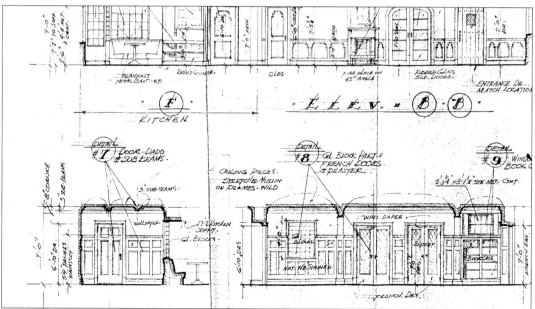

Detail from the architectural plans drawn up by Dean Tavoularis for the Don's home in Long Beach.

Don Corleone's 'den' as designed by Dean Tavoularis.

joking, and suddenly Brando walks in, and they just turned to ice. It was as though Christ had come down from the Cross. That's how much he was held in awe.'

5 Filming in New York

'Political power grows out of the barrel of a gun' – Mao Zedong

A plot to oust Francis Coppola from the director's chair began germinating during the very first days of principal photography.

The confusion of even the first day's shooting contributed to the tension and anxiety on the part of Paramount executives. Snow flurries did not fall as everyone had hoped, and snow-blowing machines were called into play. Coppola also filmed the shots outside Radio City Music Hall, as Michael and Kay chat and then learn from a newspaper headline of the attempt on the Don's life. The front-of-house neon at Radio City featured *The Bells of St Mary's* (which really had been screening there in December 1945), and ushers from the theatre informed what patrons they could that Elaine May's *A New Leaf* was showing inside that day. Finally, before the crew wrapped at 2 a.m., some filming was done on the corner of Fifth Avenue and Thirty-first Street.

As the rushes from the first days of shooting began to unfurl on the thirty-third floor of the Gulf + Western Building in Manhattan, and then, a day later, in the screening room at the rear of 202 North Cañon Drive in Beverly Hills, the whispering campaign against Coppola gathered momentum. Bob Evans, unable to attend the shooting in person, sent Jack Ballard to New York to oversee operations on behalf of the studio. Ballard, then an executive production manager, was promoted to Vice-president by Evans in August 1971. Mario Puzo had appraised him as 'a Yul Brynner-headed guy who keeps track of production costs on a movie. Self-effacing, but producers and directors shook in their boots when he totalled tabs on their costs.'

'From day one,' recalls Coppola, 'this guy

Ballard had been my hawk, and he wanted me off the picture so that he could take over. As did my friend, Aram Avakian, who was editing it.' Bob Evans concedes that there were rumblings afoot, but maintains that 'Avakian and Steve Keston tried to get Francis thrown off so that Steve Keston would become the producer and Avakian would direct it. They went to Al Ruddy and Ruddy came to me and suggested it.' As Peter Bart comments, 'Francis at that time was impoverished, very insecure, and very neurotic.'

Avakian's argument focused on Coppola's inability to think in terms of continuity; he conceded that he 'could get great performances from his actors' but claimed to Tavoularis and others that the picture would be essentially uncuttable if Coppola were to pursue his current methods. '[Avakian] wanted to present himself as the director,' recalls Tavoularis, 'and of course he'd just directed a film [*The End of the Road*].'

Gordon Willis, while in no way a part of the conspiracy to dismiss Coppola despite serving as Avakian's director of photography on *The End of the Road*, had several fights with the director on set. 'I wasn't the most beloved person on this movie,' he admits with hindsight. 'I was very dogmatic, and argued many times with Francis. If there *was* tension between us [in the early weeks] it was because of what I perceived as Francis's lack of discipline, his wanting to fly off and do something else, when I have a more contained and specific kind of thinking. We went from hot to cold, and cold to hot [. . .] I'm sure that he thought he was locked in a room with Attila the Hun at some junctures! There's a film

school part of Francis that he won't give up, whereas I like to cut to the chase – no nonsense. But I'll always be grateful to Francis. Underneath it all he was very, very good [as a director].'

After the first week, Coppola recognized that he was 'in deep trouble, because the studio felt the rushes weren't good enough; they were too dark'. In his view, these were not bad scenes: Michael and Kay in front of Best & Co. in New York, and Tom Hagen being picked up by Sollozzo on the street, and Sollozzo meeting with Don Vito to talk about his drugs plans, and Sonny sounding off, and then the scene in which Michael shoots Sollozzo in the restaurant. 'All the top Paramount folk felt that Brando was not as impressive as he had been in his test.'

Eleanor Coppola remembers that 'Right from the beginning the studio was unhappy, saying the picture was too dark . . . And Francis was sleeping on Jimmy Caan's couch in L.A. and going to the Knicks. He was staying there to save his per diem instead of going to a hotel because there was still no inkling that the film would be a success.'

Tom Luddy, now a producer at American Zoetrope and then in the throes of founding the Pacific Film Archive in Berkeley, recalls visiting New York, emerging from a subway station and literally bumping into Coppola, who was already a friend. 'Francis told me how he had been taking a crap, and overheard members of the crew saying that perhaps they could get rid of this director. So he knew that a plot was being hatched against him.'

Peter Bart regards the first days of shooting as 'dismal. I never felt that Jack Ballard was out to get Francis. It was clear that there was a loss of confidence in him, and clear that Aram Avakian was manœuvring in that way. Most of the [footage] was useless, and was so dark that I kept thinking I'd brought my sunglasses into the screening room!' Also involved in the lobby to oust Coppola was Steve Keston, 'rather a noisy and aggressive chap', recalls Bart, who had produced *The End of the Road* and had been signed up as an assistant director on *The Godfather* as a favour to Avakian.

'There was general alarm about Francis,' continues Bart. 'He was coming off *Finian's Rainbow*, he had no track record, and had never done anything like [*The Godfather*].

And his main advocate, namely me, was in Los Angeles. Because I was involved in the other pictures we were doing, perhaps foolishly I did not go to New York. Bob Evans was in L.A. too.'

On the morning of 12 April, panic swept through the crew when Marlon Brando failed to appear for his 8 a.m. call on his first day of shooting. He had missed the overnight plane from Los Angeles, and finally arrived at 2 p.m., too late for any photography to be done that afternoon. Dick Smith, the legendary make-up specialist (*Little Big Man*), knew that he would need two to three hours just to fix Brando's face. He had created a thin steel bar denture, which would be placed in front of the

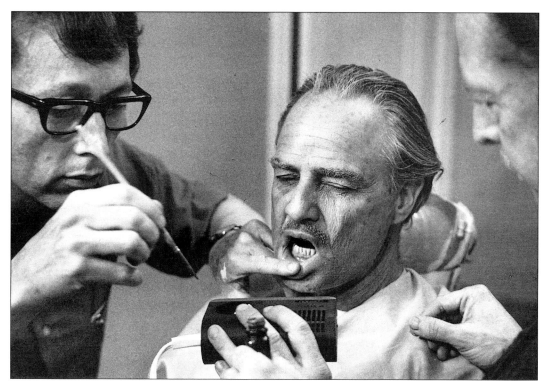

Marlon Brando being prepared by make-up consultant Philip Rhodes for his role as Don Corleone.

actor's lower teeth and near the gum-line, stretching right round to his molars where it was clipped in place. Attached to this were a couple of resin blobs to bulge out his cheeks. 'On the first day we spent hours trying to reshape them,' says Smith, 'and I kept tinkering with them all through the first week, gradually reducing the bulginess of the resin pads.' This explains Brando's bulldog look in early scenes and his less puffy expression in the final scenes with Pacino and his grandson.

The studio's suspicions increased when Bob Evans saw Brando mumbling away in the first rushes. He called Al Ruddy: 'What the fuck's going on? Are we going to put subtitles on this movie?'

By 15 April production was falling behind at an average of two days a week. According to one eyewitness, 'It is the general opinion of the crew that Coppola is overcovering scenes by shooting many more takes than necessary.'

For Coppola, the only person 'who was nice to me was Gray Frederickson, who took me aside and virtually told me that they were going to fire me. Now they didn't want to let me go in midweek, because if you did that you lost two days. Much better to fire someone at the weekend. They didn't want me to reshoot any scenes, because they'd have double expense if my replacement was going to shoot them anyway. So on the Thursday I fired Avakian and Steve Keston and then I went and reshot the scenes with Brando myself.' Bob Evans confirms that he authorized the dismissal of Avakian 'and his coterie of production assistants'. He also ordered Jack Ballard back to the West Coast. He did so in the wake of a session in his private

screening room during the third weekend of April with editor Peter Zinner, when they viewed a dozen reels of material, and decided that what they were watching 'was not just good, but brilliant'.

Word had also reached Coppola that Elia Kazan had been approached to replace him, given his skill at directing violence in pictures such as *On the Waterfront* and *Viva Zapata!*. 'I kept dreaming that Kazan would arrive on the set and would say to me, "Uh, Francis, I've been asked to . . ." But Marlon, who knew about this, was very supportive, and said he would not continue to work on the film if I was fired.' Brando confirms this in his autobiography: 'At one point Charles Bluhdorn threatened to fire Francis Coppola – I don't remember why – but I said, "If you fire Francis, I'll walk off the picture." I strongly believe that directors are entitled to independence and freedom to realize their vision.'

When Bart heard that Kazan's agent had been contacted, he grew anxious, and was delighted when highly regarded production designer Richard Sylbert told him that he had been speaking to Kazan on the phone and thought he was semi-senile, way past his prime. Bart ushered Dick Sylbert into Bob Evans's office and casually asked him to repeat his comments. 'Bob, ever-tanned, looked a little pale,' smiles Bart, 'and so that slowed down the Kazan bandwagon.'

Coppola directed with particular relish the scene when Carlo and Connie quarrel and all the dishes are smashed. 'At the end of the day,' recalls Fred Roos, 'two people supported Francis: Peter Bart and Gray Frederickson.' And it was Frederickson who found himself having to mediate between Ruddy and Coppola when tempers were at their most frayed.

On 19 April Gray Frederickson compiled a revised schedule for producer Al Ruddy. There would be sixty-four camera days, starting Tuesday 23 March in New York and ending in Sicily on Saturday 17 July. Dubbing was due to commence on Monday 11 October, the first preview would be held on Friday 5 November, a final answer print would be to hand on Friday 10 December, and *The Godfather* would be released on Friday 17 December.

Dean Tavoularis remembers being bemused when, after a few weeks' shooting, Coppola asked him and Gordon Willis to go through the script with him. 'I'll tell you my ideas, and we can talk about everything,' said the director. 'We went to his apartment,' recalls Tavoularis, 'and sat down, and he had a court reporter taking down everything we said, which rather surprised me. And we took the script, and started at page one, and Francis talks about how he sees the film, the style of the picture, the tableaux; "don't let's shoot like this, shoot like that . . .".' Although he trusted Willis and Tavoularis, Coppola had clearly inhaled the general air of paranoia on the film.

Mario Puzo remained blithely unaware of these developments, for in March he had discharged himself from Duke University's dietary clinic for weight control in Durham, North Carolina, and taken a plane to his favourite gambling mecca, Las Vegas.

Al Pacino had sprained his ankle while jumping on to the running board of the getaway car after dashing from the scene of Sollozzo's murder, and had to limp around on crutches. And nearly every scene posed a challenge to the crew. When make-up man Dick Smith used a stuffed horse's head prepared by a local taxidermist for the scene in Woltz's bedroom, it looked false. 'So we ordered [a real] one that would be slaughtered the night before being delivered, packed in dry ice, to the set. Well, it arrived, and we used Karo corn syrup, which, when mixed with red food colouring, creates realistic-looking blood. We started with the blood around John Marley's ankles in these golden-yellow sheets. After each take I had to spray water on the syrup to stop it clinging to the actor. By the time Francis had finished about a dozen takes, the bedclothes were a sea of blood. I was glad I'd started with such a small quantity!' The next day a rumour swept the crew that the unfortunate horse (which had been due to be slaughtered for pet food) had been suffering from encephalitis. 'Luckily it was untrue,' laughs Dick Smith, 'but there were some scary moments.'

Smith's ingenuity came to the rescue in the scene of Luca Brasi's murder. 'For the knife that pins Brasi's hand to the bar, the prop man presented me with a cut-off blade embedded in a heavy, rectangular plate of brass,' he remembers. 'It was difficult to manœuvre; I'd have made it of plastic, but anyway, I worked away as well as I could, applying it to Lenny Montana's hand with mortician's wax. Lenny had to keep his hand absolutely still. One false move and the knife might well have fallen away from his hand. But he was terrific. He'd been a wrestler and knew how to hold his breath, and thus fill his head with blood.

We'd tried spraying his face with a mist of dye that would turn purplish, but it just wasn't as convincing as his own effort.'

The murder of Sonny at the tollbooths takes place in the novel on the Jones Beach Causeway, on the road out to Long Beach. Although Coppola managed to do the scene in a single take, the preparations exacted a mighty price ($100,000) and three days (20–22 June). For Dean Tavoularis, it rekindled memories of the bloody finale of *Bonnie and Clyde*, on which he had worked as art director. On a runway at Floyd Bennett airfield, the special-effects crew devoted their attentions to a well-preserved 1941 Lincoln Continental. 'We riddled [it] with bullet holes,' said Ruddy. 'Before the scene we bored 200 separate holes into the car. Each hole was puttied over, painted, then filled with an explosive charge that could be touched off by remote control. And it took about two hours for special-effects man A. D. Flowers and make-up man Dick Smith to rig Jimmy [Caan] for the scene – he was sort of a walking bomb.' More than a hundred brass casings containing gunpower squibs and sacs of blood were deployed on Caan's body, face and hair. Some were attached by hidden wires, and would be 'exploded' by technicians out of camera range. Others were controlled by electric wires that ran up the actor's legs to a cable concealed behind his back, and from there to an electrical console. 'When those guys started firing the tommy-guns,' said Caan, 'a special-effects man at the console began hitting the buttons fast; each one touched off a little explosion that made it look as if bullets were ripping into me.

Simultaneously, other men pulled the very fine wires that popped pellets on my face and head.'

Dick Smith had been asked by Coppola and his associates to set at least half a dozen explosions on Caan's face. 'I put one on his forehead,' says Smith, 'but I felt it risky to place squibs below a person's eyes, so instead I did some delicate little blisters (each the size of a bullet), which could be triggered by monofilament discs. Only one day had been allowed for this scene, and by about 2 or 3 p.m. I'd managed to put in place the set of squibs and facial blisters. But the light was failing, and so they scrapped the close-up that would have incorporated my work!'

The constant upheaval of moving from one location to another – 120 in the New York area alone – added to the pressures on director and crew alike. One day they would be in the boardroom of the Penn Central Railroad, high up on the 32nd floor above Grand Central Station, for the meeting of all the Dons. Another day would be spent in the Hotel Edison on 46th Street near Times Square, where Luca Brasi meets his end. Then it would be the New York Eye and Ear Hospital on East 14th Street for the interior hospital scenes when Don Vito is protected by Michael. Or the Bellevue Morgue, on First Avenue and 29th Street, for the scene in which the Don brings Sonny's shattered corpse to Bonasera's funeral parlour. At the 118th Street and Pleasant Avenue location where Sonny batters Carlo into submission, representatives of the Italian-American League armed with sawn-off broom handles conveniently controlled the crowds of onlookers. Such crowds needed superintendence, and one early morning scene shot on Wall Street drew an estimated 15,000 throng, and created traffic chaos.

Other locations included the Old St Patrick's Cathedral on Mulberry Street for the climactic christening sequence, the Guggenheim Estate at Sands Point, Long Island, for the scenes at Woltz's mansion, and Staten Island for the wedding sequence.

As manifested in the finished film, this wedding celebration reflected a buoyant Coppola at his confident best. A wealth of detail enriches the sequence with authenticity, whether it be Clemenza dancing the *tarantella*, or Connie slyly slipping cash-filled envelopes from the guests into her immense silk purse. Eleanor Coppola mentions 'the two characters who are throwing these kind of sandwiches back and forth, and that's something [Francis] remembers as a child – throwing these football wedding sandwiches as they were called. They would be prosciutto on a roll wrapped up in some wax paper, and they would like to throw them across the room to each other.'

Lighter moments, most involving Marlon Brando, relieved the tension. When the Don is brought home from hospital, the family has to carry him upstairs on a stretcher. As the shot was being prepared, Brando asked the cameraman to give him 300 pounds of lead

Al Martino as Johnny Fontane and Talia Shire as Connie.

weights. These he hid beneath his blankets, which raised the weight of the stretcher to some 500 pounds. 'My family started carrying me up the stairs,' writes Brando, 'but they couldn't make it; they were strong, but before long they were wringing with sweat, huffing and puffing and unable to get up the stairs [. . .] After five or six takes, I raised the blanket and showed them the lead weights.' The star joined with Duvall and Caan in 'mooning' at embarrassing moments – dropping his trousers and turning his back on whoever happened to be looking.

Brando, for so long despised by the Hollywood establishment during the 1960s, found himself an object of adulation in the streets of Manhattan. The citizens of Little Italy turned out in droves to watch every moment of the shooting on Mott Street, where the screenplay called for Don Vito to be shot while coming out of a fruit store. 'When he fell to the street,' said Ruddy, 'there were gasps from the crowd and a horrified silence. When Marlon stood up after Coppola yelled "Cut!" the crowd cheered – and Brando made a low, sweeping bow. He loved the people on Mott Street and they loved him.'

Gray Frederickson summons up the moment when he, as Associate Producer, first believed that the film would be great. 'I saw the dailies of the scene when Marlon visits the undertaker and views Caan's body. It sent chills down my spine, and when I heard [Bob] Evans complaining that Francis couldn't even get a decent performance out of Brando in that scene, I wondered why these guys couldn't see the light.'

Brando's flair for improvisation also improved what would be the opening scene of the film, as the Don listens to Bonasera's

Family visit: Francis Coppola, his mother Italia, his sister Talia and his father Carmine, during the shooting of *The Godfather.*

Marlon Brando enjoying the role of his life
between takes on *The Godfather*.

plea for justice. During rehearsals, a stray cat had been discovered in the studio, and Coppola put it in Brando's hands without warning, so he could caress it on his lap as the camera was running. Al Ruddy remembers the cat purring so loudly that Brando's words were indistinguishable on the sound tapes. But the presence of the feline adds an immediate dimension to the Don's character, and a symbolic sense of the claws beneath an amiable exterior. Salvatore Corsitto, the actor playing Bonasera, had been tested by Coppola for the role of the Don. He struck the director as such an arresting actor that he gave him the part of Bonasera, which he knew would set the tone of the entire film.

This scene was harder to set up than it appears in the film. Gordon Willis attached a

computerized zoom to the BNC Mitchell reflex camera. 'You could programme it to run, say, twenty seconds, or thirty seconds. No other zoom was used in the picture, but this one had to be.' Willis had determined that *The Godfather* should be 'brown and black in feeling'. He intended to stretch the limits of what could and could not be seen by using an inky blue-black with a translucent quality that should be 'read'. This was achieved by underexposing the negative and allowing the lab very little latitude in printing the release. 'It should look like a newspaper photograph in bad colour,' said Willis. He and his crew used Eastmancolor negative, but Willis 'wanted a retrospective, 1940s kind of feel to it. The wedding sequence was very Kodachromey, the rest of [the film] was [given its structure through] lighting and the use of colour and exposure.'

One scene caused Coppola interminable heartache. He knew that Michael and his father must share a rich, intimate and eloquent scene together before the Don's death. No such conversation existed in the novel. In desperation, he turned to Robert Towne, already secure as one of Hollywood's best screenwriters, and three years away from his greatest triumph, *Chinatown*. 'I'd already met Bob on my first film, *Dementia 13*,' says Coppola, 'and he'd given me some rather lofty advice on it; but I had accepted that because he reminded me of my elder brother.' The resulting scene shows, according to Towne, 'the transfer of power from [the Don] to [Michael]. [It] was successful because Francis had done wonderful work, he knew what he wanted, but he didn't really know at

Brando's make-up is freshened by Dick Smith prior to the garden scene with Pacino in *The Godfather*.
Coppola looks on and an assistant prepares cue-cards for Brando to read.

that point, for a variety of reasons, how to do it. He was exhausted, he wasn't sure what to do, he was about to lose Marlon, and so in the course of a couple of meetings between Marlon and Francis, that worked.'

Coppola's fatigue also stemmed from the strain of awaiting the birth of his third child. On 13 May, George Lucas and his wife had come to dinner at the Coppolas' apartment, because they were on their way to Europe to go backpacking around Europe. 'We were sitting at the table,' recalls Eleanor, 'waiting for them to leave on a midnight plane. Then they left around 9 p.m., and the next day George was due to celebrate his birthday. I started to go into labour that night and had to call Francis, who was viewing rushes, and get him to come back at around 11 p.m. We arranged for the boys to go to his folks, and then he took me to the hospital, and Sofia was born at around 2 a.m. on George's birthday!' A few weeks later, Coppola used Sofia as the infant Michael Rizzo in the christening sequence.

The studio's contract with Brando called for the actor to be paid a punitive $40,000 for each week beyond the six he had agreed to perform. Coppola had scheduled the Don's death scene for the final day of Brando's stint. He had arranged for plum tomatoes to be grown and reach ripeness during that week, in the garden where the Don thrashes about before succumbing to a heart attack in front of his horrified grandson. 'But a squall had struck Staten Island and flattened the plants right before we were due to shoot the scene,' recalls Al Ruddy. 'So I went to Marlon, and said, "I'll pay you an air trip to L.A. and then back to New York if you'll return when the plants are ready again." He did come back, and for free, after four or five weeks [on May 28]. His agent was pissed! But Marlon loved Francis and had great admiration for him.' The actor tipped the scales at 250 pounds when he departed the shoot, another tribute to Coppola. 'He makes the best spaghetti in the world,' said Brando.

The film's travails in New York had not

ended, however. On 28 June, while the crew was shooting at the St Regis Hotel, life imitated art. Joseph Colombo was shot down by gangland enemies just outside the Gulf + Western skyscraper on Columbus Circle during an Italian-American Unity Day celebration. The Mafia Don was rushed to Roosevelt Hospital, and police sealed off the facility because they feared another attempt on the Don's life. Colombo recovered but died in 1978 from the effects of the attack.

Coppola felt elated on 2 July as he rehearsed the scene of Sollozzo's car picking up Michael in front of Jack Dempsey's restau-

Coppola discusses the 'garden' scene with Brando.

rant on Broadway. This was the final scene to be shot in New York, and the director knew that Paramount had acceded to his insistence that he travel to Sicily to shoot on location.

During the few days before he departed for Italy, Coppola was able to inspect a rough assembly of the footage to date.

6 Sicily and the Trauma of Post-production

'This is a long, bad trailer for a really good film' – Robert Evans

On 17 July 1971 Coppola settled into the Hotel Parco dei Principi in Rome. Awaiting him in his suite was a letter of welcome from the production office that the local Paramount and CIC head, Luigi Laraschi, had established for Ruddy on the Viale Manlio Gelsomini: 'Please be sure to bring your passport when you come to the production office on Monday so that we can obtain your sojourn permit before you leave for Sicily.'

The same letter furnished Coppola with a mini-schedule of the Sicily shoot. After preparations in Rome, the key personnel would transfer to Sicily on 22 July, followed by trucks of equipment and then, on Saturday 24 July the cast and crew would depart for the island. The schedule called for two weeks of shooting, with everyone back in Rome by Saturday 7 August after a wrap party on the Thursday evening.

Most of the locations had been recommended or found by Gray Frederickson. He had attended school in Switzerland and then found a job as an engineer, stationed in Catania, on the eastern coast of Sicily. 'So I got to know Catania, and especially the beautiful resort of Taormina,' he says. 'When we all went over to scout locations, I told them, "You don't want to shoot in Corleone, that's a dirty little town. Much better to use Taormina and the villages inland." So we found Forza d'Agro, and the whole cast and crew lived in Taormina.'

Dean Tavoularis asked to see the town of Corleone anyway. But locals cautioned him against doing so. Filming would be impossible, they said, 'because someone who shot a judge is hiding out there, and the cops refuse to go up there to bring matters to a head.' Despite these warnings Tavoularis motored up to Corleone, and took clandestine photographs of the streets from his car. He conceded, eventually, that the towns and villages near Catania would be more favourable for shooting.

Although the crew experienced little pressure from the Mafia during the two-week visit, their choice of location proved prudent, given the strength of the organization in and around Palermo. As Puzo wrote in the novel, Michael 'was to learn later that this small poverty-stricken town [Corleone] had the highest murder rate of any place in the world.' Coppola concedes that, 'Taormina is not like Palermo. For a hundred years it's been a tourist place and the reactions of the Sicilians in Taormina and all around Etna are different; it's not a particular hotbed of Mafia activity.' One director who had made numerous films in Sicily was quoted as saying that only low-ranking *mafiosi* asked for payment in cash for protecting the shoot and providing extras. The bosses preferred simply to be acknowledged, and eventually invoked favours in return.

The areas used in *The Godfather* comprised Savoca, Forza d'Agro, Francavilla, Nunziata and a villa owned in the film by Don Tomassino. Forza d'Agro, the setting for the wedding of Michael and Apollonia and most of the village scenes, lies less than 15 km north of Taormina, along the coast road and then 4 km up a spiralling road into the hills. Picturesque, with its Norman-influenced buildings, the tiny town attracts few tourists, which made it ideal for Coppola and his crew.

Simonetta Stefanelli as Apollonia. Only sixteen at the time of filming, 'I met him, I married him, I died,' she told *Time* magazine in 1997.

Fred Roos supervised the casting of local people for the Sicilian sequences, assisted by Mario Cottone, the production manager. For the role of Apollonia they had considered some of Italy's most famous young actresses, among them Ornella Muti and Stefania Sandrelli; Olivia Hussey, who had starred in Zeffirelli's *Romeo and Juliet*, was the first name on Roos's original list. Coppola opted for the unknown, timid features of Simonetta Stefanelli. 'I cast her because after we met, when she turned to walk away, she skipped like a young girl.'

Gordon Willis had only a few days to adapt his photographic equipment to the glassy, shimmering light. 'I maintained that all the scenes in Sicily should be sunny, far off, mythical, a more romantic land,' he asserts. 'So all the material shot there was grounded in this sunny landscape.' The exposure levels and filters were entirely different on the Sicilian sequences – in Willis's words, 'Softer, more romantic, in contrast to the harder, newspaper look of the New York scenes.'

The film adheres almost precisely to the novel during these Sicilian sequences. Pacino trudges through the streets and fields, 'dressed in old clothes and a billed cap', as Puzo writes. When he is 'struck by the thunderbolt' – or love at first sight – Puzo's narrative description of Apollonia and her gestures and Michael's reactions all leap to life on the screen. As Michael, who throughout his life addresses problems without preamble, asks Apollonia's father for a meeting with the girl, his dialogue springs from the book: 'You can inform the police and make a fortune, but then your daughter would lose a father rather than gain a husband.'

The wedding procession, achieved without dialogue as Coppola had first planned so many months before, also mirrors Puzo's account: 'The wedding was the usual peasant one. The villagers stood in the streets and threw flowers as the bridal party, principals and guests, went on foot from the church to the bride's home.'

Al Pacino, about to ask for a meeting with Apollonia in *The Godfather*.

By travelling to Sicily and filming on location, Coppola fulfilled his intentions of producing an authentic picture of Italian-American roots. How ironic that Mario Puzo 'didn't go to Sicily until after the film came out, and then to research my novel *The Sicilian* for about a week. It was a question of whether or not they would find out who I was before I actually left the island!'

On 21 July 1971 *Variety* ran a story quoting Paramount President-in-waiting Frank Yablans: '*The Godfather* will not be available until some time between next March and June.' This indicates that the studio already knew that it had a major release on its hands and that the sheer weight of material would probably not permit the film to be in theatres for Christmas. Yablans told the paper that he was 'insisting on a slow and careful procedure in the post-production work and the marketing approach. We will not sacrifice one tenth of 1 per cent of the quality just to hit a release date.' The budget at that juncture was being quoted as 'a little over $5 million'. Meanwhile, boasted Yablans, 'the rushes have such a fantastic look'. Two months later, however, Yablans was lamenting the costs that had been incurred by shooting in New York. 'Our below-the-line [labour] costs were around $1,500,000 to $1,700,000 when they should have been around $600,000 to $750,000.' Besides, unions in New York did not work on Saturdays, whereas those in Los Angeles did.

By early September, Coppola and Paramount had agreed to screen a first assembly of *The Godfather*, start collecting sound effects and begin manufacturing those not available from libraries. Looping and scoring would be completed by Christmas 1971. Yet there is little doubt that Bob Evans still hoped to open the film in time for the holiday season. Paramount had booked it into 800 theatres, and Evans waited nervously to see the rough cut.

Coppola was editing the film up at his Folsom Street facility in San Francisco. In the wake of Avakian's firing, two editors were hired, Bill Reynolds and Peter Zinner. Walter Murch, one of Coppola's original band of brothers at American Zoetrope and who was hired by the director as Post-production Consultant on *The Godfather*, takes up the story: 'The decision [after the original editor had departed] was made to reconstitute what had been done up to that point and start again, but because they had effectively lost those months, and it looked as though the film was going to be almost three hours long with an inflexible deadline, it made sense to hire two editors. The film was still shooting and there was just a lot of work to do: each editor had a ninety-minute film to complete in twenty-four weeks.'

When principal photography had finished in New York, Zinner and Reynolds flew west and took up office residence in the airy, colourful Folsom Street facility. In July 1971 there was a first, informal screening of all the material in sequence at Coppola's house. 'There was so much film to deal with,' recalls Zinner, 'so Bill and I tossed a coin. Bill won, and chose the first part, including the wedding sequence. We worked for four months or more up there, we even premixed up there. Francis wanted the entire post-production to be handled in San Francisco, but of course it just wasn't feasible, we didn't have the machinery off the lot. It was very unusual for a film to be edited off the lot anyway in those days.'

Bill Reynolds, whose 'half' of the picture ended with the murder of Sollozzo, remembers that 'Francis had been adlibbing the wedding sequence when he shot it – it turned out to be much longer than it was in the original screenplay. He simply staged a typical Italian wedding. Now all of a sudden at the editing table I saw Marlon Brando there in shot, and I turned to Francis and said, "But I just left him upstairs!" So Francis got around it by having little shots of Brando greeting the guests and so on.'

Since the second week of shooting, Coppola had been referring to the climax of the film, with the intercutting between the christening and the murder of Michael's enemies. But this posed nerve-racking problems of choreography on the cutting table. 'It was desperation time,' sighs Zinner. 'We had eight or nine 1,000-foot reels of the priest, the baby and others, but nothing had been really completed. Francis was off to Sicily and before he left he said, "See what you can do, Peter."

'When we had our second or third cut, and we could see *some* light at the end of the tunnel, we decided to put some temporary music over it, because we had so little sound. I'd been a music editor at MGM for eleven years, and now I spent an entire day in the San Francisco Library listening to music, particularly organ music, because I felt that an organ had to carry that theme.

'Well, finally I came up with the idea of let-

ting the priest's voice run on over the murders and the baptism, so there was a kind of continuity. Bob Evans wanted to keep the music like that, so we redid some of these things in the final version.'

The montage of newspaper headlines rotating and gliding over images of the Corleone Family at war with its rivals harked back to the classic gangster movies of the 1930s. George Lucas helped Coppola achieve this sequence, with its cadenza-like effect.

Almost without warning, the length of the film became a pressing issue. It may have appeared initially as an unequal struggle. Bob Evans, by late 1971, had become the longest-serving production chief on the West Coast. *Love Story* had become a worldwide smash hit for him, and he already had eight original screenplays on various burners, including a proposed sequel to *The Godfather* written by Puzo. In the other corner, Francis Ford Coppola did not have his name above the title, did not have the right of final cut, and had escaped being fired by the skin of his teeth.

Yet neither side would yield to the other where the length of the picture was concerned. Coppola: 'We were told by Bob Evans that if we brought in a film longer than two hours fifteen minutes, Paramount would take the print away from us in San Francisco and edit it down in Los Angeles. I think we'd come in with a running time of around two hours fifty minutes, and so we cut out lots of scenes and then ran the picture. And Evans declares that we'd taken out the best things in the film and that we had to put them back in again!' Every studio head Coppola had known always said, 'Cut! Cut!'

Al Ruddy's recollection is that 'Francis was cutting the film up in San Francisco, and brought it in at two hours fifty-three minutes. Bob Evans liked it, but when Frank Yablans – who was running the studio from New York – heard about it, he flipped out, and said he wanted it down to two hours fifteen minutes.'

Evans maintains in his book, *The Kid Stays in the Picture*, and in a more recent interview with this author, that he found himself under brutal pressure from the Paramount high command to bring *The Godfather* out at Christmas 1971. He claims that 'the first screening took place four months prior to the presumed Christmas opening. Lasted two hrs six mins. At a meeting afterwards, [he] rounded on Coppola: "You shot a saga, and you turned in a trailer."'

This runs counter to press reports of the period. As noted above, Frank Yablans, President of Paramount, had already conceded that *The Godfather* would be best held over until 1972. In an interview with *Variety* on 17 November 1971, he mapped out his strategy for an Easter release. The film would open simultaneously in two or three theatres rather than in the mass-density 'showcase' concept in a single territory. In New York, Yablans intended to screen the film at Loews State I along with Loews Orpheum and possibly one or two other theatres.

'Francis and I had a perfect record,' declares Robert Evans. 'We didn't agree on anything – from editing to music and sound.' They still do not agree, Evans claiming that Coppola 'had as much authority to cut the

picture in San Francisco as I did to walk into the White House and sit behind the chair in the Oval Office'. However, Coppola and colleagues on the picture, such as Fred Roos, Peter Zinner and Bill Reynolds, all point to the long editing hours done at the Zoetrope offices on Folsom Street in San Francisco. Walter Murch remembers: '*The Godfather* existed in a two hours fifty minutes version, and it was painful for Zinner and Reynolds to reduce it, but they did get it down to two hours twenty, for the celebrated screening when Evans and Francis clashed. I believe that a lot of the Italian sequence was cut to meet that length. I remember Bob Evans saying that "This is a long, bad trailer for a really good film."' Bill Reynolds remembers only that 'We made eliminations all the way through the film to meet the required length.'

The crisis boiled over on a Sunday in October 1971. Coppola, Fred Roos and others descended at Evans's behest on his luxurious home in Beverly Hills. There, in a guest cottage once used by Greta Garbo and now converted into a screening room, the latest version unspooled – at two hours eleven minutes. As the lights came up, Evans turned to Coppola and commented with a shrewd eye, 'This movie is longer at two hours fifteen than it was at two hours fifty-three.' Reynolds recalls him exclaiming, 'I remember lots of wonderful things you shot. They're not there. Put 'em back.'

Standing in the same room, twenty-five years later, Evans conjures up the moment: 'I told him, we can't release this film. It's just a glamorized version of *The Untouchables* – there's no texture in it. I gave him instructions: "You either add fifteen minutes to the picture, or I'm firing you."' While Coppola consulted with his team, Ali MacGraw, who was about to receive an award that evening from the Hollywood Press Association, and leave the next morning for Texas to shoot *The Getaway* with her future husband, Steve McQueen, kept pressing Bob Evans to accompany her to the ceremony.

Suddenly Coppola turned to Evans and asked him to go outside for a minute. They chatted beside the egg-shaped pool, with its slender, curling fountains arching over the water. Out of ear-shot of the others, Coppola turned to his producer and agreed to restore the original footage.

'Bob did have a tactile instinct for what made a picture work,' comments Peter Bart, 'and he did sense that when the attenuated version was screened, some of the scenes and characters should have been more developed. I recall Bob making countless brilliant suggestions to Francis, and Francis accepted them.' Al Ruddy concurs. '[Bob] is never arbitrary about cuts. He gave in a lot of areas and the picture is better because of him. He didn't have to give up anything.' In fairness to Evans, who devoted day after day to supervising the final mix of the film, he suffered throughout these months from acute sciatica, which forced him to be wheeled on a stretcher from one part of the studio to the other. 'We rigged up two hospital beds on the stages at Goldwyn Studios, where we did the mix,' says Peter Zinner.

Coppola transferred to the Goldwyn Studios and set about restoring whole stretches of dialogue and 'the non-narrative, family ambience type parts of scenes'. When he brought a two hours fifty-five minutes version to Bob Evans, everyone agreed that the film played superbly. Evans screened the picture for Frank Yablans. The President of Paramount looked at him and said, 'Bob, don't cut a frame.'

During the winter the choice of composer of the score became a question of controversy. Ruddy and Evans both acknowledge that Coppola had the idea of approaching Nino Rota, the Italian composer for such films as Visconti's *The Leopard* and Fellini's *La Dolce Vita*. 'Quite honestly,' admits Al Ruddy, 'I didn't know who Rota was at the time. He sent over a tape, with the main tune played on the piano.' During a casting trip to Rome, Coppola and Fred Roos had gone to Rota's home, and persuaded him to score the picture. Later Coppola hand-carried a set of cans to Italy so that Rota could begin composing.

'When Francis first mentioned Nino Rota I thought he was taking a terrible risk,' says Peter Zinner. 'We'd only known Rota from the Fellini films. I was afraid that it was just too far removed from Hollywood, because *The Godfather* was a truly Hollywood picture even if it had Italian themes. But to his eternal credit, Francis was right, and the music was wonderful for the film.'

Unbeknown to Coppola, though, Paramount had commissioned Henry Mancini to write the score for *The Godfather*. Mancini, a household name after 'Moon River' in *Breakfast at Tiffany's*, had continued to score Blake Edwards's movies throughout the 1960s, culminating in *Darling Lili* – which, of course, Paramount had produced with much fanfare. Evans denies that he personally

Nino Rota, composer of the score for *The Godfather.* (Photo courtesy of CAM.)

wanted Mancini (he had used Francis Lai for *Love Story* the previous year). 'We wanted more source music in it, songs of the time,' he says. Peter Bart speculates that someone in business affairs must have cut a deal with Mancini, because the composer definitely believed he was about to score the film.

The debate over the music reached ignition point in January 1972. 'Bob Evans and I had a big fight,' says Coppola, 'and they all wanted me to take Rota's score off the picture. I refused, and each day for five days Walter Murch and I went to Bob's house in Beverly Hills and sat by the pool waiting for Paramount to change their minds. But they didn't. So finally, I said, "Okay, if at a preview the audience all say that the music is lousy, then let's get rid of it." And Evans said, "Who makes the call?" And I said, "You do."

'So we showed the picture on the Paramount lot, to about thirty or forty people, and they all came out loving the picture, the acting and everything, and when asked if they liked the music, they said, "Oh it was terrific, and especially that great theme." And so Paramount kept it.'

Al Ruddy showed his wife the scene when Brando talks to Michael just before his death.

'And I thought, "Shall I bring up the [Rota] refrain?" And as I did so I could see tears streaming down my wife's face. That's how powerful the music was.' Ruddy tells another anecdote in this vein: 'Once I got a call from the guy who was running Famous Music, Paramount's music company. I go to his office and he plays me a bad rumba tune. They wanted me to use it in *The Godfather*. I said, "You can't use that lousy modern recording, Francis has been spending weeks getting the period atmosphere just right." Anyway, the next day a limo shows up, with Charlie Bluhdorn and Bob Evans, and Bluhdorn was clutching a record of this rumba. So Francis and I explain that we can't use the music, and Bluhdorn is screaming, and Bob Evans says, "Charlie, I resent your getting heavy with the boys." So as Bluhdorn left with the record, he cried, "I'm running a democracy here, and yet I own the fucking company!"'

Coppola's flautist father, Carmine, composed the *tarantella* that enlivens the wedding sequence at the start of the film, as well as a foxtrot and a mazurka that contributed to the flavour of that celebration.

The final note of discord was struck by Mario Puzo. 'I was opposed to the ending they used,' he wrote. 'I wanted an additional thirty seconds of Kay lighting the candles in church to save Michael's soul, but I was alone on this.' He also reiterated his desire to see his favourite line somewhere in the movie: 'A lawyer with his briefcase can steal more than a hundred men with guns.' When he referred this to Bob Evans, the producer immediately informed Ruddy, Coppola and the editors that the line *must* be in the film. 'So much for being head of a studio,' he says of Evans. 'It still is not in there.' Nancy Tonery, in charge of continuity, remembers that 'Brando said [the line] was too preachy and he persuaded Francis to cut it'. Coppola still regrets the omission. 'I love the line – we just couldn't find a place for it.'

Behind all the snarling and resentment, however, there seems to have been a universal belief that *The Godfather* aspired to greatness. 'Why do you get tears in your eyes when the Don dies?' asks Evans. 'It's because of the brilliance of the making of it.'

Coppola, too, relaxed with each passing day. Ruddy remembers a moment during the mixing at Paramount. 'The screen went dark, and up comes the face of Bonasera, and he's saying, "I luvva the Mafia!" I nearly had a heart attack, swung around and there was Francis grinning his Cheshire cat grin. He and his team had done it as a prank.'

7 Opening Campaign

'Don't just stand there, you fool, raise the prices!' – Charles Bluhdorn

In February 1972 Frank Yablans claimed that Paramount already had $11 million guaranteed for *The Godfather* in 241 US theatres, and that by the time of the pre-Easter saturation bookings, they would have $13.8 million in box-office advances from 350 locations. The studio spent some $1 million on a pre-release campaign, much of it targeting irregular filmgoers. On television, and in full-page ads in *TV Guide*, the catchphrase was '*The Godfather* Is Now a Movie'.

Paramount decided to bypass the sneak preview tradition, and instead arranged a screening for the nation's top 500 exhibitors at the Directors Guild of America theatre on Sunset Boulevard on 23 February, during the studio's three-day sales convention. 'It played a little slow,' recalls Bob Evans, 'and there was no applause. The exhibitors had walked in thinking it was a problem picture, because we'd pulled it at Christmas and they resented that.' Coppola stood nervously beside the exit: 'One guy came out and I asked him how he liked it, and he said, "A *Love Story* it is not", and walked on.'

Many exhibitors felt that the picture had no action, too much dialogue, and no prospects overseas. Sumner Redstone, then a major exhibitor and now head of the mighty Viacom empire (including Paramount Pictures), told Evans that the exhibitors resented the fact that *The Godfather* ran without intermission – which was when they made their profits on sale of concessions. (Paramount refused to bend, however, and even deployed a task-force to tour the country and cancel a screening if any theatre attempted to interrupt the screening artificially.) Nor was this the only

Henry Kissinger, Robert Evans and Ali MacGraw arriving for the première of *The Godfather* in Manhattan.

bad augury. Peter Bart remembers a screening at which Paramount's two foreign-affairs executives emerged complaining that the film would make very little at all in Europe.

Most of the exhibitors came away stunned from the screening, however, and Paramount spirits were lifted by a rave review written by Ivor Davis in London's *Daily Express*. The notice appeared on 25 February in the *New York Post*. Davis extolled what he called 'Brando's greatest film.'

On Tuesday 14 March 1972 *The Godfather* premièred at New York's Loews State I Theatre on Broadway and Times Square. Guests arrived in pouring rain, and after the screening set off for two parties – one for those who had purchased $100 tickets for the benefit of the Boys' Club of New York, and the other for friends of Paramount at the St. Regis Roof restaurant. 'The Boys' Club bash included supper at "21",' noted *Variety*, 'with the Paramount brass shuttling between the two spots, aided by a fleet of limos for VIP guests which [Frank] Yablans farsightedly recruited in advance, regardless of the inclement weather.'

Francis Coppola and his wife Eleanor attending the première of *The Godfather*.

Bob Evans had orchestrated the occasion down to the last detail. He had even persuaded Henry Kissinger, then Secretary of State, to accompany him to the screening, and had spent hours at the St Regis checking the food, the music and the appurtenances.

Although the film had not roused the audience to applause, the mood at the festivities afterwards was triumphant, with Coppola, Evans, and even Mario Puzo (who had been in Italy writing the first draft of the sequel) acknowledging the acclaim of the crowd. Evans found even greater consolation when 'Francis Coppola, the director whom

I'd hired over Paramount's objections and then personally fired four times during the post-production editing, came over to hug me, closing the book on two years of terrible battles.'

On the eve of the première, Evans had arranged for *Time* to interview an unshaven Al Pacino for a cover story, following one of Charlie Bluhdorn's characteristic phone calls, to the effect that *Newsweek* and *Life* had appeared featuring cover stories, but where was *Time*? 'I felt the picture made a useful commentary on corporate thinking in this country,' mumbled Brando in his *Life* profile. 'I mean, if Cosa Nostra had been black or socialist, Corleone would have been dead or in jail. But because the Mafia patterned itself so closely on the corporation, and dealt in a hard-nosed way with money, and with politics, it prospered. The Mafia is so . . . AMERICAN!'

The reviews reflected the delight and excitement that a Hollywood film could reach so deep into the roots of America's European civilization. Pauline Kael wrote in the *New Yorker* on 18 March: 'Francis Ford Coppola [. . .] has stayed very close to the book's greased-lightning sensationalism and yet has made a movie with the spaciousness and strength that popular novels such as Dickens's used to have [. . .] The direction is tenaciously intelligent.'

Vincent Canby, in the *New York Times*, described *The Godfather* as 'one of the most brutal and moving chronicles of American life ever designed within the limits of popular entertainment'. Gary Arnold in the *Washington Post* acknowledged the production as 'An extraordinary achievement: a new classic in a classic American film genre. It will take some kind of movie to prevent *The Godfather* from dominating next year's Academy Awards. A product of almost limitless commercial potential.' Charles Champlin in the *Los Angeles Times* saw it as 'probably the fastest three-hour movie in history', and Stephen Farber wrote that the 'haunting conclusion exemplifies the film's ability to enrich its melodrama with a full-scale commentary on the failures of a generation'.

Some critics harped on the film's disdain for morality. 'The success of *The Godfather* is deplorable,' wrote Robert Hatch in *The Nation*, 'if you believe that popular entertainment both reflects and modifies social morale. In a sentence, the picture forces you to take sides, to form allegiances, in a situation that is totally without moral substance . . .' Judith Crist, at that time an influential, much syndicated critic, also dismissed the picture as essentially immoral. Stanley Kauffmann, in the *New Republic*, complained of the length and the implicit endorsement of Mafia methods: 'As the picture winds on and on, episode after episode, the only real change is the Mafia's shift from "nice" gambling and prostitution to take on "dirty" narcotics. [. . .] Well, I suppose everything's going to hell, even the morality of the Mafia. But the picture certainly takes a long, long time to get there.' Many felt irritated by the length of the movie, including Arthur Schlesinger, Jr, who told *Vogue* readers that *The Godfather* had 'swelled into an overblown, pretentious, slow, and ultimately tedious three-hour quasi-epic'. Even some of the popular press journalists were dismissive:

'Far from surviving [. . .] as the *Gone With the Wind* of gangster movies, my guess is that *The Godfather* will be as quickly forgotten as it deserves to be,' thought right-wing guru William F. Buckley in the *New York Post*.

'When I saw *The Godfather* the first time,' wrote Marlon Brando, 'it made me sick; all I could see were my mistakes and I hated it. But years later, when I saw it on television from a different perspective, I decided it was a pretty good film.' Many critics abroad enjoyed Brando in particular more than the film in general. Derek Malcolm later wrote in the *Guardian*: 'Nowhere else does the film measure up to the social and political significance with which Brando miraculously invests his part, though there are a dozen other very good performances.'

But even had the reception been less fulsome, it would probably not have affected the the extraordinary box-office appeal of *The Godfather*. Rain continued on the Wednesday, but brightened for the crucial weekend screenings. Queues formed without warning, and stretched around the block behind the Loews twin theatres into 45th and 46th Streets. Screenings had been scheduled on the hour, staggered from 9 a.m. to midnight, but that allowed management a mere five minutes to clear the theatre between each show. On the first night, staff could not cope, and viewers attending the midnight screening emerged into the dawn at 4.10 a.m.

Despite these saturation screenings, managers found themselves being offered bribes of $10 or $20 to get to the head of the line at the Loews State II. Some youngsters queued up for hours on end and then sold their places near the head of the line to latecomers, for a couple of bucks.

In January of 1971, the admission price for a film in the United States averaged $1.61. Paramount decided to charge $3.50 for *The Godfather* in its opening run at 400 theatres. When executives saw the queues, they promptly jacked the tickets up to $4 for the weekend shows. Paramount were already culling 90 per cent of the gross take from exhibitors, something that only a monumental smash such as *Jurassic Park* or *Independence Day* can command today.

Peter Bart chaperoned Charlie Bluhdorn on a tour of the Manhattan theatres. 'He could see the lines around the block through the windows of the limo, and after the third theatre Charlie couldn't stand it any longer. He bolted from the car, grabbed the poor manager, and said, "Don't just stand there, you fool, raise the prices!"'

Coppola saw the phenomenon through somewhat different eyes, as his wife recalls: 'Francis thought *The Godfather* was going to be a disaster, and he'd taken the job of writing *The Great Gatsby*, and he was in his hotel room struggling with this screenplay and looking out and seeing these lines of people for *The Godfather*. He wasn't able to enjoy the success, because he was already sweating on his next project.' In his heart, Coppola may have felt that people would believe he had turned a gripping bestseller into a dark, ponderous, boring movie.

By 22 March *Variety* could pontificate: 'The estimated gross of $454,000 at the five Gotham sites in the first week ended last night represents the biggest blockbuster maneuver

and series of ploys in recent film biz history.' Not all of that cash reached the vaults. At 3 a.m. on the opening Saturday two men shot in the arm one Kenneth Holden, a relief manager at Loews theatres, and ran off with the $13,000 or so that he was about to lodge in the night depository of the Chemical Bank at 1501 Broadway.

Some portions of the Italian-American community still simmered with resentment. The Governor of New York, Mario Cuomo, refused to let his children see the film because he felt that it glorified the gangster world. In Kansas City, the local Italian-American Unification Council attempted to buy up the entire house for the opening screening of *The Godfather* on 22 March. Their intention was to ensure that nobody would be inside the theatre watching, while a demonstration outside would alert the Midwest public that the rank and file of Italian-Americans 'do not live in the way these people are portrayed in the picture'. In Des Moines, Iowa, an Italian-American restaurant proprietor erected a sign outside the Paramount Theatre that read, 'Don't Judge us All by the Godfathers'.

One week later, the destiny of *The Godfather* was assured. On 29 March Bob Evans had his contract prolonged for a further five years and was also allowed to engage in five of his own independent pictures, for release through Paramount. The studio purchased eight-page ad units in the trades headlined: '$7,457,691, *The Godfather* Is Now a Phenomenon', followed by a list of grosses at some 300 theatres at many of which records had been broken after anything from thirteen to a mere three days.

Other films had not been quelled by the arrival of *The Godfather*. *What's Up Doc?* set a new, single-day, all-time record at Radio City Music Hall on 25 March, and *Cabaret, A Clockwork Orange* and *Diamonds are Forever* all enjoyed excellent box-office.

But by the next week, Paramount's gross ads in *Variety* and the *Hollywood Reporter* were quoting a nationwide haul of $17,291,705, and *Variety*'s respected editor, Abel Green, took to his typewriter in a rare major article, one year before his death: 'That Paramount's *The Godfather* is an historic smash of unprecedented proportions is not only generally conceded within the trade but it has also generated a new-found optimism of proportions rarely if ever experienced before.'

By 12 April the film's gross had climbed to $26 million, and that week Gulf + Western stock reached $44.50 after touching just $28 earlier in the year. By 3 May, *The Godfather* had surged $5 million ahead of *Love Story* in a comparable period. Paramount executives hesitated to exult, but felt that by July they would know if their film would top *The Sound of Music* and *Gone With the Wind* (the latter having already been rereleased six times since 1939).

On 17 May Frank Yablans sent cheques for $500 each to twenty-seven Loews theatre managers, district managers and the division manager in New York, with thanks for their overtime commitment and handling the crowds at the five Loews theatres in Manhattan. In that week's *Variety*, the studio gross ad proclaimed a staggering total of $53,302,439 after a mere nine weeks.

Peter Bart wrote a wry letter to Coppola:

I just wanted to let you know how you are influencing manners and mores.

A veritable deluge of Mafia screenplays and novels has descended on me, which is not especially surprising. But what is noteworthy is the fact that the heavy of the latest Mafia piece is named Coppola – and the hero of another is named Francis.

That's what it means to be a legend in your time.

Frank Capra, who had known the same kind of adulation in the 1930s, took time to write to Coppola: 'It's the best film I've seen in the last ten years. The acting was superb, the script one of the finest, and the directing? Out of this world. I cheered inwardly at scene after scene.'

On 16 April, only a month after the première, Paramount announced that a sequel – provisionally called *Don Michael, The Death of Michael Corleone* or *The Son of Don Corleone* – had been commissioned from Mario Puzo for $150,000. Puzo revelled in the torrent of royalties. The print-run of the tie-in film edition of his paperback was an unprecedented 1,300,000 copies. Glancing back from the vantage point of 1996, the novelist reckons that he received royalties on 14,500,000 copies of *The Godfather* in paperback.

Bob Evans told the press: 'I'd like to have [Coppola direct the sequel]. He just has a number of other things he wants to do. However, Francis will be very much involved with the sequel. It might even be a co-production between him and Al Ruddy. In any case, I want Francis's stamp on it – there were a thousand nuances in *The Godfather* that made it different from all other gangster pictures, and I owe that all to Francis.' Evans then departed for Europe with editor Peter Zinner to supervise the first four foreign-language versions of the film. 'We hired real directors and real actors, and paid much more than anyone else to get good foreign-language versions,' he says. 'We made our pictures indigenous to the countries they played in, flying in the face of our own distribution guys. That's why the American film is number one in every country in the world. In those days the Italian film was number one in Italy, the French film number one in France, and so on.'

Peter Zinner assumed responsibility for casting the dubbed versions in Germany, Italy and Spain. It took him a week in each territory to test the various actors, with the Don's voice posing a pronounced challenge to all comers. His work would be partly reflected in a unique exercise that summer in Munich, where the Olympic Games took place. Paramount arranged for the film to open simultaneously in five versions across the city: one in English, one dubbed in German, and prints subtitled in French, Spanish and Italian.

A young Englishman named Ian Scorer had joined Paramount in the wake of the 1968 events in France, during which as an accountant with Ernst & Young in Paris he had driven two Gulf + Western executives around France. 'Bob Evans was the embodiment of success,' he reminisces. 'When I was working at North Cañon Drive, I'd look out the window and see him and Ali MacGraw arriving for work around 11 a.m. He already had the reputation of being incredibly good around

the back end of the movie, the editing and post-production stage.'

Sent back to Paris because of his knowledge of French and France, Scorer became nominal head of Marianne Productions, established by Paramount and its partners in CIC to produce potential blockbusters for the local market. They had already been involved with two films directed by Louis Malle, *Lacombe Lucien* and *Le Souffle au cœur*. So Bluhdorn and Evans talked with Malle and offered him half a million francs ($100,000 and probably around $400,000 today) to supervise the dubbing. Malle bypassed the usual pool of actors who specialized in dubbing American pictures and chose instead respected players such as Michel Duchaussoy (Don Corleone), Claude Dauphin (Woltz), and newcomer Sylvain Joubert (Michael), for their suitability and persuasiveness. Malle felt that audiences would prefer an accurate translation of the dialogue, even if it was at the expense of flawless lip-synching. The dialogue was adapted by Eric Kahane, who translated all of Harold Pinter's plays for the French theatre.

Danny Goldman at CIC in Paris and Philippe Selz, head of publicity for Paramount in France, embarked on a launch campaign with obsessive eagerness. Ian Scorer: 'This was before the autoroutes were built, and from 14 July [1972] onwards, the CIC marketing team put up posters every two kilometres or so down the old RN7 to the Riviera from Paris. They found farmhouses, old buildings, whatever was available, and so drivers southbound would see these posters announcing *The Godfather* as opening after the *rentrée*. And as people returned from holiday along the same road, they'd be confronted with a similar succession of posters in the other direction!'

The première was a resplendent affair at the old Opéra Garnier in Paris on 17 October. The wife of President Georges Pompidou had declared her intention of attending the evening's festivities, but at the last moment she withdrew. This was in response to an outcry in the Italian press, where editors felt it unseemly that a film about the Mafia should be graced by the French First Family, especially on the eve of Italian high-level talks in Paris. But the essentially diplomatic snag failed to detract from the première, for which virtually the entire team came over, and the screening was followed by a dinner of Italian cuisine. Within a matter of weeks that autumn, *The Godfather* had become the largest-grossing Hollywood film of all time in France.

In neighbouring Italy, where Dino De Laurentiis had said the picture would die with Brando above the title, the story was the same: an all-time box-office triumph for *The Godfather*. *Corriere della Sera* did not welcome it in flattering terms, and the Communist papers also seemed ranged against it. But in each successive city, opening records tumbled – Turin, Bologna, Florence, Naples . . . In early October, the film finally received its Sicilian première, opening in Palermo's two largest cinemas. 'Roberto Ciuni, the young and handsome editor of the *Giornale di Sicilia*, said Brando is 'the envy of the real *padrinos*, because he represents the "old way of doing things" and the island's

younger generation of Cosa Nostra is giving the old men a hard time, even setting up hits and jobs without their approval.'

The Italian-dubbed version contained Sicilian, Calabrian and Neapolitan accents along with American Mafia phrases and this contributed to the film's instant acceptance among local audiences – despite a 25 per cent increase in ticket prices in all the major venues. By 11 November 1972 the film had grossed $4,375,000 in seventeen Italian cities.

The international grosses exceeded anything in Hollywood history. In Japan, *The Godfather* attracted one million people in its first seven weeks – even though the opening had been overshadowed by typhoons and torrential storms in Tokyo and Osaka. Explaining the unexpected success, a distinguished Japanese critic, Tadao Sato, commented that 'Behind the popularity of the movie, I can see Japanese nostalgia for the old family system, which modern Japanese society has lost.'

In London, all-time house records were established at all four flagship theatres in the West End, and grosses reached the then-magical plateau of $3 million in the UK. Records had been devoured in Australia, Mexico and just about everywhere the picture opened. The only disappointment concerned the 'GI circuit'. US forces in Europe did not flock to *The Godfather*, partly because of the high ticket prices.

On 2 August 1972 Paramount bought a double-page spread in the trade papers, announcing that *The Godfather* had grossed $101,000,000 in its first eighteen weeks of release. The advertisement also formally declared that *Part II*, starring Al Pacino as Michael Corleone, would open on 27 March 1974 at the same five Loews theatres in New York where the original had performed so spectacularly. On 6 September Frank Yablans stated that 'Everyone owning a piece of *The Godfather* is a millionaire already.' Paramount could make the announcement with self-righteous satisfaction, because the studio controlled eighty-four of the film's 100 'points' – a situation almost unknown in today's world of package deals and director-producer 'shingles' (or independent entities) within the purlieu of each major studio.

Love Story had peaked at $50 million in rentals. *The Sound of Music* had gone to the top of the tree with $72 million, and then been leapfrogged by *Gone With the Wind* at $74.2 million. *The Godfather* passed all of them over the Labor Day weekend, and as of October 1996 had posted $86,250,000. It now lies a sorry thirty-fourth in the all-time chart, but in terms of today's money ranks twenty-seventh with $352.3 million (*Gone With the Wind*, by the same yardstick, has 'taken' a phenomenal $1,250,600,000).

In an ironic finale to the campaign, Bob Evans received a bill for a new Mercedes 600, the most luxurious limousine available, purchased by Coppola on the very day that *The Godfather*'s gross passed $50 million. Months earlier, the director had suggested that the studio should purchase the vehicle, because while shooting the film he had been saddled with an old station wagon. Paramount now informed the press that the car, big enough to house President Nixon and all his bodyguards, was a bonus to Coppola. The director's stream of cheques from his agent Jeff Berg at CMA allowed him to invest in San Francisco. He paid off all his debts, bought an apartment building, and also the fabled, sea-green Sentinel Building in North Beach as a headquarters for American Zoetrope. Coppola acquired the Fox Theater in San Francisco, and refurbished his twenty-two-room home with relish, installing a screening room in the basement. '*The Godfather* launched Francis into a world-class director,' says his wife, 'from a promising young guy to an internationally acclaimed film-maker. It also showed how well a film could do internationally; nobody had ever thought of that before.'

8 The Mother of All Sequels

'Ah, but a man's reach should exceed his grasp, or what's a heaven for?'
– Robert Browning (1812–1889), quoted by Al Pacino in reference to Francis Ford Coppola

To everyone's surprise, Coppola expressed disinterest when the studio broached the idea of a sequel to *The Godfather*. He wanted nothing so much as the financial independence that would enable him to return to intense, personal film-making, with *The Conversation* high among his priorities.

Peter Bart persisted. 'I said to Francis, "*You* were the star of *The Godfather.*" So what does the biggest star in Hollywood get now? The million-dollar barrier had just been broken, so I said to him, "If someone offered you a mllion dollars to direct the sequel, would you do it?" He looked absolutely shocked, and then he said, "I th-think so." So I said, "Okay, consider it done." Bob Evans was overseas or somewhere, so I called Charlie Bluhdorn in New York and he went crazy. "I'll talk him down in price," he promised. But of course he never did.'

Bluhdorn invited Francis and his father Carmine Coppola out to dinner at the Palm restaurant in Manhattan, to show his approval. 'He persuaded me to do the sequel,' Coppola maintains. 'I gave my arguments against the project, and finally he said, "Listen, when you've got a licence to make Coca-Cola, make Coca-Cola!" So I agreed to produce it, and I demanded three conditions: a ton of money, complete freedom and control, with none of the Paramount corporate types involved, and the title *The Godfather Part II*. The first two conditions they agreed to pretty quickly, but they couldn't take the third. They said, "You can't call it Part II, the audience will mix the films up, etc. Boy, if I'd had a penny for every film with a Part II or III after its name, I'd have been able to retire by now." Anyway, to distinguish between the two parts, I created letterheads bearing the logo in red, as opposed to black!

'I said I would select a director, and I chose Martin Scorsese. But the guys at Paramount didn't want him.'

Coppola's deal for *Part II* consisted of $1 million plus 13 per cent of the studio's gross rental profits. Paramount conceded to his wish to delay shooting until October the following year. This hiatus would enable Coppola to shoot *The Conversation* during the winter of 1972–3, and then leave sound and post-production in the capable hands of Walter Murch while he threw himself into pre-production on *The Godfather Part II*.

Already in May 1972 Francis had a tentative schedule drawn up for the next twenty-two months. This called for him to start shooting *Part II* in May 1973 and to release the picture at Easter 1974. A revised version of the schedule shows the first day of shooting commencing on 1 October 1973 (the scene of Anthony having his first communion inside a church). The 101st day of shooting was to take place on 6 February 1974 (interiors in the Ellis Island processing room). On 8 November the team would begin shooting in Las Vegas. On 14 November they would move on to Los Angeles and, on 8 December, fly to Puerto Rico for the Havana casino interiors. On 13 December everyone would transfer to the Dominican Republic. There would be a two-day break for Christmas, and then on 6 January the crew and cast was slated to film in New York. Finally, on 27 January Coppola would lead the troupe to Italy.

Many changes were made in detail, if not in

sequence, to this schedule, which had been constructed before Coppola and Puzo had sat down together to work on a screenplay. Puzo himself had signed a first draft on 5 May 1972, but the first draft bearing Francis's name is dated 4 July. Then comes a gap of over a full year before the emergence of a third draft by Coppola containing the first 105 pages (up to the Senate hearings). This screenplay opened on a scene in Sicily with young Vito being identified as a fine shot and seen with his father in a sequence with three Mafia men and Don Francesco (later Don Ciccio). Then Andolini is killed, and there is the funeral procession over the rocky river bank.

Although eager to return to the intimacy of *The Conversation*, Coppola continued to commute to Hollywood from the Bay area, discussing the logistics of *The Godfather Part II*. On 9 June he wrote a memo to Peter Bart, summarizing the work to be undertaken until the start of pre-production on *Part II*. 'We have engaged Harry [*sic*] Korshak as Special Consultant for preparation period on flat deal [. . .] Have set up offices in Beverly Hills to accommodate all research and preparation. My own office will remain in San Francisco, with secretarial help as discussed in budget [. . .]' A comprehensive list of all characters in *The Godfather* who were left alive and therefore might figure in *Part II*, had been prepared, comprising the actors who played their roles and their estimated ages for the period in *Part II*. A family chart of all children in *The Godfather* cast had been drawn up, determining their ages in *Part II* so that the script could include these new characters.

Coppola went on to say that he had

already 'done a casual location search in the Lake Tahoe area where I've found an exceptionally strong location for Michael's estate. It is the former Kaiser Estate on the Lake and its mall-like setting can be used extensively in script. After approved draft, we will move to secure right to shoot at this location.'

He informed Bart that Jack Wheeler would be going through the out-takes of the first *Godfather* to determine if any sequences shot but not used might be included in *Part II*. But, as Paramount's Vice-president and West Coast Counsel, Eugene H. Frank, noted in a memo dated 12 June, 'none of the photography or soundtrack of an actor can be used other than the picture for which he was employed, without the approval of SAG [Screen Actors Guild] and separately bargaining with the actor and reaching an agreement with him.'

Coppola also complained to Bart that he needed a 16 mm print of *The Godfather* for ready reference, a plea easy to sympathize with in the pre-video era. 'I think you can understand,' he writes, 'how essential it is that I be able to refer to the original film easily and at any hour I might be working. I understand [Frank] Yablans' desire to control the prints of the film, but surely the film-maker who after all had the work-print of it in his safe-keeping for six months, can be trusted with a 16-mm print. It is essential to my writing the script.'

The same day, 12 June, a note from Coppola to Bart lists the budget projections for pre-production on *Part II* as $98,370. Charlie Bluhdorn, at his request, was still copied on all such matters.

The retention of Sidney Korshak, a friend of Bob Evans and a respected deal-maker with contacts in the Mafia, almost at *consigliere* level, would enable Coppola to monitor underworld reactions to *The Godfather*, and to gain access to unfamiliar facts about the Mafia for his new screenplay.

Unorthodox in everything from his taste in shirts to his choice of pasta, Francis Ford Coppola would find it almost impossible to succumb to 'sequelitis'. The conformist approach to *The Godfather Part II* would have placed Michael Corleone at centre stage, taking the Corleone Family into the modern era of drugs and gambling. Instead, Coppola – aided and abetted by a pliant Puzo – opted for a majestic saga that would veer through time from the earliest years of the century to the late 1950s – and demand infinitely more of its audience than the original. It would become, in his own words, 'two parallel stories, two generations, two men at the same point in their life – they both have young children, and they are learning to deal with power.'

This audacious sequel was thus conceived as a meditation on crime and nemesis, with the Corleone Family mired in political venality and contract killing. Yet such activity would appear a side-show by comparison with Don Michael's appalling urge to cleanse his Family of everyone who refused to bow in fealty before his will. This mission justifies in Michael's eyes the murder of his younger brother, Fredo, the expulsion of Kay and the side-lining of his foster-brother, Tom Hagen.

Focusing his thoughts, Coppola sat at the portable typewriter he took everywhere with him and and tapped out a long shopping list of themes and incidents he wanted to include in *Part II* – 'listed randomly':

1. A great party on Michael's estate on Tahoe, 1962. The ties and resonances from his Italian background have strained, but one can still sense them there. Much more whitebread than Connie's wedding, probably due to Kay's influence. Cocktails . . . wealthy, influential people from L.A., Tahoe, S.F. Young college students in white jackets serving drinks on the great lawns that border the lake. Water sports, speed boats, water-skiing, tennis etc. The occasion? Something to do with Michael's twelve-year-old son . . . Vito Anthony . . . Tony. A beautiful quiet, unspoilt child. [*At this juncture Coppola mentions Hyman Roth and Sammy Davis Jr as new characters.*]

2. Possibility of Michael's second child born a cripple à la [Meyer] Lansky and Kaiser [original owner of the estate that would be used as a location on Lake Tahoe].

3. Michael's focus turning from Cuba . . . to the Bahamas and Haiti . . . and therein lies his meeting with Hyman Roth, whom Michael respects enormously.

4. Fredo has married a movie star à la Raquel or Ann-Margret, who gives him trouble.

5. Hagen has made several big blunders in the Cuban deals. A closet alcoholic . . .

6. Michael has taken on more of his father's qualities . . . less ruthless than when he was younger. More mellow, philosophical . . . though still not so much as his old man before he died. His enterprises steadily move out of 'rackets' and into more Real Estate, high finance, big time resort, gambling development in partnership with the wily 'Joe Meyer' alias Hyman Roth.

7. Fabrizzio, in return for the assassination of Apollonia, is in N.Y. or somewhere, Michael must plot his revenge.

8. Fredo runs the new legalized brothels in Nevada. A girl is found sadistically murdered in one, and Michael knows that the last person she spent the night with was someone prominent in politics.

9. Connie remarries. Irony of this cross-juxtaposed with the big wedding in Part One.

10. Sammy Davis Jr (Al Freeman Jr) as a jester and link between Michael and big politicians.

11. Something to do with a kidnapping of Tony as a boy.

12. Fredo's wife making trouble [. . .]

13. A son of one of Michael's defeated enemies tries a reprisal.

14. Clemenza talks to a Senate Committee à la Valachi and Puzo's [initial draft] script.

15. A new 'Luca Brasi', the whole Neri story [fully developed towards the close of Puzo's original novel] . . . but retold. The policeman who didn't get justice comes into Michael's employ. New casting. Whole segment?

16. In the first Michael segment . . . he triumphs with Roth's assistance.

17. In the second, Roth turns against him. And Tony is twenty-two. Götterdämmerung. Michael makes a mistake: he underestimates Roth because he is old.

18. Fredo stupidly (through his wife) violates the Family thing with Roth? Michael cannot order him killed. Does it himself. Beginning of the end.

19. Michael a diabetic . . . eyes begin to go.

20. Michael caught at Appalachin. Perhaps transplant to his place at Tahoe.

21. Connie defiantly marries someone Michael doesn't approve of, in a secret dumb civil ceremony in Las Vegas. Talks about Carlo and never forgave Michael.

22. Michael divorces Kay.

23. Michael imports an Italian killer, specialist à la Buscetta to kill Hyman Meyer during what for all

purposes is a vacation to Sicily with his family. All plush.
24. Someone marries another family's daughter à la Rosalie Profaci.

While a majority of these ingredients emerges in *Part II*, the character of Michael takes on a more ruthless, implacable streak. He *will* prove capable of ordering the death of Fredo. And he will suffer from hubris, not diabetes.

The mention of various real-life *mafiosi* indicates the extent to which Coppola wanted to anchor the story of the Corleone Family in post-war America. The confessions of Joseph Valachi had fascinated Mario Puzo and now Coppola would find inspiration in the antics and machinations of real-life *mafiosi* and supergrasses. Seizing full advantage of the twelve months prior to serious pre-production on *The Godfather Part II*, Coppola not only filmed *The Conversation* but also initiated a research programme beyond the ken of most Hollywood studios. He demanded details about a host of subjects and personalities: Meyer Lansky, Fulgéncio Batista, the construction of the New York subway, vaudeville, tenements, Ellis Island, festas, garment workers, hospitals and health clinics, the Statue of Liberty, and the Brooklyn Bridge.

'I had other beautiful scenes in mind,' said Coppola afterwards. '[. . .] In one of them, Caruso was singing "Over There", a patriotic song of World War I that encouraged young men to enlist. Others included Italian construction workers building the New York subway, and Vito Corleone courting his fiancée and joining his friends for a drink.' Another sequence would have shown Italian

labourers putting up the mosaics in Times Square (as Joey Zasa boasts to his fellow *mafiosi* in *Part III*, 'We laid the bricks that built this city!').

Faded clippings and manila files in the bowels of Coppola's research facility in the Napa Valley attest to the meticulous efforts of the Zoetrope staff during late 1972 and early 1973. The preliminary list of props provides a hint of the team's passion for detail: Cuban cigarettes, blood-pressure apparatus, instruments for a ten-piece Italian band, street knife-sharpener stands, a 1956 blue Cadillac sedan, leg manacles and $3 million in prop money. When Coppola insisted that the cars in the film should make the authentic sounds of vehicles from the 1950s, Walter Murch visited an automobile museum in San Francisco, and recorded the appropriate models in all manner of situations. 'Francis gave me a cassette of music from the end of that decade,' recalls Murch, 'that a devotee had assembled in New York, and so for a number of weeks I just listened and thought of ways of fitting it into the background of the film.' As a consequence, *Part II* possessed the texture, rather than the mere sheen, of authenticity.

As the character of Hyman Roth was largely inspired by the late gangster Meyer Lansky, the writers wanted to include sequences in Latin America that would resonate as profoundly as the Sicilian scenes had in *The Godfather*. An unsigned, original typed report in the Zoetrope archives summarized Lansky's role in Cuba, for example:

Lansky had met Batista during the 1930s, and had run raw molasses for making illicit alcohol. Lansky also once ran the Havana race track and had a finger in the old Casino Nacional. When a turn in Batista's political fortunes forced him into temporary exile in 1944, he enjoyed it in Florida where his friendship with Meyer Lansky [developed]. 'Bigger than US Steel' [used by Roth in *Part II*] is Lansky's own phrase. He started his life of crime at sixteen, later hooked up with Bugsy Siegel and started the Bugs and Meyer Mob [. . .] The Kefauver hearings threw light on Lansky's power for the first time, forcing his casinos to close down [. . .] Lansky fled Cuba in January 1959, as did Batista, but left his brother behind to negotiate a deal with Castro.

Zoetrope staffers also studied the congressional hearings into organized crime, and the special committees and subcommittees involved, from the year-long 1950-51 Estes Kefauver inquiries and some 400 witnesses, to an investigation into the 'Heroin Paraphernalia Trade' of 1970. Hyman Roth refers scornfully to Kefauver in the film, and much of the testimony in the Senate hearing in *Part II* owes its flavour to these transcripts.

All Hyman Roth's dialogue was close to what Lansky actually said or was reported to have said, the only variation being that at the time *Part II* was made, Lansky was out on bail and awaiting trial for income tax evasion.

Former Cuban dictator Fulgéncio Batista's second wife, Marta, was still alive when the film opened, along with six of his eight children. Batista himself had died in 1973. The Batista family sent letters to Paramount because they were afraid that certain scenes might sully 'the good name' of the late dictator. Paramount and Zoetrope conceded that all references to the Batista family would be deleted from the screenplay, as was a reference to the Lieutenant-General of Nevada (probably because of the sleazy character of Senator Geary 'of Nevada').

The Valachi revelations were to stimulate a wealth of incident and dialogue in *The Godfather Part II*. Dino De Laurentiis had produced a fictional screen version of Peter Maas's book, *The Valachi Papers*. Starring Charles Bronson and directed by Terence (*From Russia with Love*) Young, the film had been announced by a beaming De Laurentiis at a reception at '21' in New York, just two days after the première of *The Godfather*. Paradoxically, Coppola's film captured more of the flavour of the Valachi confessions than the official adaptation.

The screenplay gestated spasmodically throughout late 1972 and all of 1973. In the early stages, the greater responsibility fell to Mario Puzo, for Coppola concentrated his energies on *The Conversation*, filmed on location in San Francisco from November 1972 to March 1973 (on 22 September 1972 he received a cheque for $102,125 as his first payment from the studio for *Part II*). When Coppola did focus on the screenplay, he looked to the novel only for its pre-war section (in essence, that boils down to Chapter 14). This covers the youth of the Don in New York, and contains many evocative scenes and characters that would be retained in *Part II*: Fanucci, for example, 'a heavy-set, fierce-looking Italian who wore expensive light-coloured suits and a cream-coloured fedora', and who urges Vito to let him moisten his beak – 'fari vagnari a pizzu'; or Clemenza, who 'even then [. . .] liked to wear loose clothes'; or Signor Roberto, the landlord 'in a constant state of irritation', worry having 'worn his nerves to a frazzle'. And, above all, the fast-maturing, worldly wise Vito Corleone, who soon recognized that 'without political influence, without the camouflage of society, [Al] Capone's world, and others like it, could be easily destroyed.'

Coppola wanted to cover the Corleone past in the following stages:

1) The Don as a boy in Sicily.
2) Young man in Hell's Kitchen (and the killing of Fanucci).
3) Becoming a man of respect.
4) The Marazano War (and Al Capone).
5) Consolidating, and plans for the future.

He typed notes to remind himself of certain key themes: 'Mafia is a form of government. Vito as observer, observes the consequences of the violence (in Little Italy). The concept of Vito having a real "family", small, but with only him to take care of it. Crime provides the only way to American luxury. The Mafia, "not an organization, but a philosophy". Essential premise: America does not take care of its people. Don Corleone does!'

The lineaments of the film take shape from the various letters exchanged between Puzo, typing away in his Long Island residence, and Coppola, in his newly acquired mansion on Pacific Heights in San Francisco. Puzo agreed that Lansky should loom large, but that 'Michael should destroy Lansky's power by helping Castro against Batista. Reason: Michael is a hero. Too many people side with Castro. [. . .] Society is unjust to Cuba. Therefore Michael and Family are against Batista and for Castro. For practical and not

liberal reason.' He also reminds Coppola of the importance of adhering to myth. 'In myth, Hagen can't screw Sonny's widow . . . Also in myth Michael can never be close to his sister, Connie. Reasons: from story and emotional pay-off to what the hell can you do with a brother–sister relationship.'

Coppola to Puzo, one week later: 'I think now that Fredo should be important in this movie. With his characterization changed slightly, he is more mature, more important to the family – but still has that fatal flaw of some weakness in character, some softness, maybe more humanity. This can cause Michael a lot of trouble and so he would be helpful to the plot [. . .]

'Also, in going through the opening I think that the three men wandering through the streets [of Corleone] warning against helping Vito would be tremendously effective on film.'

On 17 September 1973 Puzo contributed the final scene of the Christmas reunion with all the Family and the Godfather in flashback, with Brando reproaching his son gently for having volunteered to join the army in the wake of Pearl Harbor. 'I don't understand why you want to die for strangers. Well, you're a man now. You do what you want. But when the time comes, come to me as a son should come to his father. Let me help you with your life.'

Eight days later, Puzo sent Coppola his evaluation of their joint efforts: 'First – I have every confidence you'll make the script work. Second – I feel very much like a rear-echelon soldier telling infantrymen how to go out and get killed. Third – I hate to [do] this kind of writing where other considerations, call them political, financial or whatever, affect what I think should be done [. . .]

'What pleases the audience is the Family Bond. Since everything is breaking down, there should be one unquestioned Family Unit in the picture. One person we and Michael can trust absolutely. That person should be Hagen.

'[Fredo] should *not* know he is going to die which I assume he does [in the screenplay] because he is reciting a prayer. This gives him a false dignity. It also in a funny way takes away his humanity. His tragedy is that he is so human, so fallible, so ignoble. He would not believe his brother would have him dead.'

In both the first and the second draft, there is a closing scene showing Michael meeting his son Anthony, now eighteen, with Connie in attendance in 'the role of a surrogate mother–wife.' Michael 'seems older than his years, as though his illness – diabetes – has taken its toll.'

Al Ruddy was out of the picture, electing to concentrate instead on *The Longest Yard*, based on his own original eight-page story with a screenplay by Tracy Keenan Wynn, son of actor Keenan Wynn. Besides, Coppola preferred to be surrounded by people he could trust – and command. Back in the dark days of shooting *The Godfather* in New York, he had told an observer on the set: 'Always remember three things: have the definitive script ready before you begin to shoot. There'll always be some changes, but they should be small ones. Second, work with people you trust and feel secure with. Remember good crew people you've worked

with on other films and get them for your film. Third, make your actors feel very secure so that they can do their job well.'

He maintained this attitude when preparing *Part II*, and indeed *Part III*. Loyal lieutenants such as Fred Roos and Gray Frederickson joined him to set up the sequel. He urged his actors to return to the fold, and promised to reward them more handsomely to compensate for their miserable deals on the original *Godfather*. He hired the same technicians, such as production designer Dean Tavoularis and make-up wizard Dick Smith, at up to $1,500 a week. Theodora Van Runkle agreed to design the innumerable costumes for a flat fee of $45,000. Bill Reynolds, who had just edited *The Sting*, was unavailable to rejoin the crew.

The talent deserved recognition beyond the norm, felt Coppola, because none of the performers on *The Godfather* had benefited from the unforeseen box-office bonanza. He urged Frank Yablans, and by extension Bluhdorn, to let them have a percentage of the potential good fortune ahead. Al Pacino would receive $500,000; Robert Duvall $150,000 plus a $25,000 bonus when gross receipts reached $25 million, and a further $25,000 when they hit $30 million; Diane Keaton's fee was set at $50,000; John Cazale settled for $35,000, of which $25,000 was to be deferred until the box-office touched $25 million; while Talia Shire, who had been paid a beggarly $1,500 on *The Godfather*, signed a contract for $30,000 plus $10,000 when receipts breached the $27.5 million mark.

Gordon Willis returned to the fold, and matched almost anybody's purse except

Gordon Willis and Francis Coppola discuss a scene for *The Godfather*.

Pacino's, with a contract offering him a guaranteed twenty weeks' employment for $70,000, with a $40,000 bonus should receipts reach $25 million, and a further $40,000 when receipts went through the $50 million mark (they never did). 'When we made *Part II*,' says Willis, 'I wanted to use the same lenses.

They were good for that movie.'

The one major dispute involved Richard Castellano, who had been paid handsomely for the role of Clemenza in the original, and who now insisted on too tough a deal – including his own wife's prerogative to write his lines for him. At last, Francis wrote him a personal note: 'Dear Ritchie, [. . .] keep in light the fact that we have to make deals with over twenty actors, all of whom feel basically screwed by Godfather One, and who have favoured nations clauses of one sort or another; which is to say that their deals are somewhat based on the deals of the other actors.'

Castellano and his agent stood firm, and Puzo and Coppola responded by announcing the unfortunate passing of Clemenza in the opening sequence of *Part II*, and replacing him with the character of Pentangeli. Sensitive as always, Francis even wrote a poignant letter to Richard Castellano after the first previews of the film: 'Many people mentioned how much they missed you, and wished you were in the film. Gazzo does a very good job, but it's clear that no one could replace you. [. . .] If you would drop me a note telling me your preference I would tell [journalists] what you want me to tell them.' In fact, Michael V. Gazzo as Pentangeli did project the right image of sly, self-obsessed fallibility that is associated with minor Mafia figures.

Newcomer Robert De Niro (as the young Don Vito) claimed $35,000. Francis had seen his performance in Martin Scorsese's *Mean Streets* but, long before that, he and Fred Roos had cast De Niro as one of the button-men, Paulie Gatto, in *The Godfather* (a role that other commitments prevented him from taking).

'We had this notion about his playing the Don in his early life,' says Roos, 'and at the time it was a crazy idea because he had made movies where he played dimwits, like *Bang the Drum Slowly*. So we invited him out to dinner socially in New York, with two or three other people, and that was his audition, and during the entire dinner we studied his face to see if it could look like Brando's when he was young. Could we make the audience believe that this guy was Brando when young? De Niro doesn't know to this day that that was his audition. It was a controversial casting, because nobody had seen that side of him.'

For the part of Hyman Roth, both Coppola and Roos thought of approaching Lee Strasberg, legendary head of the Actors Studio in New York. 'I remember we were not sure about it,' says Roos, 'and we really couldn't audition him because he was too much of an icon. So we persuaded Sally Kirkland, who was part of the Actors Studio, part of the Strasberg circle, to host a party to which he would be invited. Francis and I went to this party and Lee was there, and we just kind of circled round him, talked to him and he didn't realize that was his audition.' Other actors considered for the role ('a small, wizened man in his sixties') included Elia Kazan, George C. Scott, Fredric March, Luther Adler, Harold Clurman, Dalton Trumbo, Abraham Polonsky and even Laurence Olivier.

Martin Scorsese, a fellow Italian-American whose *Mean Streets* had aroused considerable admiration among the cognoscenti, auditioned for the part of the young Genco ('a Sicilian extrovert type') or the young Clemenza. Coppola loved the thought of non-professional actors enhancing scenes in *Part II*, but they must not be household celebrities, only vaguely familiar faces. So when Roos cast the Senate hearings sequence, he considered veteran director William Wellman, screenwriter Niven Busch, and Western B director A. C. Lyles – in addition to Roger Corman (Coppola's early mentor and backer of *Dementia 13*), Bill Bowers (a Hollywood writer-producer who had co-written *The Gunfighter* in 1950) and Phil Feldman (producer of *The Wild Bunch* and Coppola's first agent), who did appear on the Senate bench.

On Monday 26 March 1973 the Academy Awards ceremony brought some of the rewards that had been predicted. Nino Rota's melodic score, forever associated with the film's appeal, had been ruled out of contention by the committee just three weeks before because a seven-minute section, in the love theme, had been used (in a different orchestration) by Rota in the 1958 Italian film, *Fortunella*. If self-plagiarism were a sin, it was ironic that the eventual Award should have gone to Chaplin's score for *Limelight*, itself already some twenty years old.

The evening in the Dorothy Chandler Pavilion did not run according to expectations. Both *The Godfather* and *Cabaret* had been nominated in nine categories. As Bob Fosse's film about 1920s Berlin scooped the statuettes for sound, editing, supporting actor, art direction, adapted score and cinematography, Coppola and Bob Evans grew nervous. Then *The Godfather* won its first major award, for Best Adapted Screenplay. Coppola, wearing a red tuxedo jacket, mounted the stage with Mario Puzo's daugh-

ter to accept the Oscar from Jack Lemmon, and expressed his gratitude to Bob Towne for writing the garden scene between Brando and Pacino.

The Award for Best Actor, which many assumed would be a coronation for Marlon Brando, provoked the controversy of the decade. Army Archerd, the *Variety* columnist who interviewed celebrities as they arrived at the Pavilion, received a tip that an Indian princess, Sacheen Littlefeather, would be attending the ceremonies in Brando's stead. Once the proceedings had begun, Archerd slipped into the wings to inform the show's producer, Howard Koch. But it was too late to save the situation. Jeers and applause greeted the diminutive Indian as she ascended to the stage in full regalia. 'Dignified amid the heckling and confusion, she paraphrased a prepared text from the actor who said his refusal of the Award was based on the industry's "demeaning and degrading" treatment of the Indian in films and television.' That evening Brando himself was at Wounded Knee, where a dispute had developed over reservation rights.

Coppola had won the prestigious Directors Guild of America award a few weeks earlier, and traditionally the DGA laureate went on to take the Academy Award. In 1973 Bob Fosse turned the tables, however, and as Clint Eastwood opened the envelope containing the identity of the Best Film Award, Coppola and the Paramount contingent braced themselves for a major disappointment. But a few seconds later a delighted Al Ruddy could climb the stairs to the stage and accept *The Godfather*'s third statuette of the evening. 'I was beginning to wonder if I would get up here at all,' he commented with a nervous grin, before using the opportunity to make what *Variety* sniffily described as 'one of those Horatio Alger speeches about how anyone can make it in America if they work at it.'

Backstage with the press after the ceremony, Ruddy admitted that when Fosse was announced as Best Director, 'I was ready to tear up my speech'. Beside him, Coppola kept shaking his head and muttering: 'I was so sure I was going to win Best Director . . .'

9 Shooting *Part II*

*'If only we'd had two more weeks,
it could have been great!'*
– Francis Coppola

As the shape and extent of *Part II* evolved before their eyes, Coppola's Zoetrope team had to scout locations, negotiate terms with actors and technicians, and generally cope with the prospect of a production costing more than twice its forebear. On 1 May 1973 researcher and assistant Debbie Fine ordered fifty block lessons in basic Sicilian for Al Pacino, Richard Bright, John Cazale, Tom Rosqui, Morgana King and Richard Castellano (replaced by Michael Gazzo), which cost the production $600. De Niro was accorded even more intensive coaching; in September the actor flew to Sicily for three weeks to research his role, and Paramount paid him $1,500 in living expenses. Sonya Friedman of Texture Films in New York was signed to prepare subtitling for the Sicilian sequences for $3,500 plus expenses.

Dean Tavoularis had begun his labours at an early stage, before a screenplay even existed. 'But Francis said that art-direction-wise he wanted this and that. He wanted to see the Italians who came first to America coming off ships, entering the army, marching back in a World War One parade, etc.

'The street where young Vito set up shop was the most difficult to do. As we drove around New York looking, I kept on the dashboard a picture of one of the famous streets, Mott or Mulberry, with push-carts and Italian grocery stores circa 1912. One day I was with Jack English, a location guy, and we drove down through the Ukrainian area and suddenly came on this nice street. We stopped, walked around and started chatting to people. Fortunately, the second and third generation of these Ukrainians wanted to resurrect the history of this particular street – B Street – and they took us down a basement and showed us all these photos they had researched.

'The construction work took months. We had to approach everyone on the street, some three hundred people from the grocer to the mortician. We had to measure everything, photograph everything, and then change everything. Building the grocery store, putting gravel on the roads, changing all the lights – it took around six months all told.'

Carroll Ballard, who had attended film school at UCLA with Coppola and would make his own reputation with *The Black Stallion*, had been requested to go up to the Kaiser Estate at Lake Tahoe. 'I went out there one Saturday with my old and trusted cam-

era,' says Ballard. 'Francis wanted images of destruction, and certainly the estate had been run down. The place was falling apart, rotting bathrooms, cobwebs, the lot.' The footage shot by Ballard that day would not appear in *Part II* – but when Walter Murch was casting around for some spare material with which to open *Part III* and make the bridge between Michael's days at Lake Tahoe and his new life in Manhattan, he came upon Ballard's work – and used it.

On the eve of the commencement of principal photography in October 1973, Fred Roos had timed the 199-page screenplay as coming out to three hours fifty-six minutes, a daunting prospect that would place *The Godfather Part II* equal with *Gone With the Wind* and *Lawrence of Arabia*.

The main street dressed by Dean Tavoularis in *Part II*.

Shooting *Part II* at the Kaiser Estate. Coppola watches John Cazale and Mariana Hill.

The cast budget was estimated that month as $1,449,558 (including stunts, looping, a large overtime contingency, etc.). Twelve actors had returned from *Part I*, and were paid $816,750 as opposed to $102,300 on the original. Also, there were more speaking roles (146 as against 52) and a longer schedule (101 days against 77).

Behind the scenes, a nerve-racking situation had developed. The company was well advanced on building the sets at Lake Tahoe, because to achieve the required look, shooting had to begin by a certain time. But Al Pacino would not approve the script. So Coppola, conscious of spending his own money as the days ticked by, finally insisted that matters had to come to a head. He and Pacino flew to San Francisco, and huddled together, working through the screenplay until the actor was satisfied.

The Lake Tahoe compound, including cottages, was leased for $7,500 a month. As the opening shots were filmed on 1 October and the winter had already set in, extras were obliged to wear thermal underwear beneath their summer clothing. Coppola and his family lived in one of the houses on the estate, and Eleanor recalls how 'They would be shooting right outside the door, and the cables would be running through the kitchen. We were living literally "in the set". Sofia, our daughter, was a toddler, so she would run around among the crew. She was like the pet monkey, and they would give her candy!'

While shooting proceeded at Lake Tahoe, a memo from co-producer Gray Frederickson, dated 9 October 1973, indicates that Coppola, anxious about the escalating budget, had laid down an edict that 'every department in the production company is to cut 10 per cent across the board'.

A touching private note was injected into the scene in which Michael says goodnight to his son Anthony. Lying in bed, the youngster asks Michael: 'Did you see the picture of the car?' The drawing had been done by the Coppolas' son Gio. 'It was me in a limousine,' says Francis, 'and then it said, "Do you like it, yes or no?" We asked him to draw ten copies of it, and we used his drawing in the film . . .' On 26 May 1986 Gio died in a gruesome speedboat accident near Annapolis, while his father was shooting *Gardens of Stone*. In an affecting reprise, Michael hands the carefully preserved drawing to Anthony on the eve of his operatic début in Sicily in *Part III*, like a talisman to bring him luck.

From 8 November the production filmed in Las Vegas, using the Tropicana Hotel as a main location, and working from midnight until noon each day for more than a week. Then everyone flew back to Los Angeles for studio shooting. The final scene in the film called for a flashback to the 1940s, with Marlon Brando surrounded by his family. Negotiations lurched along between the actor and his agent on the one side, and Zoetrope and Paramount on the other. Considerable sums had been committed to Jimmy Caan and other actors to return to the studio for just one Monday of shooting. In fairness to Brando, he had always intimated that he would not participate in the sequel. 'Marlon was mad at Paramount because of the deal

they forced him to take on *The Godfather*,' says Fred Roos, 'but we thought of him as appearing in the film in some shape or form. The script was loose and flexible enough, as was the cut.'

'I'd been calling Brando from phone booths, hoping he'd show,' says Coppola. 'But he couldn't work out his deal, and I heard this on the Friday. So I thought about it for a couple of days, and then came down to my hotel in Los Angeles on Sunday night and rewrote the scene, using the idea of the surprise party, so we could shoot on the Monday.'

Decamping at dawn like some itinerant circus troupe, Coppola and his crew traversed the nation, first to Miami for some exteriors, and then on 2 January 1974 to Santo Domingo. For Mona Skager, who had assisted on the production of *The Rain People*, and for Francis himself, this style of working came as second nature. 'When we made *The Rain People*,' says Coppola, 'we had this unusual format of this very small caravan that could strike anywhere, and we began to feel like Robin Hood and his band. We really had the film-making machine in our hands and it didn't need to be in Hollywood, it could be anywhere.' Gray Frederickson recalls, 'We filmed in so many different places that it was a miracle that people showed up [. . .] We were preparing places while we were wrapping in other places, while we were shooting in other places. It was almost like a TV series.'

Paramount had suggested using the Dominican Republic as an alternative to Cuba because Gulf + Western owned a large portion of the island. Charlie Bluhdorn used to fly his better guests down to the company's hotel there, and pumped hundreds of thousands of dollars into the improvement of social and educational conditions in the Republic. Trujillo's mansion would serve as an exterior for the presidential palace of the Batista regime. But although the harsh light and the rather faded architecture proved ideal as a substitute for Havana, the shoot ran into difficulty almost at once.

Dick Smith, who was present as make-up supervisor, says that 'the food was appalling, and the crew came close to mutiny'. Even Eleanor Coppola, who was in Santo Domingo for about half the time, smiles as she remembers 'One of my profound moments of parenthood occurring there. I was walking with Sofia across the lobby of this hotel where we were staying, and I had her over my shoulder, and she was vomiting down my back and having diarrhœa down the front!' More threatening was Al Pacino's sudden collapse on Wednesday 16 January. He had been caught in a downpour, and, feeling 'faint and fatigued', succumbed to what was officially described as exhaustion and pneumonia. For almost two weeks Coppola had to prepare sets or simply do nothing. The studio's insurance claim spells out the situation:

[Pacino's] condition became worse on the 17th, however he did report to work. From Friday, the 18th of January through Monday, the 4th of February, Mr Pacino was incapacitated and unable to work with us.

In addition to the days that the Francis Ford Coppola Company was shut down due to Al Pacino's illness, additional times were lost because of schedule adjustments and his unavailability.

[Pacino returned to work on February 5] but as indicated on the medical report, was in a weakened condition and could only complete half a day's work. Company lost half day. [On the following morning] Al Pacino complained of dehydration due to his weakened condition and company shut down in early afternoon.

In general, when Al Pacino returned for work in Santo Domingo with a chronic weakened condition, the balance of our filming involving him was at a much slower pace resulting in additional time lost.

Pacino's illness may have been caused by the pressure of containing himself for the monstrous role of Michael in *Part II*. As Coppola commented, 'He's the same man from beginning to end, very rarely having a big climactic scene where an actor can unload, like blowing the spittle out of the tube of a trombone.'

By this juncture, *Part II* was languishing several weeks behind schedule. Casting dilemmas, which should have been solved before the film began shooting, continued to gnaw at Coppola. Even the role of Hyman Roth seemed in jeopardy. Lee Strasberg fell sick almost as soon as the unit reached Santo Domingo, and his inexperience as an actor before the cameras – despite his legendary reputation at the Actors Studio as a teacher – began to show. 'His performance is on the thin edge of being terrible,' concedes Fred Roos, who had agreed with Coppola in casting the seventy-three-year-old New Yorker. On his third day at the Hotel Embajador in Santo Domingo, Coppola wrote an impassioned four-page telex to Elia Kazan, all but begging him to consider taking over the role

Al Pacino, containing himself during the Senate hearings in Washington in *Part II.*

of Roth whom he described as having to be at once physically frail and psychologically menacing. Kazan responded four days later, politely declining because he was finishing a book and could not afford to lose the momentum, 'which is hard as hell to get up again once dropped'. Coppola reacted swiftly, rejigging the screenplay to present Roth as an infirm gangster whose tell-tale cough at the end of sentences echoed Strasberg's own affliction.

Strasberg, immured in his own self-reverence and clad in Dick Smith's 'Florida-style old-age tan', would sit around at lunch and regale Coppola and Pacino with his views on acting technique. He admitted that in his career as a teacher he had not himself become used to the repetition of lines and gestures. 'I had problems with my words in the party scene [on the roof of the Havana hotel],' he told them.

Strasberg deserved his Academy Award nomination, however, for just one scene – when he stares at Michael with barely controlled rage and tells the story of Moe Greene's destiny in Las Vegas, and Greene's execution by persons unknown (namely Michael). 'I didn't ask who gave the order –' he spits, '– because it had nothing to do with *business!*' Then, as he turns away he refers to the bribe that Michael had been due to bring to Havana: 'I'm going to have a nap. If the

De Niro with his 'thin, authoritative moustache' in *Part II*. Coppola in background.

money's on the table when I come back, I'll know I have a partner. If it isn't, I'll know I don't.' Elementary words, yet spoken by Strasberg with a venomous intensity.

The tribulations persisted. On 27 February, playwright and neophyte screen actor Michael Gazzo (author of *A Hatful of Rain*) received minor abrasions to the neck during the attempted strangulation of Pentangeli in a bar. On another occasion he could not report for work until 3 p.m. after a night of alcoholic indulgence. John Cazale had also suffered minor gunshot burns to the left armpit while filming his own death scene out on the water. When Morgana King hesitated at the idea of lying in an open casket on

set, Coppola screamed that he would get his own mother to do Mama Corleone's death scene. The director's short fuse was hardly surprising. He was working seven days a week without respite, often shooting *Part II* during the regular week, and then supervising the editing of *The Conversation* over Saturday and Sunday.

Much of De Niro's footage was shot in New York, where Tavoularis had converted the avenue in 'Little Ukraine' into a bustling Italian community around the year 1917. De Niro attended the same dentist as Brando and wore a similar, yet somewhat smaller, fitting in his mouth to push out his jowels. Arguments raged over whether or not he should wear a thin, authoritative moustache in his later scenes in Sicily; he did.

Gordon Willis insisted on striving for a flatter, softer light in these New York period sequences, and this caused friction on the set. For the elaborate Festa sequence, culminating in the murder of Fanucci by De Niro, Willis had his team 'cover all the windows on one side of the street to stop them from bouncing sunlight over everything'. Dean Tavoularis, meanwhile, had seen a picture of an old Madonna in *Life* magazine, and asked an Irish-Catholic friend to track down a similar model, so that it could be borne through the streets attracting dollar bills from the devoted pedestrians. 'We'd go down into basements and almost find the right one, but not quite.

Finally we located one, with this beautiful expression on her face.'

Make-up wizard Dick Smith plotted the assassination of Fanucci (Gaston Moschin). The screenplay called for the young Vito to thrust his gun right into the mouth of the gangster and literally blow his head off. 'I moulded a duplicate gun with a rubber nozzle,' says Smith, 'because actors don't relish even the concept of having a gun stuck in their mouth. A condom filled with blood was attached to the back of Moschin's neck, and was triggered by a squib, to give the impression of brain tissue splattering all over the wall behind him.'

Moschin suffered further indignities in a scene cut from the film, but reinstated by

Fanucci attacked in *Part II*.

Barry Malkin for the television omnibus edition of *The Godfather*. Two incompetent button men try to slit Fanucci's throat on a rooftop. 'I put a tube of blood under his throat,' recalls Smith, 'and then two canisters under his armpit, one with compressed air and the other containing blood – along with a switch so that the actor could turn on the flow of blood and then run towards the camera and exit left, with the result that you never saw the rigging under his right arm.' Take after take was required, and Smith and his team knelt in the back of a nearby drugstore, trying to protect Moschin's costume and hat, with the artificial blood becoming all the while stickier and stickier. 'Wardrobe had only prepared three changes of clothes,' laments Smith.

Budget concerns harassed co-producer Gray Frederickson. On 4 March he wrote to Tom de Wolf at Paramount that 'due to the rising cost of living and the overall increase of per diem to the crew and cast in New York, [my co-producer] Fred Roos and myself are taking $650 per week living advance in New York only. This is approved by Francis.' Only three days earlier Mona Skager, the associate producer, had written to the studio: 'Due to the horrendous cost of living in New York City, we find it necessary to increase the per diem for Mr. Francis Coppola to $1,350.00 per week, retroactive to 21 January 1974.'

Coppola sailed on the Italian cruise liner *Raffaello* on Wednesday 7 March, arriving in Naples seven days later. But even in Italy the final stages of the shoot were disrupted by *force majeure*. A prolonged search for a suitable equivalent to Ellis Island had ended when Dean Tavoularis settled on the old Fish Market in Trieste, which he dressed in its distinctive structure and colour to recall the landing-stage for generations of immigrants to the United States. Today the market has closed and plans are afoot to convert it into an arts centre.

The basic crew remained in Trieste for almost a month. Coppola stayed at the Hotel Duchi d'Aosta in the main Piazza Grande, overlooking the sea, and a mere 50 metres from the market location. Rigging and construction crews worked until as late as 3 a.m., responding to the reality of life in the market building, which was crowded with busy fish stalls until Saturday afternoon. Then the crew had to take out all the stalls, clean the premises, build the set and light it – and be ready to shoot on Sunday morning. Hundreds of extras were employed and then dressed; only a small proportion would appear in the final cut. But, as Gray Frederickson points out, 'We wanted the people in those scenes to look like immigrants, and extras in New York just do not look quite that way.'

Coppola and companions put their spare time to good use. Lorenzo Codelli recalls arranging a screening of *America, America*, with its early scenes in Ellis Island, and also of a documentary about the facility. Coppola, along with Tavoularis, Willis and others, attended the showing, in the La Cappella Underground, a film club that seated just seventy-two people. And it was less than half full, which was embarrassing, says Codelli. When the lights came up, Coppola climbed on stage for an informal question-and-answer session about his work.

The murder of Don Ciccio in *Part II*. Robert De Niro and Giuseppe Sillato.

About the only straightforward day of shooting in Italy involved the photographing of a boat, crammed with immigrants to the United States, outside Venice.

On 18 April call sheets show that 'due to storm conditions, equipment was delayed in shipment to Sicily so [the] company was forced to cancel filming'. Almost three weeks evaporated before Gordon Willis could line up a single shot. He had relished the chance to perfect the technique he had initiated on *The Godfather*. 'In the Sicilian sequences,' he says, 'I wanted to achieve a sense of photogravure. You can only refer to something that's a hundred years old in a visual way. Too many period films are shot in a modern manner, too "in your face". I think there should be distance between the audience and what they're looking at where the past is concerned. The usual should not feel immediate.'

Robert De Niro remembers that 'It was raining every day so we'd go to the scene where I kill Don Ciccio and there would be no sun, and we would all wait around and then we'd have a great lunch at a little restaurant that was on the side of a mountain in a little town on the way back to Taormina.'

None of the locations posed logistical problems for the Zoetrope team. There were scenes at two villas, belonging in the film to Don Tomassino and Don Ciccio; at a rural train station depicting the arrival and departure of Corleone's favourite son in the year 1922; and in the twilit streets of Don Vito's birthplace as he escapes in a covered cart. More challenging, however, was the funeral of

Vito's father, a straggling cortège picking its way across the jagged stones and boulders of a dried-up river bed.

The delays in Sicily were temporarily forgotten in the euphoria of Coppola's winning the Palme d'Or at the Cannes Festival in May for *The Conversation*. Walter Murch had been editing the sound in San Francisco right up to the last moment, talking to Francis by phone and telex, or grabbing him during the director's occasional weekend moments in the Bay area. An exultant Coppola, his wife and three children stayed up all night at Cannes after receiving the award.

By the end of May, even the executives in Hollywood were scanning the weather reports from Europe with more than usual anxiety. George Justin at Paramount sent a telex to Gray Frederickson and Fred Roos at their hotel in Taormina: 'We're all going to our various churches and synagogues praying that the good Lord will smile upon you and bring back the sun to once sunny Sicily. Give it the old allegarroo and keep fighting and tell Francis not to worry about a thing cause I'm plenty worried.' Cloud and rain in fact delayed the final day of shooting on the island until 11 June 1974. A shoot that should have occupied no more than eleven days in effect dragged on for more than fifty.

By June the overall budget for *Part II* had swelled to $12,652,937, with 158 camera days plus 21 days' hiatus – plus a further 6 days of insurance coverage. The final budget for the film peaked at $13,600,837, having been held in check by curtailing the post-production

Half a lifetime earlier: Vito's mother momentarily has the upper hand over Don Ciccio and urges her son to escape.

phase from the budgeted fifty weeks (which must always have been somewhat romantic) to twenty-five weeks. This exceeded the earliest estimates by $4,170,500 and meant that *Part II* cost more than double its predecessor.

On 8 July, having viewed a rough assembly of the material he had shot, Coppola could at least breathe more easily, and dashed off a note to Gordon Willis: 'At any rate, it certainly looks spectacular; which is due to you and Dean, so let me thank you once again for your beautiful work.' More than twenty years later, the director reflected with the detachment that comes with time: 'I had complete power on *Part II*, because the first *Godfather* had been such a success. Here was a $13–$14 million picture, and it was incredibly complex in its shooting schedule, and yet it all went smoothly and according to plan.'

Editing *The Godfather Part II* might have defeated even the most fanatical of jigsaw enthusiasts. 'Although the responsibility for editing was divided up in a checker-board pattern,' writes Walter Murch, 'scenes were initially cut and recut by the same person. But when Francis began to play with the structure of the film, people found themselves recutting what others had originally edited.' The length of the first cut differs according to the memory of those involved. For Peter Zinner, who received an editor's credit on *Part II* with Bill Marks and Barry Malkin, it reached four hours fifty-one minutes. Peter Biskind, who wrote a book on the subject, quotes a figure of six and a half hours. Gordon Willis remembers that 'By the time we finished *Part II*, we had a six-hour movie. It played great at six hours, but you couldn't exhibit it like that.'

Coppola himself told me in 1996 that his rough cut ran to 'about four hours', although in a letter to actress Julie Gregg, apologizing for the virtual excision of her role as Sandra Corleone, he wrote: 'The first cut of the film was five hours long, and I was under justified and serious pressure from Paramount to bring in the three-hour movie.'

The swirling, noble chords of Nino Rota's music had made a massive contribution to the appeal of *The Godfather* throughout the world. But Coppola knew that his father had scored much of the wedding sequence, and on *Part II* he requested Rota to allow Carmine Coppola to conduct the orchestra during the recording sessions. Carmine supplied all the source music, and Rota wrote some new music and reprised his earlier material. But Rota did not like the deal, and consented only out of affection for Francis. He received $30,000 as a fee, and eventually shared an Oscar with Carmine.

A sneak preview in San Francisco on 27 November convinced Coppola that the linear logic of the film must be improved. He commanded Barry Malkin to reduce the number of cross-cuts between past and present from around twenty to a dozen or so.

'When we previewed *Part II* in San Diego,' says Bob Evans, 'I went down there with Bob Miller and Paul Haggar [head of post-production at Paramount]. Everyone stood up as Francis walked in and applauded him; the Pope couldn't have attracted bigger applause. By the time the screening was over, half the theatre stood empty. Why? Instead of putting in the whole Havana sequence, he put in another hour of Sicily, with subtitles. Francis had felt compelled to moralize the injustices that the Mob had committed in the original.' Barry Diller, Paramount's new Chairman, attended the screening, which seemed even more protracted because the projectors broke down on four occasions.

'If only we'd had two more weeks, it could have been great!' exclaimed Coppola in the aftermath of the opening release, a complaint he would echo sixteen years later on *The Godfather Part III*. He had to concede that a 180-minute version would be best for the wider release of the film, and so the full three-hour fifteen-minute *Part II* was seen only in 160 first-run theatres in the United States.

Exhibitors were salivating with anticipation of a huge payday from *The Godfather Part II*. Some 340 theatres had committed more than $26 million in advances to Paramount's domestic distribution division – a record in the history of Hollywood. In its opening five days, *Part II* attracted 74 per cent of the business achieved by its predecessor at the box-office, and Charlie Bluhdorn, addressing his stockholders at Gulf + Western, declared that he expected the new film to outgross *The Godfather* by 20 per cent. The front-page banner headline in *Variety* confirmed his optimism: 'Like "Godfather", Like Son at B.O.' Over Christmas and the New Year the momentum continued. Three weeks after its release, the film had reaped $10,893,859 in rentals for Paramount (compared with *The Godfather*'s $42 million). But then it began to slip in the wake of new films such as *The Towering Inferno*, which after eleven weeks had comfortably outperformed *The Godfather*

Part II. The film seemed too cold-blooded and complex for a mass public, reared on the gore of *The Exorcist* and *The Godfather* itself. Only the murder of Fanucci by young Vito rivalled the bloodcurdling violence of the earlier Corleone film. Unexpectedly, the *New York Times* took Coppola to task for both pictures, noting that the original *Godfather* set 'some kind of record in the pornography of violence'.

Paradoxically, Coppola found himself extolled by the serious critics and intellectuals of the day. Pauline Kael in the *New Yorker* referred to Coppola's 'supreme confidence' as director. He was now 'the inheritor of the traditions of the novel, the theatre, and – especially – opera and movies. The sensibility at work in this film is that of a major artist.' For Kael, this 'epic vision of the corruption of America' enlarged the scope and deepened the meaning of the original. Kathleen Carroll in the New York *Daily News* anointed it with four stars (her highest rating) and called the film 'a grand courageous sweeping drama [. . .] the most ambitious American movie in terms of its size and scope in recent memory.'

Vincent Canby in the *New York Times* took a patronizing view, noting the expensive look of the film but describing it as 'spiritually desperate', and giving the impression of 'a very long, very elaborate review sketch'. Fred Roos remembers how he, Francis and others from the Zoetrope family were finishing dinner in a restaurant when word of Canby's negative notice came through, spoiling the evening. Then Gary Arnold of the *Washington Post*, who had hailed the original as a major film, dismissed *Part II* as 'fundamentally irrelevant'.

Variety, which had raved over *The Godfather* and would do so again in 1990 when *Part III* emerged, again lauded Coppola. The bold-type summary below the title at the head of its review ran: 'Masterful sequel, broadening story scope of original blockbuster. Outstanding in all respects'. Far from being 'a spin-off follow-up to its 1972 progenitor,' the unsigned review continued, '[it] is an excellent epochal drama in its own right providing book-ends in time to the earlier story'. In *Time*, with its wide national and international circulation, Richard Schickel concluded: 'Francis Ford Coppola has made a richly detailed, intelligent film that uses overorganized crime as a metaphor to comment on the coldness and corruption of an overorganized modern world.' John Simon, who had found *The Godfather* repugnant and ill-made, now bestowed some grudging praise on Coppola: 'The final argument in favour of *Part II* is that it is better made, of sounder workmanship. Coppola is getting to be a more competent director. A scene here is allowed more leisure and breathing space, is less like a guided missile trained with dumb, mechanical determinism to explode on a specific target.'

Although *Part II* received no Golden Globe awards, leaving Paramount to celebrate a sweep by *Chinatown*, the Directors Guild of America voted Coppola Best Director for the second time. When the nominations were announced for the Academy Awards, *Part II* was named in twelve categories, *The Conversation* in three. Both pictures were nominated for Best Original Screenplay and Best Picture, the first time that two films by the same director had figured among the final five in two categories. The star of Francis Ford Coppola had never gleamed more brightly.

At the ceremony in early April, *The Godfather Part II* earned the glory and recognition from the Academy that to some extent had been denied to the original two years earlier. Dean Tavoularis won for Best Art Direction, and Nino Rota and Carmine Coppola shared the statuette for Best Original Score. Francis himself mounted the stage no fewer than four times, once when Robert De Niro, absent on a shoot, was declared Best Supporting Actor. 'I'm happy that one of my boys made it,' he said breathlessly. 'I think Robert De Niro is an extraordinary actor and he's going to enrich the films that will be made in years to come.' His most satisfying moment came when the Academy named him Best Director: 'I almost won this two years ago for the first half of the same picture – but that's not why we did *Part II*.' He concluded by paying tribute to Gordon Willis, 'and thanks for giving my Dad an Oscar'. Including the Award for Best Film, Best Screenplay (shared with Mario Puzo) and Carmine's Best Original Score statuette, the Coppola family bore home that night a total of four Oscars. Had Talia Shire been named Best Supporting Actress, the triumph would have been complete. Michael V. Gazzo and Lee Strasberg had lost to De Niro in the Supporting Actor category, and Theodora Van Runkle, although given a nomination for Best Costume Design, heard Theoni

Aldredge announced as winner for *The Great Gatsby*.

On 9 April 1975 Coppola sent a personal telegram to Al Pacino, who had failed to take the Oscar for Best Actor: 'When we won Best Picture I was speechless. Now I regret not having shared the moment with you publicly. Let me do it here. We won Best Picture together. Only we know how difficult that role was. My congratulations for your performance and your talent. If you'd let me know your secret number I'd call you. Love, Francis.'

Eleanor Coppola looks back philosophically on *Part II*: 'It was a more demanding story for the audience to take, and could not have had quite such broad appeal [as *The Godfather*]. After the good critics and the Oscars, though, Francis did have a feeling of satisfaction that he hadn't succumbed to total commerciality.' And when the entire Havana sequence showing the fall of Batista and the rise of Fidel Castro was censored by Pinochet's regime in Chile, Coppola must have smiled to himself with contentment.

10 The Family on Television

The revenue accruing from sales to television often rescues an expensive film from failure. During the past decade, the income from video has surpassed that from the networks to a huge degree, but Paramount and Coppola through the years have prolonged and refreshed the existence of *The Godfather* saga on TV.

The studio deliberately kept the original film dangling before the eager networks, to maximize hype for the sequel, which had already wrapped by the time NBC agreed, on 31 July 1974, to pay $10 million for a single showing. The telecast would be spread over two evenings, Saturday 16 November and Monday 18 November. The network charged advertisers $225,000 for a one-minute spot, the highest rate in TV history, exceeding by $10,000 a minute the cost of ads aired during the Super Bowl.

On 10 July 1975 it was reported that NBC had leased both *The Godfather* and its sequel for a nine- to ten-hour presentation, aired in four separate segments. Robert Howard, President of NBC-TV, commented that Coppola 'will, in effect, start all over again. He will reassemble all the material of both films – and utilize several hours of film not shown in theatres because of time limitations – to present the "Godfather" story chronologically in what will essentially be a new treatment.'

The idea of a reconstruction had struck Coppola while trying to impress a couple of girls in his office in San Francisco. 'All I could find to show off [my new VCR] system was a big box of the tapes of all *The Godfather* stuff. I fed in the first tape, and after a while I realized that we ought to cut the movie together just the way it was. So I called Blackie Malkin, and he came out to California, and I just showed him the reels, one after another in a row, and told him with notes and comments how to assemble it.'

All of Zoetrope's energies, however, were concentrated on *Apocalypse Now*, due to start filming on location in the spring of 1976. By November of that year, Coppola's people in California were concerned that he had not yet approved the actual editing by Barry Malkin for the proposed mega-screening on NBC. The assembly was in the form that Coppola had requested when he met Malkin in San Francisco in July, but it remained *merely* an assembly. Then there were such issues as dubbing, subtitle preparation, sound effects and opticals to be addressed.

'I had begun *Apocalypse Now* and left for personal reasons about the time of the first shut-down in the summer of 1976,' recalls Malkin. 'I knew that NBC were expecting this omnibus version, and somehow felt it incumbent upon me to do it, so I said I would, providing that I could work in my home town, New York. I edited the material in the Brill Building, which contains a lot of mixing studios and editing rooms. I was pretty much left to my own devices. I requested the inventories of both films to be sent to NYC and assembled the film in chronological order, as well as finding appropriate "act" breaks for NBC. Then I went back to the Philippines with a tape of what I'd done. I hung around for a weekend, but *Apocalypse* was still so chaotic that Francis never had a chance to look at the *Godfather* tapes. I returned to the States and

the next week Francis did look at it, and sent me his comments via telex and phone line.'

Malkin notes that the original script of *Part II* did not resemble the finished film in terms of continuity and flashbacks, and that the intercutting between periods developed during the post-production phase. 'So for the omnibus, I took all the early-1900 scenes and put them up-front, etc. I had compiled a much longer cut than NBC wanted, and I was disappointed that it wouldn't fit their format. But when it was screened it was met with such affirmation that they wanted more. But I said no, it had taken up so much of my time.'

Mario Puzo's The Godfather: The Complete Novel for Television eventually appeared on NBC on the evenings of 12, 13, 14 and 15 November 1977. Together, the two *Godfather* films had run six hours and fifteen minutes. Around one hour of discarded material found its way back into this new version, and the TV features amounted to a total of seven hours fourteen minutes, plus copious commercial breaks.

Three days after the telecast, the press could announce that the *Godfather* omnibus had become the most widely viewed theatrical movie on television, according to NBC research. The network estimated that an average 100 million viewers watched the nine-hour, four-night presentation. On its first telecast in 1974, *The Godfather* itself had ranked only fourteenth in the all-time list; *Part II* fared better, ranking fifth.

Part II had grown willy-nilly, and a first cut of almost five hours obliged Coppola and his editors to omit several choice morsels. But the original *Godfather* had also been chopped about in the final weeks before release, and the Paramount vaults contained numerous cans of discarded material. It took Malkin months of steady work to re-edit the two pictures into an almost seamless whole, even if nothing short of a third film could bridge the twenty-year gulf between De Niro's final scenes as Don Vito and the first appearance of Marlon Brando at his daughter's wedding.

After the first title card of *The Complete Novel for Television,* an elliptical opening montage includes a 'No Trespassing' sign on the fence of the Corleone compound, and shots of a decaying and abandoned house, with its evocation of *Citizen Kane.* Over the notorious final shot of *Part II* – Michael brooding in close-up on his destiny – Coppola's director credit is superimposed. Then the scene dissolves to the opening funeral cortège in Sicily, and the narrative proper commences. Throughout the presentation, small details are added – beginnings and endings of scenes, an extra sentence or two here and there, a fleeting appearance by a young man who will become Hyman Roth and who is given his name by Vito, after an 'Arnold Rothstein' whom the boy admires. A charming scene depicts one 'Augustine Coppola' and his little son who plays the flute in front of Tessio, Clemenza and Vito Corleone; the director's father, Carmine Coppola, became first flute under Toscanini and began his days in New York's westside district known as Hell's Kitchen. There is additional footage of Vito and Clemenza in Little Italy, with Fanucci being attacked behind the tenements by two clumsy hit-men, and staggering away like a wounded bull.

Some restored scenes improve the continuity: for example, the Don listening to Hagen's report of his expedition to Hollywood and the home of the intransigent film producer, Woltz. He says he will send the lethal Luca Brasi to 'reason' with the man. This bridges the rather abrupt cut from Hagen's leaving the Woltz mansion to the producer's waking to discover the stallion's head in his sheets. The compassion of Don Vito marks a restored sequence in the hospital where the Family's aged *consigliere,* Genco Abbandando, lies stricken with cancer.

Throughout the full version, Malkin succeeds in smoothing the rough edges that the pressures of time and budget had imposed on Coppola when releasing the original films. When the Don is ambushed in Little Italy, Sonny receives a phone call from a police informer, and then goes to his mother in the kitchen and tells her that the Don 'has been hurt real bad'. She preserves her unpretentious dignity and goes to change in case they are allowed to see him in hospital. Sonny, alone in the kitchen, tears off a hunk of bread, thrusts it into some sauce and starts eating it as he marches back to the den.

Paulie, a marginal victim in the original film, takes on a stronger profile in the TV version. He drives Clemenza and Rocco around the city before he is despatched on an open stretch of road. One restored segment shows an irritable Clemenza obliging Paulie and Rocco to wait in the car while he goes into a neighbourhood restaurant and enjoys a relaxed meal, knowing all the time that the unsuspecting Paulie will soon be executed.

Michael Corleone spends more time talk-

De Niro's Don Vito after clubbing an old Family adversary to death in Sicily (a scene cut from the theatrical version of *Part II*, but seen on TV).

ing with his bodyguards in Sicily, and also dominates a meeting with a wealthy young man who wants to marry Sonny's daughter, Francesca. When Don Vito returns to Sicily to avenge his mother, we see him murder not only Don Ciccio but also two other men, one of whom is stabbed as he lies semi-nude beneath a mosquito net and the other clubbed over the head in an open fishing boat.

Mario Puzo's original ending to both novel and screenplay of *The Godfather*, showing Kay lighting candles in church and by implication praying for the soul of Michael Corleone, at last comes into its own in the TV version.

The demands of a network screening involved some excisions too. Shots were trimmed from sequences in which Sonny screws his mistress at Connie's wedding, and is massacred at the tollbooths; when the blood streams down Moe Greene's face as he is shot in the temple while lying on a massage table; when a prostitute is 'killed' by Senator Geary at the brothel in Nevada; and when Vito brutally inserts his pistol into Fanucci's mouth on the landing outside his apartment. NBC also baulked at the percentage of foreign-language material, and Malkin was obliged to modify some of the Italian-Sicilian verbal exchanges by inserting certain English phrases mixed with Sicilian.

11 The Quest for *Part III*

'It's almost the story of the studio that was producing it!' – Francis Coppola

Almost fourteen years elapsed between the première of *The Godfather Part II* and the commitment by Francis Coppola to direct yet another sequel. For many observers, the ceaseless efforts of Paramount to resurrect the Corleone chronicle demonstrated to perfection Robert Louis Stevenson's dictum that to travel hopefully is a better thing than to arrive.

Coppola himself scaled new heights with *Apocalypse Now* and then plunged recklessly into such box-office failures as *One from the Heart* and *The Cotton Club*. He survived as a journeyman director, thanks to *The Outsiders* and *Peggy Sue Got Married*, but could not seduce the wider audience for personal, experimental works such as *Rumble Fish* and *Tucker, The Man and His Dream*. As late as November 1987 he told this author: 'I'm not at all interested in *Godfather III*. Because I know that if I had to do it, I would do what they do on these sequels, and just take the story and tell it again. I'm not really interested in gangsters any more.'

Yet it was not until 1988 that Paramount's Chairman and CEO, Frank Mancuso, gave Coppola an offer he could not refuse – a simple combination of a huge financial reward and artistic liberty to proceed with the sequel according to his wishes and not the preconceptions of the studio.

Tracing the various efforts to create a viable screenplay throws much light on the corporate obsession of the studio as well as on the perception of international gangsterism during the late 1970s and early 1980s.

As far back as 5 May 1972, Mario Puzo had signed a draft screenplay entitled *The Death of Michael Corleone*, intended as the basis for a sequel to the original *Godfather*. Apart from a few scenes, it did not fit the bill, and only some elements of the screenplay would be resuscitated for use in the eventual *Part III*.

Gulf + Western Chairman Charlie Bluhdorn remained beset by the Holy Grail of a *Part III* until his premature death from cancer in 1983, and would regularly fly directors down to the Dominican Republic in his private jet, wooing them in his thick Austrian accent to embark on another *Godfather* movie. Despite this, it was not until July 1977 that the studio registered a specific attempt to refresh the story. Michael Eisner, then a production chief with Paramount, and subsequently head of the Walt Disney Company, wrote a brief 'story arena' dated July 1977. A CIA agent persuades an imprisoned Mafia Don to eliminate a Communist dictator in Costa Rica. In return, the CIA will help the Don's cronies in drug trafficking. Agent and *mafiosi* would, at the close of the film, kill each other.

In the same month, Alexander Jacobs was commissioned by Paramount to submit first a treatment and then a first-draft screenplay (dated 30 May 1978). Michael Corleone has succumbed to cancer and his son Anthony seeks to cleanse the family name by selling the illicit gaming and hotel operations in Las Vegas (a theme that does in fact predominate in *Part III*). The headstrong Tomasso, Sonny Corleone's heir, involves the Family in renewed warfare with its foes, and in the first draft Tomasso assumes the role of Godfather so that Anthony can work behind the scenes to achieve respectability for the Corleones.

In late June of 1978 Charlie Bluhdorn himself allied with Mario Puzo to produce a draft treatment. An elaborate concoction of killings and betrayals, this would have placed Anthony again in the spotlight, entering into a deal with the CIA to assassinate a Communist leader in South America in return for a presidential pardon for a corrupt union boss in the pay of the Family. A mentally ailing Michael plays a subordinate role, confined to the Lake Tahoe estate and bereft of his children, who are now in the custody of Kay. Puzo relished the situation. 'Here I was the boss, and Charlie Bluhdorn took orders like a good soldier,' he says with a laugh. 'It was a sixty-page treatment, and he contributed some good ideas. But when I took it out to Hollywood to hand it to Barry Diller, who was then running Paramount studios, he was accompanied by his number two, Michael Eisner, and in the background was Jeffrey Katzenberg – all three of them destined to become huge figures in Hollywood. So, acting the wise guy since I'd collaborated with their boss, I said, "You're gonna find it pretty hard to dislike this treatment." And from the cold glare all three of them gave me, I knew that picture would never get made. They did not appreciate my New York humour!'

Later in 1978 Dean Riesner produced a treatment retaining the notion of Michael as a recluse, and having Anthony involved in a deal to assassinate the Hispanic dictator. This version would have been liberally salted with Mob executions, including the murder of Sonny's son, Santino, who has masterminded the death of Michael Corleone in a bomb explosion.

In March 1979 Riesner's first-draft screenplay developed an idea of Mario Puzo's, describing the conflict between the Corleones and both the CIA and a rival Family. Two motifs resurfaced in Coppola's and Puzo's *Part III*: the idea of a huge casino in Atlantic City, and the scene in which Anthony (Vincent Mancini) has an affair with a TV newswoman and kills two men who attack them while in bed.

More than three years later Vincent Patrick's name appeared on a treatment that placed *Part III* in the year 1964 and introduced Anthony (now estranged from Michael, whom he holds responsible for Kay's suicide) and Santino (Sonny's son) as comrades in crime, about to enter the drugs trade. Michael is killed in this version, while Tom Hagen and Santino are in Sicily.

After a hiatus that was in all likelihood due to the seismic impact on Paramount of Charlie Bluhdorn's death, a treatment emerged in September 1985 under the name of Nicholas Gage. Set in the 1970s, it shows Michael seeking to legalize the Family gambling business. However, he is brought to trial on the evidence of one Belangi, who has helped Michael to secure a casino. Michael evades the charges by pressuring a witness, and then has Tom Hagen executed for supposed treachery. 'Having eliminated all his enemies, supposed and real,' concludes the document, 'Michael discovers he's also eliminated the love and respect of his son, Anthony, his one hope for the future.'

In the same month, yet another treatment surfaced at the studio, written by Nick Marino and Thomas Lee Wright. It begins with Anthony's graduation. Vincent is a hotheaded family chieftain like his father, Sonny. Connie's son, Victor, hates Michael for having ordered the murder of his father, Carlo. So Connie schemes with him to assassinate Michael, eventually blackmailing Neri so that he poisons his master. Anthony wants revenge and kills Victor and others. He becomes Don, and the Family completes a new casino in Las Vegas. The same authors moved forward to an initial draft of a screenplay, dated 10 November 1985, with an expanded role for Anthony's girlfriend, Anne. She becomes his fiancée and their relationship somewhat parallels the marriage of Michael and Kay many years earlier. Literally days before *The Godfather Part III* eventually opened in December 1990, Marino failed to win an arbitration decision by the Writers Guild of America on a credit for the picture. He alleged that the script written by Wright and himself was used as a basis for the final draft by Coppola and Puzo.

Yet the likelihood of a plausible sequel continued to retreat like a mirage before successive Paramount managements. Not until 1986, when Mario Puzo was again requested to create a draft screenplay, did one or two of the essential ingredients of the film begin to emerge. Puzo sought inspiration in the decade that had always fascinated Francis and himself – the 1930s. He focused on Don Vito's struggles with Maranzano to keep the peace for the Families on the East Coast. Here we also have Michael's yearning to 'legitimize' the Family business, his wanting to retire and his final agreement that Vincent should inherit his mantle as Don.

Francis Coppola with Paramount president Frank Mancuso on location in New York for *Part III*.

Clearly the studio appreciated Puzo's effort, for he was paid to do a second draft (dated 30 November 1986), with a 'little more emphasis on the present rather than the flash-backs'. Tom Hagen dies at the outset, and Vincent is more aggressive about retaining the Family.

In the third draft, co-signed Nicholas Gage (17 January 1987), Anthony discovers that his father had lied about his past, and decides to quit. Against Michael's wishes, Vincent takes control of the Family, and Mary – Michael's young daughter – becomes pregnant and ready to marry. Yet a fourth draft, dated 26 March 1987, resembles its pre-

decessor in all but 'minor dialogue and scene changes'.

In the early autumn of 1988 Frank Mancuso decided to take the initiative. Sid Ganis, his deputy at Paramount, had known Coppola since the late 1960s, and having worked for George Lucas he also knew many of the director's friends in the Bay area. Using Ganis as an introduction, Mancuso phoned Coppola at his home in the Napa Valley and told him that his talent had been the common denominator of both *Godfather* movies. Now, said Mancuso, the studio recognized that only a film directed by Coppola would have sufficient richness and credibility to justify the revival of the saga.

Just as Coppola had been burdened with financial obligations in 1970, so eighteen years later he needed the money to sustain his independence at Zoetrope. *Tucker, The Man and His Dream*, although produced by George Lucas, had not done well at the box-office, and Coppola had already spent a considerable amount on pre-production on his epic about Republican Rome and latterday New York – *Megalopolis* – which would have been shot at Cinecittà in Rome.

Worse still, the threat of bankruptcy imperilled both him and Zoetrope, arising from a loan for $3 million that Coppola had accepted from the wealthy Singer family of Canada in the early 1980s. Gathering interest over the years, the debt now amounted to some $8 million, and this, added to the money owed to the Chase Manhattan Bank for *One from the Heart*, meant that Coppola might have to post a personal bond for $12 million, thus losing control of his company and his possessions, including the vineyard in the Napa Valley that had been bought with the earnings from *The Godfather*.

Although the exact dimensions of a deal may not have been worked out at that juncture, Frank Mancuso left Coppola in no doubt that if he agreed to co-write and direct *Part III* he would receive a hefty advance against gross points in the picture. Coppola played hard to get, and suggested that for $40,000 Zoetrope should draw up a 'feasibility study' for the studio, costing the new film in the light of current production exigencies.

Fred Fuchs, a rising executive in charge of production at Zoetrope's offices in San Francisco, worked around the clock to complete the report for Paramount by 15 December 1988. However, the first evidence of Coppola's intention to consider the project himself comes from notes (made by his librarian and researcher Anahid Nazarian) on a meeting held on 25 October: 'Pacino is sixty. So son is in thirties. So grandson is around twenty? Figure out exact ages. Set movie in 1960s to 1980s. Pacino's son like Fredo. Set mainly in NY and Italy.'

When Fuchs presented his report, he began with a ringing commitment: 'The movie will be written, directed, performed, designed and executed by the same talent that made the first two *Godfather* films cinema classics. *Godfather III* will be of the same texture and style as the first two parts, although closer in spirit to the first *Godfather* film in terms of scope, and will have a single linear story line. The intention is to produce a film no longer than two hours and twenty minutes so that it can be released in standard distribution patterns.'

Fuchs offered Paramount a choice between basing the film at the studios in Los Angeles and then leaving for location shooting after the stage work had been done; or shooting at Cinecittà studios in Rome, on location in Italy and finishing in other locations. He pointed out that Paramount could save some $2 million by choosing the second option, as lab costs, set building and other items cost much less than in Los Angeles.

The Zoetrope budget reserved $3,645,600 for Coppola's services, and $864,500 for the 'producer'. The 'story' would cost $2,040,900.

The 'cast' would run to $9,677,500. Including below-the-line outgoings, the total proposed budget was $36,984,205 – almost three times as high as that of *Part II*, but by no means astronomical in 1989. Pacino's fee had been provisionally set at $4 million, with Diane Keaton likely to receive $1,500,000 and Robert Duvall $1 million.

At this juncture the studio had not told Zoetrope that it would saddle the film with the accumulated and abortive costs of development since the mid-1970s. By the time Coppola began principal photography on 27 November 1989, the budget had risen to $44 million, of which $20 million was above the line (director, stars, producers, plus the accrued expenses).

The schedule assembled by Fuchs named 15 January as a date for completing negotiations with Coppola and Zoetrope, 10 August 1989 for the delivery of a finished script from Mario Puzo and Coppola and 1 March 1990 as the start of principal photography. Shooting would consume ninety-six days, and would be followed by thirty-four weeks of post-production. On 1 March 1991 Zoetrope would deliver a finished answer print of the picture. Three major locations would be used: Cuba, Italy and New York. 'The basic concept of the story [. . .],' wrote Fuchs, 'revolves around Michael Corleone. The setting is roughly contemporary and takes place in New York, Italy, Cuba and Las Vegas.'

Instead of focusing on superficial current obsessions such as drug cartels in Latin America and CIA death squads, Coppola believed that success would hinge on the way the character of Michael Corleone manifested itself en route to his inevitable demise, 'because that's where the tragedy lies', he said.

On Christmas Day 1988 Francis Coppola decided that '*The Death of Michael Corleone* will be written for fourteen reels, two hours and twenty minutes.' It would start with a close-up of a hand belonging to a plain-clothes detective, listening to a tapped phone conversation. Ten storeys up, in Las Vegas, Johnny Fontane sings a number 'for my Godfather'. Then we cut to Michael's suite, where he is being greeted by Neri and Hagen.

In early meetings with his associates, Coppola made it clear that Michael should be presented at about the same age (sixty) as Brando was in the original *Godfather*. A return to Sicily would also be intrinsic to the plot: 'In Sicily what you're always looking for is the contrast of that hot, fertile territory from which all this comes, juxtaposed with the stark scenes of conspiracy.' Coppola wanted at first to include Havana, because the Family had always conducted business there. He longed to study such corporate raiders as Boesky, Icahn, Milken and – in a first reference to the eventual film's most gripping theme – the Vatican Bank and its murky dealings on the world investment market.

'The idea [in the original *Godfather*] was that the Don split his attributes through his three kids,' declared Coppola at this gathering in Napa. 'Sonny had the warmth and the temper. Michael had the coldness, and Fredo had the kind of lovability. Brando was lovable too.'

He began to hint at various key motifs in *Part III*: 'Opera, murder backstage, Michael's son being talented at something. I had a funny idea that if you really get Frank Sinatra as some character, it would be a great scene if Sinatra slaps Johnny Fontane around!' Sinatra would later consent to play Don Altobello, only to withdraw when he learned that he would be required for two months on set and location.

Coppola suggested that Michael should die in the arms of Tom Hagen, the foster-brother whose shadow would dominate *Part III*. Gian Maria Volonté entered his thinking as a new-minted, more lethal version of Sollozzo, the Turkish drug dealer in *The Godfather*. There would also be a small role for Gene Hackman as a wiretapper, Harry Caul reincarnate.

Mancuso continued to be encouraging, and in March 1989 Coppola flew to Reno, Nevada, to spend a week in the Peppermill Hotel Casino with Mario Puzo. Their conversation was recorded by Francis's librarian, Anahid Nazarian, and whenever the suite became too stuffy, the two men would descend to the gambling levels. Coppola: 'I kept telling Mario, "We're losing thousands down here at the tables, but we're making millions upstairs."' During this conclave for two, many of the principal ideas and details would be born.

Coppola wanted to call the film *Mario Puzo's The Death of Michael Corleone* (and still does!). Kay would somehow have retrieved her kids, Michael having given them to her as they became older.

Puzo: '[Michael] is in legitimate gambling. He still has troops at his command, but he now has so much money that he has set up foundations like the Rockefellers. A couple of enormous foundations in memory of his father who established the Family – credentials to American tradition so his children and grandchildren could go into the mainstream – become senators, presidents . . .'

Coppola conceived the notion of including the Vatican theme. Various characters fascinated him: Bishop Paul Marcinkus, in charge of the Pope's finances, Cardinal Ottaviani, and even Licio Gelli, 'that crazy Italian involved with the Masonic P2'. He enjoyed Marcinkus's famous line: 'You can't run the Church on Hail Marys.' Puzo suggested a big meeting inside the Vatican attended by Michael.

He felt that Michael should be suffering from diabetes (rather than blindness, which would be 'really Grecian'). Also that Vincent would be Sonny's illegitimate son, like Edmund in *King Lear*. 'Handsome and sharply dressed like [gangster] John Gotti.'

He also liked the parallels with *Timon of Athens*, 'about a guy who's really rich and he's so generous and so powerful that when people come back' to repay loans, he refuses.

Coppola put forward the wild idea that Michael might be seen in some prison sequences after being arrested by the FBI. He wanted to begin the film with a wiretapping scene in a basement, like the Bonasera episode in *The Godfather*.

Puzo thought up the scene in which Vincent kills the burglars, which had been in the first or second draft of his own earlier script.

Both men believed that there should be 'a majestic death and funeral for Michael at the end. This is the epitome,' said Puzo. The film would begin in one of the Corleone hotels in Las Vegas on the seventieth birthday of Tom Hagen. At this stage, the character of Hagen was intended to receive the award, and the dignity, that because of Robert Duvall's refusal to participate in the production, would fall to Michael. Anahid Nazarian pointed out that Roberto Calvi, the Vatican banker found hanging beneath Blackfriars Bridge in 1982, had been a Knight of Malta, and that Tom/Michael could be given such an honour.

Coppola had lost his enthusiasm for the complex flashback structure of *Part II*. 'It's hard to juggle back and forth. It's like fighting a boxing match with one arm tied behind your back. You get the audience really going and then you've got to say, "Okay, now we're going to stop and we're going to go back and we're going to start telling you a whole other movie".'

Gene Hackman was again mentioned, and Coppola considered writing a cameo for comedian Eddie Murphy as a black gangster drug-dealer. He also wanted a new Sonny, in his twenties, and mentioned Eric Roberts for the part.

Coppola kept harping on his idea for a big boxing match in Las Vegas to open the film. Much time was spent on talk about reviving the role of Johnny Fontane.

'I think Vincent should die in this movie,' mused Coppola. 'That'll be a real shocker . . .' He also began to see Connie Corleone as resembling Winnie Mandela, at once protective and scheming.

After three days of intensive discussion in

Reno, Coppola and Puzo sent a jointly signed 'wish list' for *Part III* to Frank Mancuso:

1980, Straight Timing, Great Action Sequences, Authenticity, Great Villain, High-Placed Corruption, Big Believable Characters, Shakespearian Scale, Family/Business, Broadly Accessible, Vatican, Italian-American, Morality Tale, Old/New Morality, Loyalty, Michael's Power/Soul, Redemption for Michael (Rebirth, Resurrection), Talent, Opera, Young Person – New Era of Mafiosos [sic], Michael Love Interest, Las Vegas (Show Business), Death of the Empire, Rituals, Misdirection, Women, Living Style, Memorable Phrases, Music, Roman Empire Rituals, Timeless Themes, Intro New Talent, Erotic Moments, Big Money, Period Look and Texture.

With the exception of Las Vegas, every one of those themes appears in *The Godfather Part III*.

By the end of that March, Coppola was planning to write two reels a week. Puzo would work on the final four reels, so they agreed to meet and do the middle together, the section concerning the Vito Corleone Foundation. In conversations by phone and e-mail, they exchanged further ideas. They wanted, for example, to give the Don's old desk to Hagen on his seventieth birthday, all wrapped up, and opened to ooh's and aah's. They thought about dropping something heavy on Michael during a post-opera party on the stage, or having him stabbed or even tripping over a hole in the floor. Puzo believed passionately that Michael should be killed coming down the steps of a grandiose opera house – and this scene, one of the finest in *Part III*, testifies to his savvy. Coppola wanted *Cavalleria Rusticana* for the climactic opera sequence and had opted to make Tony an opera singer with this Sicilian classic in mind.

On 31 May Coppola flew down to Hollywood with Fred Fuchs and Anahad Nazarian to attend a crucial gathering at Paramount. Present for the studio were Frank Mancuso, Sid Ganis, Garry Lucchesi and a couple of other executives. Coppola, the born salesman always impressive at such moments, talked about the Corleones as a 1970s version of the Rockefellers. Rockefeller, he pointed out, was hated in his lifetime and suppressed unionism, but nonetheless established a foundation for doing good works.

Several interesting conclusions were reached, among them the need to retain Michael's cold, murderous streak; making the Archbishop a wolf in sheep's clothing, eternally corrupted; and having Michael refusing to endow Vincent Corleone with the Family name until the end – he would have to earn it like a knight of old. Connie would become like a *caporegime*, like Clemenza, like Lady Macbeth, said Coppola. He also likened her to the wife of Mao Zedong.

'There's something about the [Catholic] Church and its ancient medieval tradition that's great stuff for fiction,' Coppola told the meeting, and Sid Ganis recalled that Charlie Bluhdorn had sold half of Paramount's Marathon Street lot to Società Generale Immobiliare in the summer of 1970, in return

'Connie would become like a *caporegime*, like Clemenza, like Lady Macbeth . . .' Talia Shire with Eli Wallach in *Part III*.

for a 10 per cent stock investment in the 'worldwide real estate and construction firm'. Coppola remembered that when he asked Bluhdorn who this organization was, the Chairman of Gulf + Western had responded, 'Oh, it's the Pope.'

In fact, Immobiliare had a reasonably respectable pedigree as a long-established construction company that controlled real estate around the world, from shops and offices on the Champs-Elysées to the Watergate Hotel in Washington. The Vatican owned some 15 per cent of the shares, and thus exercised more than just a casual influence over the enterprise. Under Bishop Paul Marcinkus, a native of Chicago, the Istituto per le Opere di Religioni (more commonly known as the Vatican Bank) had prospered – not always via legitimate or orthodox methods. According to Richard Hammer, author of *The Vatican Connection*, the Vatican Bank was involved in the early 1970s 'with the potential effective "laundering" of almost $1 billion in immaculately forged securities [. . .] for which it paid a maximum of 65 per cent and then the sellers would give huge kickbacks to Marcinkus and others'. Marcinkus, not just your friendly neighbourhood Bishop but 'a hulking, burly man, towering more than six feet four inches and weighing well over two hundred pounds', was known throughout the Vatican as 'The Gorilla' and usually took charge of the Pope's personal security.

The link between Paramount and the Vatican may be traced to one man – Michele Sindona. A financier whose empire would crash in spectacular circumstances in 1974,

Sindona had bought a massive one-third segment of Immobiliare in 1969. Pope Paul VI, counselled by Marcinkus, had personally selected Sindona to serve as an adviser to the Vatican on things fiscal. His ties with the Gambino and Inzerillo Families made him a tempting prize, for Sindona effectively held sway over the 'cleansing' of around $500 million a year, which the Families derived from smuggling heroin out of Sicily. The Pope believed that by using the discretion of Sindona, the Vatican could tiptoe out of the financial limelight in Italy. Marcinkus held him in close friendship, and stated in public that he regarded Sindona as 'well ahead of his time as far as financial matters are concerned'.

Michele Sindona considered Gulf + Western as the model for a well-balanced and widely dispersed conglomerate. His silver tongue persuaded Charlie Bluhdorn to do what he assured him would be a painless deal over the Paramount lot, and at a single stroke Sindona had found a niche for Marcinkus in the forever alluring world of Hollywood. When Bluhdorn and his colleagues learned of the true nature of Immobiliare, they immediately bought back their property. Peter Bart remembers seeing Sindona walking the corridors at Gulf + Western's building in New York, and Coppola had been introduced to Sindona in the elevator by none other than Bluhdorn himself. 'I like *Part III* because it's almost the story of the studio that was producing it!' laughs the director.

Sindona's good fortune did not last long. After offering a reputed $1 million in cash in a briefcase to Maurice Stans, head of Nixon's

The menacing figure of Lucchesi (Enzo Robutti), with Don Altobello (Eli Wallach) and Vincent (Andy Garcia) in *Part III*.

Campaign to Re-elect the President fund (and being refused because Federal regulations did not permit anonymous donations), Sindona found it harder and harder to juggle his nefarious exploits. On 8 October 1974 his Franklin Bank closed its doors. It was the largest bank failure in US history, and left the FDIC (Federal Deposit Insurance Corporation) facing a $2 billion payout. For year after year throughout the late 1970s, Sindona fought a tenacious battle with the Italian authorities, who wanted him extradited to face charges of fraudulent diversion of funds. But he had friends in high places, none more powerful than Licio Gelli. This suave, 'unctuously

intimidating man', on whom the character of Lucchesi in *Part III* is obviously modelled, headed the notorious P2 Masonic Lodge. A significant number of Italy's top industrialists belonged to the Lodge, as did Roberto Calvi (Keinszig in the film), whose administration of the Vatican-owned Banco Ambrosiano provided P2 with a conduit towards respectability whenever a financial crisis loomed for one of its members.

When Gelli's protective network finally collapsed, police found a list of 962 members of the P2 Lodge in his office at the Gio-Le textile factory. Today he remains under investigation for occult and terrorist activities, as well as fraud involving Banco Ambrosiano.

Calvi had spent almost his entire career at Banco Ambrosiano, but his final decade would prove exasperating and his career crumbled to the point at which, having fled his home and office in Milan, he came to London and met his death by hanging beneath Blackfriars Bridge in 1982 – whether by his own hand or that of an assassin, such as Francesco Di Carlo, has still not been established. The Vatican's declared budget deficit had climbed to a disturbing $25 million by 1980, a situation improved only briefly by the popularity of Pope John Paul II. The earnings of the Vatican Bank became more and more indispensable, and Banco Ambrosiano could handle the necessary transactions, 'spiriting money out of the country as the lira weakened and currency regulations tightened' and investing them in offshore concerns.

Licio Gelli, the master manipulator, tightened the vice on Calvi at the turn of the 1980s, 'mixing promises of help with half-spoken threats to let spill other of the banker's embarrassing secrets'. Small shareholders in the Banco Ambrosiano protested in a formal letter to the Pope himself that the bank 'had strayed from the ideals of its founders'. Calvi, they stated, 'was the point where Sindona's Mafia legacy and degenerate freemasonry met'. It transpired that Ambrosiano had more than $1.25 billion in unsecured loans to Latin American subsidiaries. The bank was de facto ruled by four unidentified Panamanian corporations through Ambrosiano's subsidiary in the Bahamas, the Cisalpine Overseas Bank of Nassau – of which Marcinkus was a board member.

Calvi, vulnerable to arrest and already psychologically unstable, surrounded himself with a retinue of bodyguards, and drove only in a bullet-proof Alfa Romeo. In June 1982 his resolve cracked, and he travelled by night to Klagenfurt in Austria, staying in the home of the Keinszig sisters (from which Coppola and Puzo presumably took the name for Calvi's equivalent in *Part III*). From there he flew to his demise in London, perhaps unaware that his secretary had committed suicide by leaping from her fourth-floor office window in Milan, leaving a note denouncing Calvi for his cowardice in running away and for the damage he had inflicted on the bank.

The ill-fated Calvi was reputed to carry with him everywhere a copy of *The Godfather*, 'rather like a priest with his Bible', and admired Puzo's work for its grasp of 'the ways of the world'.

Michele Sindona lost his struggle against the law, although not before staging his own 'kidnap' by the agents of *mafiosi* in Sicily and the US, in a last frantic effort to trigger aid from his political pals in Italy. In the company of John Gambino, he left New York under cover in 1979 and went to ground in Palermo. But he soon felt compelled to return to the States, and the following year appeared in court on sixty-seven counts. Marcinkus and two cardinals offered to testify to his character (on videotape, not in person), but this was vetoed by the Vatican Secretary of State, 'who felt it would be neither fitting nor proper'. Convicted, and sentenced to twenty-five years in jail, and having failed to kill himself with an overdose of digitalis, Sindona ended his days in Otisville Penitentiary, where he was a model prisoner, and spent much of his time immersed in the pages of Nietzsche. Marcinkus, however, continued at the Vatican until October 1990, when at the age of sixty-eight he 'retired' voluntarily to return to his native Illinois, where he would focus on parish work. In his final years in Rome he knew that to stray beyond the walls of the Vatican would be to invite instant arraignment for financial improprieties.

Trawling these turgid waters, Coppola and Puzo found a dramatic hook – the death of Pope John Paul I in bizarre circumstances in 1978. Albino Luciani had served only thirty-three days as Supreme Pontiff before succumbing during one night to a mysterious ailment. He was embalmed with unseemly haste, before any post-mortem or autopsy could be performed. Shocked by what he saw as a negation of his Catholic ideal of grace through poverty, the new Pope had demanded that the ostentatious wealth of the Vatican be investigated. For individuals such as Gelli, Calvi, Marcinkus and even Sindona, this would have proved disastrous. Marcinkus had called Calvi a few days after Luciani's election and told him that he would do well to remember that 'this Pope has different ideas from the last one'.

Speculation over the legitimacy of the stated cause of the Pope's death had continued to fascinate writers and religious commentators throughout the 1980s. Coppola was drawn to the whiff of conspiracy that lingered about the affair, and decided to develop a story line that could reach a climax with the passing of both the Pope and Michael

Corleone. He and Puzo invented some characters, and based others on real-life villains such as Gelli, Calvi and, to some extent, Marcinkus (who, ironically, had been promoted to Archbishop only under the benign Pope John Paul II). New York gangster Johnny Zasa had his origins in Johnny Eboli or Johnny Pineapples, 'a good-looking, dapper dan who wears hand-tailored clothes, drives a big black Lincoln and likes good restaurants'.

Once Martin Davis, then head of Gulf + Western, had given the project the green light, Coppola plunged into the process of casting and pre-production, hoping to have more time for rehearsals than he had on the earlier *Godfather* films. 'Davis was so completely different to Charlie Bluhdorn,' said Coppola. 'The reason Nicholas Gage had been involved in a screenplay for *Godfather III*, and then came aboard our film as an executive producer, was that he knew Martin Davis.'

Old friends such as co-producer Gray Frederickson recommended that Coppola should shoot on the Paramount lot. The director even visited the Disney Studios in Orlando, but, as Frederickson recalls, 'Francis insisted; he knew Italy, liked living there and so we built all these New York sets in Cinecittà. Even the light switches had to be American-style switches!'

In June, things started to go awry. Robert Duvall, one of the two key figures in the newly minted *Part III*, did not relish Zoetrope's offer of $1 million to play Tom Hagen. On 27 June 1989 his agent, Bill Robinson, complained, and Coppola replied

Friends from the beginning. Coppola with Fred Roos, who has cast or co-produced all the *Godfather* movies.

directly to Duvall that the total above-the-line budget had been set at $17,188,366, involving $4 million for Al Pacino, $1.5 million for Diane Keaton, $1 million for Duvall, $500,000 for Talia Shire, and $3 million for the director himself. 'I appreciate that you might not choose to do this film, and certainly there will be no hard feelings,' he wrote. He told the actor that he was continuing to work on his role, including 'some good scenes with the banker Vanni in which they behave like dirty old men. I like the idea that each character in *The Godfather* now be touched by sin.'

Duvall did not reply. Instead, his agent said that his client 'of course is interested in con-tinuing the creative process with the hopes that you two can work together again'. But, 'a million dollar offer for this project is simply not acceptable'. Like many actors, Robert Duvall had achieved star status thanks to Coppola's belief in his talent (in *The Rain People*, *The Godfather*, *The Godfather Part II* and *Apocalypse Now*) and he could not tran-scend his pride to join the Zoetrope band for one more gig. Coppola remodelled the part on numerous occasions, constructing scenes so that Duvall need be available for only two or three weeks – but to no avail. Duvall declined every offer.

Throughout the summer of 1989 Fred

Andy Garcia as Vincent accepts the homage of Al Neri (Richard Bright) and Calo (Franco Citti) in *Part III*.

Roos had been testing some exciting new talent for *Part III*. Over one hundred actors auditioned and tested for the role of Vincent, mindful that this could propel a young performer to star status in the way Pacino had been in the original *Godfather*. Paramount felt enthusiastic about Alec Baldwin, but he was unavailable. Matt Dillon sniffed eagerly at the part, and Sean Penn and Coppola's nephew Nicolas Cage were also interviewed. A young Val Kilmer did a screen test for Vincent on 20 July. But both Roos and Coppola were in the end to plump for Andy Garcia, whose dusky charisma as Michael Douglas's side-kick in the thriller *Black Rain*

had caught the attention of everyone in Hollywood. An inspired choice, Garcia would move through the film with the easy, watchful grace of a closet assassin, like the young De Niro in *Part II*.

The casting of George Hamilton as Michael's financial guru, B. J. Harrison, provoked scorn among many industry observers. Hamilton, although beginning his career thirty years earlier on such intriguing films as *Home from the Hill* and *The Victors*, had become a familiar presence on talk shows, known for his deep suntan and his gigolo-esque good looks. Now, as a 'middle-aged, Waspy, investment banker', he would delight

Coppola: 'He's been an unused resource, and this film will have people reconsidering his image.'

Bridget Fonda won the small part of Grace, the journalist who sleeps with Vincent, against competition from Diane Lane and Rebecca De Mornay, but Michael's daughter (and Vincent's girlfriend) Mary would prove to be the role most difficult to cast and difficult to play – and one that in the eyes of most critics undermined the eventual film. Roos's original casting list for Mary included: Uma Thurman, Winona Ryder, Diane Lane, Mary Stuart Masterson, Madonna, Madeleine Stowe, Jennifer Grey and Molly Ringwald. His papers show that on 21 July he also tested the twenty-one-year-old unknown, Julia Roberts, in the wake of other stars of the future such as Gina Gershon, Marisa Tomei and Sandra Bullock. The choice would fall on Winona Ryder, a mere seventeen at the time, and yet a veteran with seven film appearances to her name, starting with *Lucas* in 1986.

Coppola had felt especially tempted by the potential partnership of Robert De Niro as Vincent and Madonna as Mary. But on second thoughts, the director decided that Vincent should be a younger personality; that meant Andy Garcia for sure. It also meant no Madonna. He described his dilemma in an e-mail to Paramount Chairman, Frank Mancuso, on 15 September:

We are at work, and I feel pulling the elements together. We are presently in Napa, with Al Pacino, Bob De Niro, Talia [Shire] and others . . . (Bob De Niro, of course, is working informally with us to see if idea can work.) We screen-tested Madonna (for Mary Corleone), and she did great.

We screen-tested Andy Garcia, and he did great . . . [De Niro] in fact did the test with Madonna, so we have a little of him on film, though without special hair or make-up. He looks good – forty at youngest, the question is whether with effort and work, [he] can come down to thirty-five. Fact that he was in Godfather II as Vito definite PLUS. Madonna looks twenty-five [. . .]

Diane [Keaton], who's not here yet, trepidatious about things like age (Madonna makes her hit ceiling as her daughter, although would work fine). I hope to have a real one-to-one with Diane, hear her thoughts, and hopefully make her more comfortable with her role (ageing wife).
Group read through script this morning and it felt very promising. More next week. Best, F.

On 6 August, Coppola had informed Mario Puzo that Duvall would not appear in the picture and that he, Coppola, was reconsidering the script. Michael becomes 'a powerful guy like Kirk Kerkorian – too big to risk or desire being involved in the Mob [. . .] I've wondered about starting the story maybe with a christening – and then the news of Hagen's death. Maybe even a suicide if it gives some momentum to the mystery.' Over the next two months, Coppola kept in touch with Duvall, but the actor insisted on a fee – as high as $3.5 million at one point – beyond the range of the budget agreed with Paramount. Not until 6 October did Francis abandon the campaign; he advised Puzo, 'It looks like we're not going to get Hagen – at any rate I don't think it worth going any higher.' He then outlined his idea for changing the opening scene and bringing the Archbishop into the limelight as a major character.

On 15 August Coppola e-mailed the novelist at his Long Island residence. 'We are going to do a full cast READING AND REHEARSAL, this coming Tuesday morning. If you were to be able to spend only three days with us, you would see things you couldn't otherwise see. You could help us to write and SET scenes right on the spot. Your contribution would be so powerful, that you would have definite IMPACT on your gross points [in the] movie [. . .] This will be a great chance, and your contributions mean $$$$$$$$ to all of us. The new scenes you sent were a GREAT HELP. Please try to fit us in for a days [sic] – your children will thank you –'

The novelist answered this plea, climbing aboard a plane, and driving up to Napa where Coppola had converted a large barn in the ravine to the north of his house in Rutherford. Reached by a winding lane, the air-conditioned barn permitted readings and rehearsals, even some primitive set-dressing, to take place. As the broiling sun worked on the vineyards in Coppola's Niebaum Estate, Al Pacino, Diane Keaton, Eli Wallach, Andy Garcia, costume designer Milena Canonero and Zoetrope executive Fred Fuchs relaxed in the informal surroundings and began to familiarize themselves with their roles in the production. Joe Mantegna, accorded the eye-catching if insalubrious role of Joey Zasa, enjoyed the get-together. 'If there is one image that I think I have of Francis, it is with an apron, either at the head of a table, heading a big dinner, and singing, or behind a stove.' Andy Garcia also helped in the kitchen, and the scene in the film when he shows Mary how to cook in the kitchen of his apartment stemmed from those days in Napa, when

Coppola had noted the actor's interest in food.

Al Pacino's deal, although agreed only in August 1989 and serving as the studio's signal to green-light the project, had never been in question. The actor spent day after day in Rutherford, keeping up with his other commitments by phone, and trying to focus on the changing role that Coppola and Puzo had created for him. In a letter to Coppola, he said, 'If we could be allowed to have ample time before we actually film [. . .], I think we will only benefit from this [. . .] I will give it what I can, but I owe it to myself, to you, to the film, to let you know that I am interested in developing something that I can get behind, that has momentum and metaphor and the power I believe it should have.

'If I do stuff in a take where half of what I do is grope for words and such, valuable energy will be wasted [. . .] As you may or may not know, I hold the record for consecutive performances of *Richard III*, but it was *rehearsed*! I can do it 'til the cows come home if I know exactly what I'm doing.'

Dick Smith, whose make-up for Brando had so influenced *The Godfather*, wrote to Coppola that he 'was fascinated to be plunged once again into the labyrinthine world of the Corleone family'. In the draft screenplay mailed to him, Smith found Michael described as 'in his sixties, white hair; the face of a bulldog. He is the epitome of the American businessman. Richly dressed, exquisitely barbered.'

Smith wrote that before reading the script, 'I visualized Michael as having put on weight, having that substantial look that De Niro had

Another loyal member of the team: Dean Tavoularis, production designer on all three films.

as Al Capone, so I was pleased to see him described as having the face of a bulldog.'

'Is it your intention,' he asked Coppola, 'that he should resemble his father? We could lean that way. A moustache would help. Al's hairline might also be receded some as well as grayed. I don't think that's necessary and I remember Al hated to have his hair cut [...]

'If I can be provided with good, close-up, 8x10 colour photos of Al's face and neck, virtually head-on and slightly three-quarters, I could make some cel overlays to show various make-up approaches.' Little did the enthusi-

astic, meticulous Smith suspect that Pacino's hairstyle in *Part III* would lead to a major rift between him and Coppola.

The loyal, quiet-spoken and prodigiously gifted Dean Tavoularis, one of the first to whom Francis had mentioned the possibility of a *Part III* as long ago as September 1988, had pressed for the production to be based in Cinecittà. Now he sat on a canvas director's chair in a remote cleft in the Napa hills and pondered his sketches for sets that would be built to his specifications in the Italian studios.

12 Shooting for the Moon

'We're back to the Borgias!'
– Michael Corleone

On 7 October 1989 Francis Coppola and his family departed from Rutherford on the initial stage of their journey to Italy to make *The Godfather Part III*. They flew first to Los Angeles, and spent the night in their house there. 'Fred Roos, the casting director, was waiting on the front porch with a box of video-tapes,' wrote Eleanor in her diary. 'We settled into the living room [. . .] I fell asleep on the couch, exhausted from the last weeks of cast rehearsals in Napa and preparations to leave home for five months.'

The family took a plane to New York and there embarked on the *QE2* for the leisurely passage to Southampton. Francis spent much of the time creating a stream of e-mails, tidying up portions of the screenplay, fleshing out others. When they finally landed at Rome's Fiumicino Airport on 20 October, an escort met them on the tarmac with the words, 'Welcome to Roma. You are the director of the film *Stepfather* . . .' The Coppolas barely had time to glance at the offices created for Zoetrope in the Stage 5 building at Cinecittà, before Francis was obliged to fax the final screenplay to Paramount.

Two days later, with much more anguish than he ever conceded in public, Coppola finally eliminated the name and role of Tom Hagen from his script. Walter Murch feels that this inevitably threw the film off kilter. 'In its early script stages, *Part III* was designed to be symmetrical with the other films. Each was about the death of a brother – *The Godfather* about the death of Sonny, *Part II* about the death of Fredo and *Part III* about the death of Hagen. So when Duvall asked for more money than Paramount was prepared to pay, it knocked the structural pins out of Francis's shape. Rather than Michael's fraternal struggle with his brother there was the sound of one hand clapping.'

The issue also triggered a flurry of suggestions concerning the screenplay from just about everyone. The three Paramount executives assigned to the film, Gary Lucchesi, Bill Horberg and Bob McKinn, sent Coppola a continual stream of detailed observations on individual sequences and characters. The director seemed content to accommodate thoughts and ideas from all sides – from Gordon Willis to Fred Roos, from most of the actors (Pacino, Keaton, Garcia, Shire, Wallach) to co-writer Mario Puzo – still on

Long Island – and of course from Zoetrope's script supervisor, Wilma Garscadden-Gahret. First cousin Bruno Coppola commented on the financial intricacies spelled out at the stockholders' meeting early in the story. Veteran technician A. D. Flowers offered Coppola a disquisition on how murders could be achieved with special effects. Fred Fuchs maintained a steady bombardment of memos, often helpful, to Francis about the screenplay. Even Richard Bright, brought back to play Michael's bodyguard Al Neri for the third time, would deliver to Francis handwritten letters about his vision of the role.

Altogether the screenplay progressed through no fewer than a dozen drafts. 'The

George Lucas visiting the set of *Part III*. With Coppola and Eli Wallach.

script's like a newspaper,' joked Coppola to his actors. 'A new one comes out every day!'

Dennis Jakob, a fellow-student of Francis's at UCLA in the 1960s and his companion in crazy dreams during the *Apocalypse Now* phase, now appeared on the radar yet again. Two weeks after the commencement of principal photography, he submitted a sardonic, yet beseeching critique of the script, pleading for Kay to be developed so that she would represent the moral fulcrum of the film.

In the midst of this open-heart surgery on a picture that would begin shooting only on 27 November, Coppola managed, through some mysterious, magical authority, to keep the climactic finale concealed from all but a handful of colleagues. Each version was shredded as soon as it gave way to the next. Key technicians were instructed to read their scripts within the confines of the Cinecittà offices, turning in their copies upon completion. The original ending described Michael's death when he is gunned down on the steps of the Opera House in Palermo, followed by his lavish funeral, intercut with Calo's vengeance on the wily Lucchesi. But in the pocket-sized, green-covered screenplays issued to the crew and cast, the final five pages consisted of forty-four scenes, ending on Vincent, the surviving members of the Family and other mourners in a cemetery, all of them having witnessed the burial of Michael Corleone.

One of those privy to all the changes was Dean Tavoularis, who moved from location to location and back again to Cinecittà, building sets, sketching new ones, dressing still others – such as the lofty interior rooms of the Palazzo di Giustizia that would serve as the Vatican Bank's offices in the film. Tavoularis describes how for his purposes he penetrated the Vatican: 'One day this driver comes up to me and says, "You wanna see the Pope's apartments?" So in a day or two the driver returns and says, "We can go on Thursday." He just knew the other drivers, the chauffeurs who drive all the Cardinals. So I went with one or two other people and we saw everything, and we went into a room containing the wardrobe with all the robes and all the gifts that flow to the Pope from different continents. Just beside the window where he addresses the throngs in St Peter's Square at Easter, there was this little niche where you can sit down – somehow very touching. Now the movie company couldn't go into this part of the Vatican. So I tried to simulate something, to get the identical flavour. Well, we found [a sixteenth-century villa] in Caprarola, about forty miles north of Rome, that had the big stairway going around where the Archbishop falls to his death. We just re-dressed it, and we had to do quite a bit of work on the windows.' Also not far north of the capital lay Viterbo, where Tavoularis and Coppola set the crucial confession scene between Michael Corleone and Cardinal Lamberto. Here they found a cloister garden in the seventeenth-century church of Santa Maria della Quercia.

On 7 November Coppola told *Daily Variety*'s columnist Army Archerd that he was working seven days a week to ready the film. 'We asked Francis if it's true the *Godfather*'s Corleone Family is based on the Coppolas,' wrote Archerd. '"Yes," he laughed, "and also on the Kennedys and

Rockefellers.'" Coppola claimed that he might have started shooting as originally planned on 15 November had it not been for the difficulty of assembling the cast. Al Pacino, Diane Keaton, Winona Ryder and Talia Shire each had schedules that 'presented logistical problems for Coppola'. In fact, Paramount had pressed him hard on this point: 'Our feeling on the casting,' wrote Frank Mancuso and Sid Ganis in a joint memo, 'is that since Winona is everyone's first choice, although we would prefer not to spend the cost of a delay, we should stay with Winona, particularly since she is not the *only* scheduling problem [. . .] As you know, the delivery date of October 26th is essential to the project and to Paramount and we do have concern that dropping from the 22nd of November to the 29th of November means a real reduction in the original post production plans, including, we assume, reducing the director's cut down to ten weeks.' This last comment struck home, for Francis had always insisted on a lengthy post-production phase.

On 15 November Coppola visited Palermo on a location recce with several colleagues: Dean Tavoularis, Gordon Willis, Angelo the set dresser, an Italian grip, an Italian gaffer and various Americans. Phoning his office, he talked of Palermo as being 'the final chapter' of the film, '[at] dusk, very tragic', with a flurry of priests outside the Teatro Massimo, and the assassin managing to penetrate the Family's security net.

Back in Rome, Coppola could not decide how Pacino's hair should be cut. Dick Smith had requested two full weeks to prepare the

new-look Michael Corleone, especially as Pacino sported shoulder-length hair and refused to have it cut until he reached Italy. Not until the Friday morning, prior to the following Monday's start of principal photography, did Coppola emerge from a meeting with Pacino in the latter's trailer and announce, to Smith and others, 'It's a crew-cut.' Smith remonstrated with him, saying that a crewcut could not hold the bleach as well as a business haircut. When he continued to argue, Smith asserts that Coppola said, 'Insubordination. You're fired!' and stalked off. Two hours later, Dick Smith received a letter from the director, not apologizing but reiterating his conviction that the crewcut was most suitable for his image of Michael in late middle age. Dick Smith could stay on the set until shooting commenced. The director recalls 'a long, difficult negotiation, with Dick stubbornly resisting me and threatening to quit if I did the crewcut'.

'Sometimes I have been impressed with these guys in their fifties or sixties who have this crewcut look,' commented Coppola in 1996, 'like they're men of steel.' Diane Keaton and others told Coppola he was crazy to cut Pacino's hair, and that Michael Corleone already possessed an established image in the minds of audiences. 'But,' insisted Coppola, 'this guy is now in a different part of his life.' Michael would surely not have the same hairstyle at the age of fifty-five as he wore in his twenties.

When Coppola first called 'Action!' on the huge stage at Cinecittà less than two weeks after that Sicilian excursion, he retained a

'It's a crewcut.' Al Pacino's distinctive new hairstyle for *Part III*. With Coppola and Andy Garcia.

very clear outline of the film's primary theme. 'Michael, in effect, will look toward Europe for his salvation, finding himself confronted with the audacious new identity of that continent, and its challenge to America,' he said. '[. . .] I have always been fascinated by the effect of pure wealth, pure power. The Corleones want to be legitimate. The Vatican is legitimate. The Vatican is also a separate state that can move money around the world.'

Despite this detached concept of things, Coppola found himself mired in detail from the very first day of shooting. Al Pacino's make-up took a long time to apply, and

Gordon Willis told Dick Smith and his associate Bob Laden (who had made up the face of Max von Sydow in *The Exorcist*) in no uncertain terms that he could not photograph the actor unless more old-age stippling was used. Smith complied, but 'It doesn't suit Al,' he said, 'It makes him look like a mummy.' So the Italian make-up artist was brought in, and he applied a very delicate coat and it passed muster.

As the shooting progressed, Coppola would sit with Pacino at the end of each day, and look at the scene they had filmed, already in rough-edited form, and discuss it. The entire production had been story-boarded into a preliminary final form, with the art department creating coloured sketches of each shot, as had been done for all Coppola's films since *One from the Heart*. 'We'd time each shot,' says Dean Tavoularis, 'by moving in or out of the drawing with the camera – a ten-second scene would run ten seconds. We called it the war room; you could see the whole movie in advance. Then the actors would read the script and you'd lay that on, then you'd do the music and you'd lay that on, and you'd have kind of a sketch of the film.'

'Pre-production, production, post-production are now turning into one very powerful phase,' said Coppola. By mid-December he knew that the film would run to fourteen reels, or two hours twenty minutes. 'When you are dealing on this scale of movie-making,' he emphasized, 'you cannot afford to produce a three-hour movie and then cut out forty minutes. You have to cut the forty minutes out now.'

The early scenes impressed Frank Mancuso back on the Coast. On 14 December he wrote to Francis: 'I had the pleasure yesterday of seeing the realization of a 14-year-old dream when I saw the first dailies on THE GODFATHER. Since we have been involved on this undertaking on and off for so many years, I am hopeful that it felt as good for you when you started to shoot as the experience I had yesterday [. . .]

'I am most pleased and impressed with the way you are handling some difficult situations. Please know that you have my continuing support for both this project and your attitude towards getting it done in the deter-

mined fashion you have displayed.'

In a rare interval of serenity during this pre-Christmas period, Coppola maintained his grandiose vision of *The Godfather Part III*: 'This is the cathedral of the *Godfather* movies,' he declared in his office overlooking the lush swards of Cinecittà. 'It's bigger in scale than the other two, and a very juicy, human piece.' Behind him, on an immense bulletin board, was pinned a photograph of his idol Akira Kurosawa, alongside a chart showing every pontiff in the history of the Roman Catholic Church. 'When this film comes out,' he continued, 'it will concern what's going to be in the papers at that point: the rise of Europe and the European challenge to America. It's very classical; in the tradition of a Shakespeare play, one of the characters, Vincent Mancini, is the illegitimate son of Sonny Corleone [. . .] There are many generations within the Family. Sometimes the younger members are more into the past than the future, and sometimes the older folk are more concerned with the future than the past.

'I think this script is stronger than the ones for the first two movies. A lot of what made those films good emerged from the combination of *those* actors, and *that* material, and *that* photographer, and *that* art director, and my being the ringleader. It's much easier to work when you have freedom from the studio rather than having to write a custom job. When I made the first *Godfather*, it wasn't a lot of fun.'

Eating his dinners at small places such as Ciak in the bohemian quarter of Rome, Trastevere, he spoke robustly of the accomplishment to date: 'This is the least "oft-

E59 OVER SHOULDER
A mounted policeman working his way through stalled traffic.

F59 EXT. RESTAURANT

The mounted policeman is one block away from a restaurant. We
see a guy in a nearby doorway. He's got a walkie-talkie.

VIEW
Horse hooves on pavement.

Storyboard images for two
sequences in *Part III*.

FADE IN:

53   INT. MICHAEL'S APT./KITCHEN - NIGHT

A stormy night. Neri is searching through the newspapers like
a seasoned detective. Michael doesn't seem well. He is there
with Vincent and ROCCO LAMPONE, an older caporegime. They all
have newspapers. Also Connie and Dom. B.J. is there as well.

                                          B.J.
                              We were lucky. No one knows you
                              were in New Jersey -- the papers
                              are full of names, pictures, but
                              no mention of you.

                                        MICHAEL
                              Grazia, Vincent.

                NERI
    The old dons were pretty much
    wiped out -- those who survived
    made deals with Joey Zasa.

                                        MICHAEL
                              Altobello?

                        NERI
            Had a stroke -- but survived.
            He's with his daughters in
            Staten Island. Going to retire
            to Sicily now.

delayed" of movies – it was started right on the clock. Who else has just started, literally from scratch and without a book or anything, and seven months later is shooting a film of this size?'

On Christmas Eve, the 'Family' gathered at the rented apartment of Talia Shire. There, as they surveyed the city from a huge terrace, Mama Coppola 'made her traditional seafood sauce with octopus for the spaghetti'. Al Pacino, Diane Keaton, Andy Garcia and his family, Francis and Eleanor, Talia and the others enjoyed a characteristic Roman meal. Next morning, they opened presents galore. 'We were twenty people spending the day together in a two-roomed apartment,' wrote Eleanor in her diary.

That Christmas offered a welcome respite before the tremor that would jolt the production to its foundations on 28 December. Indeed, never again would *Part III* arouse quite the same expectations among cast, crew and, probably, deep in the heart of its director. Throughout the whole of 1990, Coppola and his team would struggle to keep on schedule, to curb budget excess and to open the picture on time.

The agitation began two days after Christmas, when Winona Ryder landed in Rome. Accompanied by her boyfriend, Johnny Depp, she drove straight to Cinecittà for costume fitting and hairdressing. Her schedule had delayed her arrival, but as Mary she would be speaking only a couple of lines on 28 December, so the production team had few qualms about her apparent fatigue.

Next morning Ryder failed to answer her call, and Johnny Depp phoned to say that she felt unwell. The Zoetrope doctor went to her bedside. He pronounced her 'too sick to work', and said that she would best return home for treatment in the United States.

At noon Eleanor Coppola received a call from Casey, the assistant director, saying that 'Francis has decided to cast Sofia in the part [of Mary]. He asked if Sofia could come to the studio immediately, because a scene with her character was scheduled to shoot in a few hours and they needed her for a costume fitting.' Sofia – like Winona Ryder still only eighteen – was just waking up. At first excited, and then concerned at the responsibility, she walked with her mother to the subway and took the A line out to its final stop – Cinecittà.

A wave of gossip and uncertainty swept through cast and crew. The director had asked Fred Roos who could be signed at short notice to replace Ryder, and he had suggested the sultry Laura San Giacomo, who had come to the fore some months earlier in Steven Soderbergh's *sex, lies, and videotape*. But on reflection, Coppola plumped for Sofia, who had read the part of Mary just for fun while the cast had been rehearsing in Napa. She had, after all, appeared in a small part in Coppola's *Rumble Fish*, in 1983, even though she had not studied acting in any formal context. Many viewed the decision as sheer nepotism. After all, Francis had a reputation for giving work to his family, whether it be father Carmine, nephew Nicolas Cage, his late son Gio and his younger son Roman, or even his uncle Anton.

To add fuel to the flames, Diane Keaton was also due to film her first scenes that day –

and the forecast called for snow which in Italy tends to disrupt filming almost from the first flake.

The following day, Coppola sent a lengthy explanation to Frank Mancuso and Sid Ganis at Paramount. He wrote:

The main thing is I feel well. I am enjoying the creative side of the work: directing, rewriting. I feel the situation is stable here, although there is a lot of the gossip, uncertainty, feet-dragging, and second-guessing that ALWAYS goes on with a big movie [. . .] We are now completing our 5th week. This will get us past the holidays and into the principal set, the Michael Corleone NY apartment; with hopefully, ALL OUR CAST in place, many of them already deep into the work.

Coppola then repeated his familiar lament about the way a November 1990 opening date had obliged Zoetrope to juggle with set building and actors' schedules, and therefore to pull

as many IMPORTANT SCENES from throughout the script (i.e. OUT OF CONTINUITY) in order to be able to start shooting with ACTORS WE HAD, and on locations that COULD BE MADE READY. [He reminded the studio of Winona Ryder's commitment to her role in *Mermaids* for Orion, and his sister Tally's tight schedule involving *Rocky V*. For the first time, he mentioned Al Pacino's late arrival on set during the first few weeks, the disputes over hair and make-up and '[his] brilliant and completely unrelenting photographer, who rightly INSISTS on moving forward in an intelligent and STRUC-TURED manner – regardless of how the SCHEDULE wishes things to proceed'. [He lamented the fact that Raf Vallone, cast as Cardinal Lamberto and Pope John Paul the First,

did not inform Zoetrope of his commitment to performing matinees in a Shakespeare play in Rome, as well as sundry aggravations such as Diane Keaton's late arrival in Italy.]

After all this CHAOS essentially created by our *EARLY START DATE IN NOVEMBER*, we have succeeded up to this point. We are exactly ON SCHEDULE. We are roughly $110,000 over BUDGET. I will reduce that next week. I AM VERY PLEASED WITH THE WORK OF THE CAST, ESPECIALLY AL – but really all our actors.

In what must have seemed the most important letter of his working life, Francis expanded on his predicament.

On a movie, everyone WANTS the director to fall behind a day, because it means they all GAIN a day. It is like an undertow, invisibly pulling you out to the dangerous waters of OVER BUDGET.

You have to set them straight: all of them, the actors especially, know that the 'Oh, look it's snowing, no school today, let's go home' mentality does not work on my production. Everyone says they go over budget together, but IT IS MY SIGNATURE on that $43,968,386 budget dated 21 November 1989.

He rejected the notion of going over budget unless it proved unavoidable.

If in Sicily, I get hurt by weather, or if in a really great scene, I need more time, I assure you I will take it, and those will be officially approved FFC overages.

If, after a MAY preview, I feel I need 2 or 5 more days of shooting, I will take them, and they will be officially approved FFC OVERAGES. I will approve no other kinds of overbudget due to ANYBODY. I will use the more or less 2 million dollar contingency that I insisted on and you graciously gave me, ONLY FOR the opportunity to fix bad scenes, fix bad casting and/or INSURE the delivery date.

Then, and only then, did he broach the matter of Sofia's casting. He described Winona Ryder's exhaustion and how she had dropped out of the picture, and then revealed that he had originally written the role of Mary for his daughter Sofia,

mainly because it was inspired by her. She is the daughter half of an Italian and half of a WASP. I didn't particularly want to go through the whole deal of explaining why I wanted my daughter to you then, but gave the order that we would TEST her and that she would read one full day with the actual CAST, which I videotaped. Bridget Fonda came in the next day and did the same, as did Madonna.

I liked Madonna, because I thought De Niro might do Vincent. Sofia at 18 was too young, and Winona at 17 was also TOO YOUNG.

[. . .] Julia Roberts was unavailable, unless we would cause tough scheduling if we waited for her till after New Year. So I chose Winona, BECAUSE OF ALL OF THEM, SHE WAS THE MOST LIKE SOFIA.

Coppola once again outlined his determination to conform with Ryder's tough schedule (a director had been replaced on her previous film, and this jeopardized her start and finish dates on *Part III*), and his exasperation when he learned from the doctor that 'This girl is in the midst of a nervous breakdown. She MUST return to the States and get immediate medical attention.'

Then, the director said, having heard from Fred Roos that only Bridget Fonda (or possibly Laura San Giacomo) was available at short notice, he returned to his video-tapes and looked at the original screen tests.

After re-acquainting myself with the tapes of Sofia reading the script with Pacino, Andy, Diane – I confirmed in my mind, that my gut reaction wanted her all along, and was fashioning Winona in her image.

Now I didn't create this Winona problem, I tried to accommodate her in every way. So you know I TRIED. But given all the GIVENS, I made my decision on a creative basis, and I stand with it.

If in the future, you SEE DAILIES that are weak, or that don't live up to the excellent standard we are creating – please let me know your feelings, and I will see that they are up to that standard in the final film, whether by re-shooting or re-casting ANYBODY in this film. (P.S. I am the guy who [. . .] fired Harvey Keitel, after 6 weeks of expensive shooting on *Apocalypse Now*.)

So. That's how I see it all – obviously when you've had a chance to digest all this, we can certainly talk. But meanwhile, I am not authorizing any OVERAGES, whether insurance MIGHT pay for them or not. I think you have a good and a BIG claim when I think of all we did to get Winona, and her illness making all that a waste. As for Sofia, she is MARY CORLEONE. She has the vulnerability, the beauty, she really is half Italian and half English. I have already worked with her in two supporting important parts in RUMBLE FISH and PEGGY SUE GOT MARRIED, so I am confident she has the experience and the talent. Also, she had a major part in Tim Burton's FRANKENWEENIE. Interestingly, she was the finalist that Jon Voight wanted for DESERT BLOOM, and got beaten out by a younger Winona Ryder. I reviewed the reading and tests she did, and liked her work very much.

Also, most important, I KNOW SHE WILL

Father and daughter. Francis Coppola with Sofia Coppola between takes on *Part III*.

COME THROUGH FOR ME – which few people, up to now, have done.

Best regards and good wishes. Anxious to know your views. Francis Coppola.

This message landed like a grenade on the screens of the Paramount hierarchy. Mancuso and Ganis drafted an immediate reply by fax. It was avuncular and cogent in tone:

In the spirit of our personal and collaborative relationship [. . .] we must talk to you about casting Sofia as Mary. From the start we've always been interested in trying to bridge the generation gap by casting a young, hot actress in Mary. That was our motivation. We have known Sofia for years and have seen her grow into a lovely young woman. Nevertheless, even though Sofia is the

inspiration for Mary, is she the correct actress to play Mary? Based on our objectives, it made good sense for Madonna and subsequently Winona to play Mary. It was the right kind of heat.

There is a secondary concern, and it's a concern that's a much more personal one. As friends and partners we have to tell you that we believe that a decision to use Sofia will possibly be viewed as less than an objective one by the world out there. We know full well the ability that the press has to work around the truth. Reality is one thing, perception is another. You, more than most, know how cruel the press can be. They would have a field day with 'Coppola casts his daughter in key GODFATHER role'.

Although the choice to use Sofia, based on everything you've said in your memo, was a spontaneously correct production decision two days ago, we must ask you to please rethink and discuss with us this extremely important decision from both the artistic and marketing points of view. We understand that a number of actresses are available and are among those that were originally considered by you to play Mary. Please let's talk about this so that together we reach the right conclusion [. . .] In the meantime, definitely keep the faith and know that we are with you all the way.

Coppola, having once made an artistic decision, rarely changes his mind. Intrepid, impulsive, he pressed on with Sofia, and the cast and crew could mutter only token opposition. In an open letter to the entire cast, the director reiterated portions of his memo to Paramount. In another, he emphasized that 'It may be that my requests are unusual, or don't fit in with other production methods, but none the less, they represent the way I work.'

Sid Ganis jumped on a plane as soon as he heard that Winona Ryder was leaving Rome. Reaching Cinecittà, he began to reason first with Coppola and then with those closest to him. But this only stiffened the director's resolve to persist with Sofia in the role. He rejected all talk of flying Madonna in to take over the part. '[She's] got to be Diane Keaton's daughter!' he exclaimed in an interview after the film had opened. '[She's] got to look like Al! If you've seen the stills, Sofia looks like their daughter. It was casting. If she had not been my daughter but had been the babysitter that I had seen on the set, I might have done the same thing.'

Incensed by Ganis's efforts to turn Pacino and others in the cast and crew against him, Coppola alerted his attorney, Barry Hirsch,

and told the Paramount executives 'in so many words, "Get out of the kitchen. Because that's not our deal." . . . Bottom line: it wasn't up to them who I cast in the movie.' The frustrated Frank Mancuso, still in thrall to Coppola's talents, now also flew to Italy. He arranged an impromptu supper for Pacino, Keaton, Garcia and others, and told them that he had full confidence in Francis's decision. 'Basically, what they said [to me], was, "Frank, if you believe in it, then we feel more assured." They felt that if anybody had a lot at risk, it was certainly the studio.' Of course, Mancuso conceded to Coppola on this particular issue in the hope that he would deliver the mother of all epics in time for Thanksgiving 1990. He also knew that his director might well explode and storm off the set as he had during the shooting of Bob Evans's ill-fated *Cotton Club* six years earlier.

Sofia, timid yet tough, and respectful of her father's talent, played chess with Al Pacino while waiting to go on camera, and he would reassure her. 'I remember he quoted Brando's line: "Whenever you get the urge to act, wait until it passes off."

'At eighteen, I was right at the stage when I wanted to break away from my parents,' says Sofia, 'and so naturally I did not want to follow [Francis's] instructions.

'I suddenly found myself in the middle of everything, attended by dialogue coaches, etc. My father doesn't have to be diplomatic when he's directing Talia Shire and me; we're family, and he can show his frustration.

'There was all this high drama with the studio, and I felt caught in the midst of it all, just as Mary Corleone felt caught in between these bigger powers.'

Coppola's granddaughter, Gia, runs into shot and joins the waltz with Al Pacino and Sofia Coppola in *Part III*.

Even while the tabloid press were sniffing around the story, trying to penetrate a closed set, Coppola had to grapple with other problems. Gordon Willis expressed himself in such blunt terms to some members of the Italian crew that the director felt obliged to write an open letter to them – in Italian – explaining that both Toscanini and von Karajan had been guilty of such behaviour, while diplomatically implying that 'Maestro' Gordon Willis's frustration had been provoked by talking during lighting and the preparatory phase for each shot. 'Each artist has his own way of working based on his personality,' continued Coppola, presumably tongue in cheek, 'and the inner struggle he goes through in the pursuit of Beauty. [Willis's] anger is not PERSONAL, it is only BUSINESS.'

On New Year's Day 1990 Winona Ryder called from California to apologize to Coppola, and promised to make it up to him in the future. She did, by playing Mina in *Bram Stoker's Dracula*. 'I was in every scene of [*Mermaids*],' she would say later, 'and I got really sick, physically overexhausted. I went to Italy and realized they'd be working with a wet noodle. It wasn't even a choice for me. I couldn't get out of bed, I was so sick. It wasn't a nervous breakdown or pregnancy or whatever the rumours are.'

For Coppola, however, the pressures were mounting. He had let his temper show, not least with two of his oldest and most valued allies, Gray Frederickson and Fred Roos, the co-producers of *Part III*. Already on 3 December he had exploded at them for an incident at the entrance to the Vatican, when his car was refused entry by the Swiss Guards, and a scene had to be shot just beyond the perimeter gates of the Holy See. Now, under fire about the casting of Sofia, he blamed his colleagues for not having anticipated the problems with Winona Ryder, and for the production's ballooning costs. Roos and Frederickson were despatched to the States, to focus on casting and locations for the extensive New York portion of the shoot. 'I asked Francis if I'd done anything wrong,' recalls Frederickson, 'and he said, "Not at all, you're still producer of the picture, but things are going to get nasty around here. You're too nice, and I want someone to scream at. I don't want you to get caught in the crossfire."'

On 8 January a despondent Coppola faxed his research assistant, Anahid Nazarian, in Napa: 'So, I guess it's back to the drawing board for me. I plan to do extensive work on the script, of course this means the Sicilian or last part especially.

'So I will probably do it in some hotel somewhere, and I will need the most up to date script in reels that we have. [. . .] So, if you can make me a work script to go through [. . .] Let me know what you advise regarding a big writing weekend for me.' That night, he 'went to sleep in a cold sweat and got up at five in the morning to go to the studio'. Sofia, meanwhile, suffered under the strain of playing Mary. Her mother wrote in her diary: 'Well-meaning people tell me I am permitting a form of child abuse. They say she is not ready, not trained for what is being asked of her, and that in the end she will be fodder for critics' bad reviews which could scar her for years.' Fred Roos arranged for a voice coach to help Sofia with her accent, and reassured her that most of her lines could be looped later in the year.

On 19 January, however, everyone enjoyed a twinkling of release during the waltz scene with Al Pacino and Sofia in front of the guests in the opening party sequence. Coppola's grand-daughter Gia ran into shot and seized Sofia's skirt. The cameras continued to roll. 'I would wager that spontaneous moment will end up in the final cut,' noted Eleanor – and it did.

By now the film had slowed to a trudge. Morale was down among the actors and crew. Talia Shire had to rush through her final shots because of her commitment to *Rocky V*. With all hopes dashed of a sneak preview in Seattle in May, Coppola acknowledged that he would have to apply the scalpel to much of the Sicilian segment. He also had to cope with the arrival on 3 January of a new co-producer, Charles 'Chuck' Mulvehill, who had been hired by Fred Fuchs at Coppola's request. Mulvehill, a veteran of twenty years in the business, had produced many of Hal Ashby's best films. When he heard on New Year's Eve that Zoetrope wanted to hire him, Mulvehill 'thought hard about it for about forty-five seconds. I thought, "It's *Godfather III*, it's Francis! Going into a situation like this is like fucking without any foreplay."' Within a month, Coppola found him 'wise and impartial'.

Mulvehill concentrated on bringing the budget under control and on ensuring that the logistics of the Italian and Sicilian shoot would proceed smoothly. Francis regarded him as a person in whom he could confide. On 24 February, for example, he e-mailed him across Cinecittà:

I know you are busy so rather than 'summon' you here to the [Silver] Fish, interrupting you, I thought I'd send you some of my feelings as to where I am.

I really felt this morning my nerve starting to go. I guess the process of changing and rewriting at such a pace, trying to deftly benefit from so many people's suggestions (when as we all know, everyone has an opinion, and sometimes two different wise people will disagree), some tough comments by fax from Barry Malkin, the main editor, who, while not actually working on the stuff, is monitoring everything on tape while finishing *The Freshman*, and the ridiculous situation I had at 6.00 a.m., where I couldn't find ANYONE's telephone number, so as to be able to call Fred Fuchs or Lisa Fruchtman, the SF editor. I got myself very frazzled, and was late this morning, which really makes me feel bad.

He expressed his shock at the continuing budgetary problems, and assured Mulvehill that he would 'keep improving the story and script'.

I hope to issue another [version] today and Friday, or just Friday. And then use the weekend TO WORK ONLY ON THE MURDERS AT THE [TEATRO] MASSIMO. In truth, I have never really worked on this sequence, but rather just keep updating current ideas. I have never really sat down and really written this. [. . .] I think my time alone writing the script is impor-

tant, because I get so much input from so many people, and all of it useful and good. But I must choose and make the decisions alone, right? So they will come from my most personal instinct and my heart.

He went on to suggest that they transfer much of what had already been shot on to video, so that it could be assembled swiftly in San Francisco, and record the revised script for the parts not yet filmed – and

begin informal previews (with the same questionnaire we will use in our May preview in a theatre). I think some small (around 30–40) groups of impartial people, or friends and those able to make clear judgement and give us valuable feedback [. . .] I think we should make this our priority, because then we'll have true feedback as to Andy's Cuban accent, Sofia's viability, Tony's viability, the Archbishop's strengths or weaknesses, Connie's role in the overall film [. . .]

At one juncture, Coppola gave serious consideration to cutting Sicily out of the film because 'I can't be finished next week, no way. So what I basically think [is of] cutting the funeral, cutting the cathedral and cutting out the Altobello orange scene, and cutting some of the action.' He also considered reducing the shoot in Palermo to just a couple of nights, to achieve the atmosphere. In a phone conversation with Mario Puzo, he conceded, 'We've shot it all out of continuity and I'm just flying by the seat of my pants.' Not the least of his worries was the sudden break-up in the long-standing off-screen romance between Al Pacino and Diane Keaton. Both actors remained in Rome, but their scenes together acquired an added friction. When

Pacino's grandmother died in the late winter, they flew to America to attend the funeral.

On 8 March the production moved at last to Sicily. The previous day, as Eleanor noted in her diary, 'Everyone was looking forward to having a piece of the cake and celebrating the final shot [at Cinecittà]. Everyone was disappointed to find that under the real icing, the cake was cardboard.'

On arrival in Palermo, Coppola was invited, along with Dean Tavoularis, to see the Mayor. 'He was a young guy, energetic, speaking perfect English,' recalls Tavoularis.

Director and cinematographer chat in front of the Teatro Massimo in Palermo during the final days of shooting in Sicily.

'He assured us there would be no problems from the Mafia, and there weren't, there were no strong-arm tactics, or any kind of innuendo.' Eleanor Coppola, though, says that 'On the first day of shooting in Palermo, I rode to the set with Francis [. . .] Outside [Michael's villa] I saw a very large man in a black suit and dark sunglasses accompanied by a smaller man dressed identically. They looked like two guys sent by Central Casting to play *mafiosi*. I asked the production manager if they were *mafiosi*. He said, "Yes, they are here to help us." Later I heard there had been two groups who had wanted to "help" the production and there had been some difficulties arranging for only one.' Coppola himself had purchased a book of Sicilian phrases and proverbs, hoping to find more gems of the 'stone in my shoe' brand – but he could not read the Sicilian, and tossed it aside!

Once again, the troupe would use Forza d'Agro as a substitute for the town of Corleone, but this time several scenes were filmed in Palermo itself, involving church exteriors, interiors, streets and so on. The Teatro Massimo in the Piazza Verdi dates from 1897, although the architect G. B. Basile began work on it in 1875. Its neoclassical façade is fronted by an imposing staircase, which formed the setting for the climax of the film. Coppola had first learned of its significance on Labor Day weekend in 1989, when cinematographer Vittorio Storaro called him in Napa and mentioned that an exhibition of his stills and photographic work was opening at the Teatro Massimo. Using the opera house as a location, however, posed logistical problems, because it was in the process of being rebuilt.

'There was a gigantic hole at the back of the proscenium,' recalls Tavoularis, 'where the rest of the building had been removed. Of course in an opera house you have an equal distance behind the stage as you do where the audience sits. German companies were installing the ultimate in elevators, computerized backdrops, etc. So there was no way to shoot. We had to build the front, the proscenium, at Cinecittà, and the first few rows of thirty seats on left and right, and shot the performance [of *Cavalleria Rusticana*] on the so-called comfort of the stage; and all the reverse shots, with the royal box, were done in Palermo.'

In a letter dated 21 March, Zoetrope's Italian production supervisor, Sandy Normann, described the death of an aged friend from diabetes, and counselled Coppola against having Michael commit suicide in the film. 'I "see" Michael, sick, "gone" with the background of life; [Mount] Etna, the orange grove, the sea or maybe even Kay there, absently. A life, Michael's life, broken, ruined, while other lives move about continuing life's cycle. Or else an image which struck me a year ago. It was the picture of [Alberto] Moravia with a huge straw hat, sitting on a chair, staring at the large empty sea, in a total emptiness, like life.'

Absorbing this and countless other recommendations, Coppola at last felt ready to decide on the ending of the film. On 27 March he faxed Mario Puzo, who was in Los Angeles:

I don't think [the] audience has come necessarily to see Michael get killed – they don't [know] what they want, but they want some kind of moving resolution. [. . .] The killing of Mary is exactly the

Working on *Part III* in the half-rebuilt opera house in Palermo.

same as killing of Apollonia [in *The Godfather*]. That was also innocence killed. But neither Apollonia's nor Mary's death has anything to do with them, but with EFFECT AND SUFFERING IT BRINGS TO MICHAEL. Killing of Apollonia and Mary is fairy tale – the audience DID and will like it.

Just to shoot Michael doesn't make him pay, he doesn't really suffer, and it's not so terribly dramatic and is expected [. . .]

The ending of Michael living to be old man in exile is good – it was one of your original ideas. It is similar to *Godfather II*, but different in that he dies. – He dies a peaceable death in a garden like his father, but with difference that he has suffered long and hard and paid for his sins.

So, unless you wish to convince me otherwise – that's how it will be.

The next day Puzo faxed his response:

We don't disagree. We only 'differ'. I always hate to disagree with you. Let me say first. Whatever you decide, I have absolute faith in you [. . .] You are the one everybody is depending on to make this hopefully a great movie. Our job is to help you, not obstruct you. Everybody feels this way [. . .]

About Michael dying of old age. That's the way it should be in a book. It is a literary ending. His getting killed violently is I believe the correct 'film' ending. Which is very funny because we both are for the endings opposite to what people would normally expect. Again here you are the guy who has to take the heat so you have to follow your own vision.

On 3 April some 450 extras gathered outside the Teatro Massimo for the first of various night shoots. Rehearsals continued until 10 p.m. Following a meal break, the crew laboured for several hours to arrange the complex lighting conceived by Gordon Willis. At around 1.30 a.m. Coppola called 'Action!' and the first shot was taken, of the crowds arriving at the opera house, with the Corleone Family emerging from their limousines and mounting the steps of the theatre. By 3 a.m. three takes were in the can, and everyone departed except for the camera crew, who had to prepare the following day's shoot. In her diary, Eleanor noted: 'Many people think the film should end with Al Pacino dying in a burst of gunfire on the steps of the Teatro Massimo, as Francis wrote it in the original script. Now Francis feels it should be more unusual; it should end like *King Lear*, where his daughter dies, though in

this case he is left to live with the horror of his life [...]'

Coppola's solution pleased the studio, at least to judge from a note he received from Sid Ganis: 'Just got finished looking at the wonderful, wonderful finale on the steps of the opera house, and it's brilliant stuff – I mean really brilliant – emotionally, theatrically, and epic-ly (if there is such a word). It's Shakespearean. It's Shakespearean tragic death. It's exactly what you said you wanted to do. Great going!'

After nine weeks in Sicily, in early May the circus transferred to New York (with a brief excursion to Atlantic City for exterior shooting at the Trump Castle Casino Resort). As late as the first ten days of May, Fred Roos was casting and testing for minor roles and spectator parts. Locations had been selected

The death of Mary, with Al Pacino and George Hamilton at right.

by Roos and Gray Frederickson throughout Manhattan, among them Old St Patrick's Cathedral on Mulberry Street, the Verrazano Narrows Bridge, the Mietz Building on Mott Street, the Waldorf Astoria Hotel, the New York University Hospital and the Red Zone night-club at 438–440 West 54th Street.

Just as the Mob had struck at Joe Colombo while *The Godfather* was being filmed on the streets of New York, so another hit occurred as Pacino and Keaton prepared for a scene in Little Italy. James Bishop, former secretary and treasurer of the painters' union, was shot and murdered as he sat in his Lincoln Continental in the select Beechhurst section of Queens.

Tavoularis and his team dressed Elizabeth Street (between Houston and Prince) for the flamboyant sequence in which Joey Zasa is assassinated by Vincent, posing as a cop on horseback. The 'real' Festival of St Anthony took place on adjacent Mott Street, in an eerie reminder of the Festa in *Part II*, when Fanucci struts his stuff and young Vito tracks him along the rooftops. Until the schedule became too tight, Coppola had intended to stage Zasa's murder during the New York Marathon. And at an even earlier stage of gestation, the attempt on Grace's life also was to have taken place amid the hectic confusion of the Marathon.

On 25 May shooting ended in Manhattan, after 125 days of principal photography. At the wrap party, however, Coppola could not abandon himself to the celebrations. Within a few weeks, he had to recall Al Pacino, Andy Garcia and others to New York for additional shots to improve the flow of the film.

Early on 16 July the Paramount hierarchy flew to San Francisco, where a morning screening of the first rough-cut had been arranged at the North Point theatre. They were met by a bleary Coppola, who had worked through the night to ensure that the last reels would be ready. Afterwards, the executives told Coppola that a new scene was needed, one in which Michael Corleone hands over power to Vincent, providing the springboard for yet another *Godfather* film. According to his wife, 'Francis responded strongly, wanting the focus of the film to be on Michael and not to be obligated to the character of Vincent. The screenplay had always included a sequence showing Michael dubbing his nephew 'Vincent *Corleone*', and so now Coppola fleshed it out with additional close-ups and shots of Neri and Rocco paying homage to the new 'Don Vincenzo Corleone', witnessed by an approving Connie.

Despite all the sophisticated technology available, the editing of *Part III* still extended throughout the summer and autumn of 1990. In September, Coppola asked his old friend Walter Murch to help him finish the film. 'There were structural problems,' recalls Murch. 'The flashback structure of *Part II* had, in a paradoxical way, given one a concept to steer by.' Lisa Fruchtman and then Barry Malkin had been working on a random-access, computer-controlled montage editing system, but when Murch came along, 'it just didn't seem practical [. . .] to add a third station, so I worked directly on film.'

The final weeks of 1990 proved nail-biting times for Frank Mancuso, Sid Ganis and everyone at Paramount. Having missed the Thanksgiving release slot, *The Godfather Part III* was rescheduled for Christmas Day. This would enable it to take advantage of the holiday crowds and also qualify for the Academy Awards. But Pacino was still looping his lines in early November, and even by the last week of the month only two reels had been mixed. Coppola's staff worked around the clock with technicians at George Lucas's Skywalker Ranch facility in Marin County. On 10 December the first answer prints were available, and two days later Paramount arranged screenings for eager journalists in both Los Angeles and New York. At the underground Loew's Astor Plaza in Manhattan, the air-conditioning could not cope with the immense crowd of critics and industry invitees. Reviewers may have had literally only hours to file their copy, but the laboratories experienced even greater pressure. Over 1,800 prints had to be manufactured and distributed throughout the United States and Canada for the opening on 25 December. Some reels arrived at theatres a mere twelve hours prior to the opening, with the soundtrack out of synch; others suffered from poor colour grading; one even had the dialogue track missing from an entire reel. Had Paramount treated the original *Godfather* with the same unseemly haste, then there might never have been one sequel, let alone two.

The task of the two Hollywood trade papers, *Variety* and the *Hollywood Reporter*, in their reviews of new films is to 'call' the likely prospects for distributors and exhibitors in America (and now beyond). Both in their enthusiasm overestimated the success of *Part III*. Todd McCarthy, one of the most seasoned reviewers on the Coast, assessed the picture in terms that would be justified with the passage of time, but that struck industry observers as hyperbolic: 'Faced with the extraordinary task of recapturing magic he created sixteen and eighteen years ago, Francis Ford Coppola has come very close to completely succeeding with *The Godfather Part III*.' He hailed the climax of the film: 'The best is yet to come. In one of the most masterful examples of sustained intercutting in cinema, Anthony's performance in *Cavalleria Rusticana* serves as the backdrop for several murderous missions.'

For Duane Byrge in the *Reporter*, Pacino's performance was 'brilliant' and he regarded Coppola's work as 'a complex depiction of Michael Corleone's dying days attempt to cement the family in the "legitimate" business world and attain spiritual redemption, this third instalment of the Corleone Family chronicle is a full-bodied, albeit sombre dramatic orchestration.'

In the early 1970s fewer consumer magazines reviewed new releases with the same high profile as they do in the 1990s. The full ridicule of the tabloid and glamour monthly press was now unleashed against Sofia Coppola, in particular, for her performance – or lack of it. Her father found himself wounded by the scornful comments about Sofia. 'He felt those criticisms were meant for him,' says Eleanor, 'and that Sofia received them the way Mary Corleone got the bullets intended for Michael.' Sofia was encouraged, however, by letters of congratulation from Woody Allen, Anjelica Huston and others in the industry. She turned her back on screen acting, instead enrolling at the California Institute of Arts and studying painting. She has since become a published stills photographer, and is involved in a clothing-design concern. 'The Sofia "spin" was created by [the article in] *Vanity Fair* and abetted, unwillingly, by Paramount. After that article, Sofia was fair game.'

When the picture opened in the UK reviewers found themselves equally divided. Alexander Walker, in the influential London *Evening Standard*, had filed a rave from a screening he had attended in New York, while Philip French in the *Observer* wanted to endorse the film, but while granting that 'this engrossing movie is conceived and executed on a grand scale [. . .] oddly enough, Michael seems to shrink in stature as the picture proceeds and the Lear-like tragedy at which Coppola aims is not realized.' Hugo Davenport in London's *Daily Telegraph* protested against being asked to accept Michael Corleone as a tragic figure after seeing him commit fratricide in *Part II*.

In the first three days, *Part III* performed, to use *Variety*'s phrase, 'like gangbusters', grossing $14,023,983, just below the all-time $14.5 million posted by *Batman* the previous summer. But business during the first full weekend was merely respectable, and after eight days the gross had reached $33.5 million. Receipts plunged by 50 per cent in the second week, and by 56 per cent in the third. The film paled to $64 million after eight weeks, and a final tally of $67 million before slipping quietly out of contention in the spring of 1991.

International grosses were on a similar level ($60 million), helped by a prestigious launch at the Berlin Film Festival in February, with Coppola in attendance. With the final budget hovering around $55 million (plus prints and advertising), even all the eager theatre owners in Japan could not save *The Godfather Part III* from proving an expensive enterprise for the studio. Television and ancillary income would gradually sweeten the balance-sheet, but came too late to spare Frank Mancuso, whose abrupt departure from the presidency of Paramount in the spring of 1991 seemed to reflect the studio's bruised expectations.

The awards season brought more frustration. Martin Scorsese's *Goodfellas* captured the Best Film accolade from the New York Film Critics' Circle and the Los Angeles Film Critics' Association, Coppola being mentioned by neither body. Laden with seven nominations at the Golden Globes and seven nominations at the Oscars, *The Godfather Part III* left both ceremonies with nothing, as *Dances with Wolves* emerged as everyone's favourite of the year.

According to the 'combined continuity and spotting list' issued by Paramount on 27 December 1990, the film ran two hours forty-one minutes thirty-three seconds. Coppola could not conceal his impatience, and for the video version he restored fourteen minutes, much of the extra footage involving scenes between Sofia and Michael, and Sofia and Vincent. 'I'd kept pleading for another few months to do the film properly,' he recalls. The original Zoetrope feasibility study had, after all, stressed the need for an extended schedule.

So *Part III* came to light in much the same mood of breathless exasperation as had its progenitor, *The Godfather* itself. Both films, felt the director, would have been enhanced had he been able to edit and mix them without duress. Coppola is no Orson Welles where protracted schedules are concerned, but he is a perfectionist who loathes releasing a film to its audience before it has – like a case of his Rubicon wine – reached maturity.

Few critics credited him with the trilogy's most unusual feature – the consistent ageing of the characters in rhyme with the narrative. Usually the actors in sequels are not those who appeared in the original, but Coppola insisted on assembling his original core of players – Pacino, Keaton, Shire, Bright – for each episode and so rendered them human

Nearing the conclusion. Coppola with Pacino in pensive mood on *Part III*.

and plausible to a striking degree. It recalls Welles's poignant, unfulfilled hope of reuniting Joseph Cotten, Tim Holt, Anne Baxter and Agnes Moorehead, to shoot a final scene for *The Magnificent Ambersons*, showing them in old age.

Part Two

1 The Family Connection

'A man has only one destiny' –
Michael Corleone in
The Godfather Part III

If a single concept prevails and abides throughout the *Godfather* trilogy, it must be the Family. It is an idea that has obsessed Mario Puzo in his novels, and its importance has marked both his life and that of Francis Ford Coppola.

Puzo's parents came from Italy, growing up 'on rocky, hilly farms in the countryside adjoining Naples', and emigrated to the United States only a little later than young Vito Andolini in *The Godfather*. Their subsistence in the tenements of Hell's Kitchen during the Depression years is reflected in the pages of Puzo's finest novel, *The Fortunate Pilgrim*. Whenever the unity of the Family comes under pressure, their survival is threatened. In *The Godfather Part III*, Michael pronounces some lines that were cut from the eventual film: 'Every family has bad memories. The father is a drunk, the mother is a whore. A son takes to drugs, somebody dies young of cancer, a child gets hit by a truck. They live in poverty, they get divorced. Somebody becomes insane. Every family has bad memories.' The hand of Puzo may be seen here, for so much of this disfigures the life of Lucia Santa, the ultimate Italian *mama,* in *The Fortunate Pilgrim.*

Coppola's own family means more to him, quite simply, than anything else on earth. His wife, children and often cousins, nephews, grandchildren, accompany him to the most remote of locations. 'We travel together like a circus family,' says Eleanor, 'with Francis on the tightrope and the rest of us holding the ropes.' His brother August recalls that, 'In our family life, there was great passion, creativity, belief in opera. The family was the literature

Family reunion in Palermo during the filming of *Part III*: Carmine Coppola, Francis Coppola, Eleanor Coppola and Italia Coppola.

incarnate.' Francis's mother came of Neapolitan stock, and her father, Francesco Pennino, established himself in Brooklyn as a theatre manager and songwriter. In 1949 he presented Francis with his first 16-mm camera as the boy lay suffering from polio. Francis's ancestors on his father's side stemmed from Basilicata, in the southernmost part of Italy; his paternal grandfather came to America and built the first Vitaphone. There is a wistful scene that pops up in the 'complete' version of the *Godfather* saga on television and home video, in which a small boy (Francis's father) plays the flute for his father (Francis's grandfather, Augustino), who is a gunsmith.

Coppola can function at full throttle only when his family surrounds him, either in their home in the Napa Valley or in the throes of a shoot, with everyone playing a part, from uncle Anton to granddaughter Gia. 'A man who doesn't spend time with his family,' intones Don Vito in *The Godfather*, 'can never be a real man.' His statement rings with hierarchical as well as sexual significance. Italian society is founded on the supremacy of the male. His 'Family' constitutes his possessions, his very estate. This macho approach to life is both stated and implied throughout the *Godfather* trilogy. Luca Brasi solemnly voices his hope that Connie's and Carlo's first child may be 'a masculine child'. Towards the end

The scene from *Part II* that made it only to TV and video, showing a small boy (i.e. Coppola's father) playing the flute for his father, the gunsmith (i.e. Coppola's grandfather).

of *Part II*, the sentiment finds an echo in Michael's urgent demand after learning of Kay's 'miscarriage': '*Was it a boy?*' Mafia members have testified that it is forbidden to speak to women about things concerning the Cosa Nostra. Apollonia, Michael's demure young bride, seems cherished by her father and village friends as a delicate, almost other-worldly icon, and not as a creature of flesh and blood who in another society would boast a will of her own.

Because the Mafia has its origins in Sicily, its fortunes also rise or fall according to the Family. John Gotti, now languishing in jail and only recently displaced as head of the Gambino Family in New York, took the same oath as all his contemporaries in the Cosa Nostra, a 'vow of fealty requiring them always to obey the boss and never to raise hands against one another, never to violate another's wife or children, and never to deal drugs'. No *mafioso* worth his salt could be seen to lead anything but an impeccable family existence. Putting down roots in the New World, the Sicilian families held together in physical as well as spiritual terms. The 'mall' seen on Long Island in *The Godfather*, or at Lake Tahoe in *Part II*, becomes not only a home where the kitchen exudes the aromas of fresh pasta, basil and meatballs, but a redoubtable refuge in time of crisis. Don Vito's sons stand at his side in any serious negotiations. The foster-son, Tom Hagen, once accepted by the Family, is admitted to its most confidential secrets.

Michael's most appalling sin in *Part II* amounts to a rejection of his Family, although even he at one point trudges through the snow in despair to ask advice of his ailing mother. By the time *Part III* begins, in 1979, Michael has seen the error of his ways and yearns not just to achieve legitimacy for his Family affairs, but also to reunite his Family and thus redeem himself. He accepts Vincent, the bastard son of his late brother Sonny, and prepares him for an accession to the supreme power as a Corleone. He longs to reconcile himself with his estranged wife, Kay, and his children, Mary and Anthony, and relies increasingly on the counsel and strength of his sister Connie.

Individual ambition must always be suppressed in favour of Family interests. When Family members disperse to all quarters of the United States, they remain responsible to the head of the Family, and woe betide those like Fredo or Moe Greene who betray the Corleone legacy in Las Vegas. 'You're my older brother, and I love you,' Michael warns Fredo after his argument with Greene, 'but don't ever take sides with anyone against the Family again – ever.' In Puzo's latest novel, *The Last Don*, the Clericuzio Family becomes embroiled in Hollywood, tempted by the prospect of multi-million-dollar profits on their investment.

Al Pacino trudging through the snow at the family compound on Lake Tahoe.

The Family 'tree' of relationships supplies the skeletal strength of the Corleone government – a structure that originated in imperial Rome. Beyond the blood relatives are the *consigliere* (first Abbandando and then Tom Hagen), the *caporegimes* (Clemenza and Tessio), the bodyguards (Neri and Rocco, and Calo in Sicily), and the 'suppliers' (Enzo the baker, Bonasera the undertaker). Loyal 'soldiers', though unrelated to the Family by kinship, may through their commitment and subservience rise to become de facto members of the Family. *The Godfather* movies boast many such associates, usually treacherous: Moe Greene, the gangster inspired by Bugsy Siegel, or Frank Pentangeli, who takes over Clemenza's regime in Brooklyn. Then there

are honorary Family members, such as Johnny Fontane, the crooner whose records, like Sinatra's, sell in millions and who kisses his Godfather whenever he needs a favour.

According to Sicilian tradition, numberless crimes may be committed in the name of the Family (as recently as 1990 Sicily, with just 9 per cent of the total Italian population, accounted for 24 per cent of the nation's robberies). Tom Hagen flies to California to deal with the film producer who has dared spurn Johnny Fontane for a starring role.

Carlo Rizzi, the cocksure bridegroom of Connie Corleone, suffers more than most from this blood loyalty. When Sonny learns of Carlo's domestic cruelty, he gives him a savage public beating. Later, when Michael

Father and daughter. Carmine Coppola conducts the orchestra while Talia Shire sings 'Eh Cumpari' in *Part III*.

detects the hand of Carlo behind the shooting of Sonny, he has no compunction in making his sister a widow. In the panic of Batista's fall in Havana, Michael plants a kiss on the lips of Fredo – the traditional Sicilian Mafia's metaphor for a death sentence. In *Part III*, the headstrong Vinnie Mancini waits for the nod from Connie before assassinating his arch-enemy Joey Zasa. In hindsight, that early shot of a trim and boyish Michael in military uniform at the Long Beach wedding, telling his fiancée about the excesses of Luca Brasi, seems almost nostalgic: 'That's my Family, Kay – it's not me.'

August Coppola feels that Brando in *The Godfather* resembled Uncle Louis, Italia Coppola's elder brother, whose bulk had greatly impressed the boys in childhood. 'If they had given *The Godfather* to a normal American director it would have taken on the stereotypes of Italian-Americans. Francis put it into everyday life, so that every aspect of the story is tied into our own family in some way – tone, coloration, rhythm. The irony is that you begin to respond to this Mafia story almost as a celebration.' Talia Shire, the director's sister, agrees: '*The Godfather* was textured, or perfumed in a way, by our memories of our Italian-American family.' Coppola insisted that Don Vito should dress and sound like a New Yorker, rather than some comic-book image of the Italian *mafioso*.

August Coppola's reference to the story as a celebration touches on the most controversial aspect of the entire trilogy. Never before in the cinema had violence been presented with such lethal glamour. Colour and sophisticated special effects had not been available

to the makers of *Public Enemy, Scarface, Little Caesar* and other gangster classics of the 1930s. The yellow and orange tones of Willis's cinematography accentuate what might be termed a 'neo-realism' in the violent scenes. Woltz finds his luxurious, gold satin sheets drenched in blood from the head of his $600,000 stallion. Luca Brasi is throttled in close-up at a wet-bar, his head seeming to expand like some grotesque balloon, and to the accompaniment not of music but of coarse, animal groaning and the crashing of glasses on the floor. Carlo Rizzi also dies by strangulation, thrashing like a landed fish until in his death throes he kicks out the windscreen of the car. When Michael shoots Sollozzo and McCluskey in the Bronx restaurant, the blood fills the air like a mist.

Although some murders occur off-screen, Coppola wants the audience to confront the violence head-on, and to comply with it. There is no escaping the slaughter of Sonny at the tollbooths; it lasts a mere thirty seconds, but to the first-time spectator it drags on relentlessly. A true Corleone executes his victim with clinical efficiency ('only business, nothing personal'), and the young Vito earns the respect of the neighbourhood by ambushing and then shooting Fanucci face to face without compunction. The cold-blooded execution of Family enemies continues in *Part III*, with Vincent firing point-blank first at masked intruders in his apartment, and then at Joey Zasa as he tries desperately to escape through a door in Little Italy. If there is any manifestly 'obscene' aspect of *The Godfather*, it must be this feeling of complicity in the act of violence.

✳

The assassination of Joey Zasa in *Part III*.

Intimations of Sicily colour all the American sequences in the trilogy. Sizeable chunks of each film take place on the island, and these authentic sights and sounds only serve to emphasize the source of the Mafia's strength. Coppola and his team punctuate the story with subtle allusions to the 'old country' – apart from the final conversation with Sollozzo rarely in dialogue, but almost invariably in deed and gesture.

The grand wedding in Long Beach that launches *The Godfather* might be taking place in Sicily. Connie clutches the traditional bride's silk purse, and her guests one by one slip into it envelopes laden with cash. There is the energetic lilt of the *tarantella*, an abun-dance of wine (Clemenza quaffing it from a glass jug), and the presence of bodyguards, sporting the dark coats and glasses associated with the *mafiosi*. Such things suggest that this is a sacred ceremony, imported from a distant land and sealed off from the outside world, and indeed Sonny and his father's arch-rival, Barzini, both take offence at the sight of press photographers trespassing on the Corleone property. Much impressed by this sequence, Mafia chieftain John Gotti later hosted a sim-ilar reception for a thousand guests to cele-brate a daughter's marriage, with Connie Francis singing love songs just as Johnny Fontane does in the Coppola movie.

Later, Puzo and Coppola gently underline

Sicilian traditions, alive and well in Long Island. The wedding sequence from *The Godfather.*

the simple origins of a true Sicilian wedding, when Michael and Apollonia walk through the village streets in smiling silence, save for the music of the local brass band. By 1958, when *Part II* begins, such ceremonies have become vulgar and bloated beyond recogni-

tion: Anthony's first-communion celebration attracts hundreds upon hundreds of guests. In *Part III*, the restraint and sincerity of the opening party reflect Michael's craving for respectability, although the *tarantella* is still sung, and the traditional cake presented by the baker, Enzo, must be solemnly cut.

Metaphorical references to Sicily sometimes need explaining to a younger generation. When a brown paper parcel arrives, containing a dead fish inside a bullet-proof vest, Tessio has to clarify its meaning for Sonny: 'Luca Brasi sleeps with the fishes.' Sonny must also vent his exasperation when he tells Tom Hagen that he really needs a Sicilian *consigliere*, because Tom, born in New York and not Italian, cannot for all his virtues offer that subtle, implacable verve needed in a crisis.

On a lighter note, Clemenza lectures a restless Michael about the true (Sicilian) way of cooking a stew for the entire Family, just as Coppola himself loves to prepare a meal in the kitchen. There is a sense of a recipe being handed down from generation to generation, and of the sublimation of self to some code of togetherness. The stew becomes a potion, the mixing of which is every bit as important as the technique of wielding a gun or a knife. (In the original screenplay, this scene included the description: 'Clemenza browns some sausage'. Puzo made a sly note in the margin:

Walking home from the church after their marriage: Michael and Apollonia in *The Godfather*.

Coppola prepares to shoot the Five Families conclave in *The Godfather*. Note the ominous oranges on the table.

'Clemenza *fries* some sausage – gangsters don't brown!'.) Clemenza also knows the Sicilian knack of garrotting, a deft flick of his pudgy hands slipping the silken noose around the neck of a victim such as Carlo.

Still other references remain implicit, such as the presence of oranges at various points in the trilogy: clustered in bowls on Woltz's table and in the boardroom where the five Families gather after the death of Sollozzo; tumbling into the street as the Don dashes for cover from his assassins; next to Fredo as he visits his father in the hospital; in the hands of first Tessio and, two films later, Don Altobello, both of whom will betray their

master. There is the single ominous orange presented mysteriously to Michael by Johnny Ola as he arrives from Miami. Oranges roll to the floor as the helicopter's down-draught makes the tables tremble in that doomed suite in Atlantic City. And an orange slips from the hand of Michael Corleone in the final shot of the entire trilogy, just as it did from the dying Don Vito's after he had filled his mouth with peel to scare his grandson. Oranges, along with olive oil, have for centuries been exported from Sicily, and protecting the orange fields was an early function of the Mafia. Richard Bright, the actor who plays Neri throughout the trilogy, may be right

Don Vito (Robert De Niro) prepares to take vengeance on yet another Sicilian foe.

when he says that, 'The symbol of evil was a fuckin' orange!', but oranges also nourish, as in the crucial scene in the cloister garden in *Part III*, when Michael collapses with weakness because of his diabetes, and calls desperately for orange juice and candy.

At a much more profound and sinister level, the tie that binds these latter-day Americans (with their 'oily hair, dressed in those silk suits' as Senator Geary sneers) is *la vendetta* – that ceaseless struggle between one Family and another, in which vengeance is wreaked from generation to generation. As soon as he learns that the Don has been shot, Sonny's reaction is to hit the Tattaglia Family

with all his might. Clemenza and Tessio listen in loyal silence; only Hagen, the ethnic outsider, dares sway an irate Sonny from his course. An ancestral impulse drives Don Vito back to Sicily to kill Don Ciccio, at whose hands his mother and father had died a generation earlier.

In *Part III*, just before the massacre in Atlantic City, Joey Zasa declares to the assembled *mafiosi*, 'As for Don Corleone, he makes it clear today, he is my enemy. You must choose between us.' Vincent Mancini, convinced that Zasa has set up the attempt to wipe out Michael and the other *mafiosi*, proceeds to hunt him down and, as his victim

Coppola rehearses the *mafiosi* gathering in *Part III*, with the ubiquitous oranges in the foreground.

sprawls in death, snarls his name, 'Zasa!' just as his grandfather had hissed, 'Don Ciccio!' into the ear of his ancient foe as he slashed his chest with a knife on a sunlit terrace in Sicily. Such vicious heavies tend to be dismissed as *pezzi'novanta*, or big shots, by the Corleone Family. Michael mutters the word under his breath like an expletive while visiting Sicily in *Part III*, and his father blames the *pezzi'novanta* and the Church for forbidding 'the ordinary people from gambling, liquor, even women, which are things people want'.

Whenever under threat, the New York Mafia calls on its Sicilian connections to preserve its inviolability. In *Part II*, the FBI smuggles Frank Pentangeli into the Senate hearings as its star witness in the case against Michael Corleone, only to be confronted by the one presence that will guarantee his silence – his brother from Sicily, flanked and minded by Tom Hagen and Michael Corleone. In the long stares exchanged by the brothers across the crowded room lies the very essence of *omertà*, the Sicilian code of silence in the face of the authorities.

Towards the end of the saga, however, Puzo and Coppola have come to terms with the Sicilian legacy. Kay, on her first visit to the island, is driven through the countryside by Michael. She sees a puppet show in a village square, and listens to its allusive, vaguely menacing language. 'It's such a beautiful country, and so violent,' she muses with the transparent naïveté of a New Hampshire

The puppet show witnessed by Michael and Kay in *Part III*.

WASP. Later, as he carves some prosciutto for her, Michael explains why he loves Sicily:

'All through history, terrible things happened to these people. Terrible injustices. But they still expect good rather than bad will happen to them.'

Then he places the carving knife against his throat and grins at her, 'Give the order!'

'That's supposed to make me not dread you?' replies Kay, and Michael utters one of the most direct and revealing lines of the trilogy: 'This is Sicily. It's opera.'

When *Apocalypse Now* appeared, some critics were perplexed by Coppola's outrageous use of coloured smoke – like the stage smoke used in countless theatres – as the helicopters land near the surf. But the brash pinks and yellows swirling so incongruously above the Vietnam shore enable Coppola to transcend the grim, unbearable reality of war. Naturalism has never been either his forte or his goal. By filtering greed, passion, violence through an essentially operatic, even melodramatic, sensibility he achieves the artistry that eludes so many of his contemporaries in their striving after high-tech realism.

The operatic tradition informs all three *Godfather* films. The camera looks down over Connie's wedding as a spectator would from the circle. The music predominates, both on- and off-screen, as it does in so much grand opera. Nothing could be more genuine Grand Guignol than Woltz's discovery of the horse's head and his repeated roars of anguish;

'This is Sicily. It's opera,' says Michael in *Part III.*

they will find an uncanny echo at the very close of the trilogy, when Michael lies, mouth agape, on the steps of the Teatro Massimo in Palermo after the murder of Mary.

If the essence of opera lies in its discreet amplification of suspense, then Coppola, like Hitchcock, knows how to transplant that to the cinema. When Michael finds his father unguarded in the hospital, he moves him to another room and awaits the arrival of the assassins. Shots of empty corridors are accompanied by the sound of approaching footfalls, growing harsher and louder in rhyme with Michael's anxiety and anticipation. It is only Enzo the gentle baker, come to pay his respects, and the audience's relief, like Michael's, has been carefully anticipated by Coppola.

The violence in *The Godfather*, so shocking in 1972, may be seen in retrospect as ever so slightly heightened. We rarely feel obliged to turn aside in pain from Coppola's killings as we do from Scorsese's; instead, the spectacle absorbs us, enthralling rather than appalling. Take, for instance, the scene in which Carlo and Connie quarrel. They scream and shout, and lurch around the apartment, sweeping food and crockery to the floor in a din of anger. But there is none of the visceral pain and brutality of similar moments in *Raging Bull*, when Robert De Niro assaults Cathy Moriarty. The same applies to the beating Sonny deals out to Carlo in the street. This time Coppola detaches us from the action by setting his camera up several metres away, even as the exaggerated sound of the blows fills the soundtrack. The effect is operatic, yet more convincing because we are not aware of the confines of the stage. Real life seems to mimic the melodramatic gestures of the theatre. When Clemenza holds a gun at the ready in case an unwanted visitor disturbs his theft of the carpet in *Part II*, Coppola almost freezes the moment and for a split second the composition looks artificial.

Of course many an explosion of violence in

the *Godfather* trilogy arrives with a ferocity that cannot be mitigated by any degree of melodrama. Sonny's death at the tollbooths, for example, is so savage that a final gruesome shot of Sonny's corpse being kicked by his killers had to be excised for TV screenings. Or the direct, unequivocal destruction of Apollonia's and Michael's romantic dreams when her car blows up in long shot.

Coppola's love of opera returns, however, in the sustained crescendo of the finale of *Part I*, with its intercutting between the christening of Connie's baby and the systematic slaughter of the Family's enemies. Again, reality becomes almost seductive in its terrible, concocted beauty: Moe Greene raising his head quizzically from a massage table, removing his glasses so that the assassin's bullet can enter his temple and release an ironic trickle of blood. And a semi-nude and flailing Philip Tattaglia, gunned down in bed with his mistress. And, most dramatic of all, the shooting of Barzini as he tries to escape by running up the exposed steps of a classical building in Manhattan.

Part II begins with a funeral procession that looks and sounds as though it belongs to a Verdi opera (or *Cavalleria Rusticana* itself), with the mourners straggling over a rocky river bed, the musicians blasting away at their brass and a sudden burst of gunfire sending everyone scurrying for shelter.

The opening sequence of *Part II*.

Once established in New York, young Vito Andolini shares the daily life of the Italian community. With his pal Genco Abbandando he attends a tear-jerking musical, *Senza Mama*, a melodrama about the immigrant experience written by Francesco Pennino, Coppola's maternal grandfather. Amounting almost to a lampoon on the Italian love of family, *Senza Mama* is just one of several quasi-operatic, quasi-theatrical intermezzi in the *Godfather* trilogy. Like the puppet show observed by Kay and Michael towards the end of *Part III*, its naive plot sheds some light on the real-life characters in the audience.

Fanucci, the *mafioso* who terrorizes Mulberry Street, struts his stuff like some penny-dreadful rogue. His extravagant white suit and cream fedora, his fastidious, feminine manners, and his sudden flickers of anger combine to make him the perfect stage villain, as though recollected with nostalgia rather than dread by some future member of the Corleone Family. He too pauses to watch a puppet show during the Festa ('far too violent for me!' he declares sardonically to those within ear-shot) and then marches to his

Fanucci, 'the perfect stage villain', in *Part II*.

Fanucci trying to intimidate Vito in *Part II*.

doom like some character from Verdi or Puccini. The pompous, repetitive music of the Festa grows louder, accompanying Fanucci's leisurely progress through the streets with an air of foreboding. As Fanucci climbs the stairs to his apartment, the sounds of the band retreat into the background, obeying a familiar dictate of *opera seria*, so that the audience's attention can concentrate on the horror of a dramatic moment. Coppola 'rhymes' the explosion of fireworks at the climax of the Festa with the blast of Vito's gun as he shoots Fanucci through the chest and mouth. Thus Vito becomes a kind of Sparafucile in Verdi's *Rigoletto*, who has been called 'opera's prototype of the honourable hit-man'.

Part III marks a definitive return to Sicily for Michael and the Family. The entire second half of the film unfolds on the island, and concludes with Michael's death in old age, seated in a country courtyard there. The violence and passion of late nineteenth-century Italian opera prevail throughout the sustained climax at the Teatro Massimo, with a performance of *Cavalleria Rusticana* intercut with Mosca's attempt on Michael's life and Michael's revenge on the Vatican officials who have betrayed him in the Immobiliare affair. It's intriguing to reflect that the composer of *Cavalleria Rusticana*, Pietro Mascagni, was himself not only a Sicilian but also a trainee lawyer who – exactly like Anthony Corleone

Art imitates life. The staging of *Cavalleria Rusticana* in *Part III*.

in the film – studied music on the quiet in order to rebel against a traditional profession.

On stage, the young soldier, Turiddu (played by Michael's son Anthony in his operatic début as a tenor) has his ear bitten by his foe, Alfio, a scene identical to, if more stylized than, the scene in *Part III* in which Vincent bites the ear of Joey Zasa in New York. Acknowledging the reference, Vincent allows himself a sly grin as he watches from the royal box with the Corleone Family. When the statue of the Madonna is borne on stage by men in white, hooded robes, we think back to the scene in Little Italy, with Zasa being hunted down in the confusion of the Festa, and even to *Part II*, in which

Fanucci strolls through the procession like a prince of the city.

Coppola's formidable talent for assimilating the *verismo* of Italian operatic tradition also surfaces in the mayhem involving Mosca, the assassin. Dressed as a priest, he flits from box to box, and kills both the 'Twins', regarded by the Corleone Family as the best bodyguards in the region. He overpowers one and deceives the other by pretending to be dead, eyes bulging, mouth agape in frozen agony. Then, as the unsuspecting bodyguard approaches, Mosca plunges his dagger deep into his heart. Nothing could be more melodramatic, or more in tune with the music of Mascagni. Meanwhile, a guard murdered earlier lies on the floor, two streams of blood from his mouth congealed with obvious – and quite appropriate – artifice.

Coppola allows Michael to express his grief for his murdered daughter in one of the starkest shots of his entire career. Pacino opens his lips to scream, but the sound refuses to emerge. Slumped on the steps of the theatre, holding his head in his hand, he rocks back and forth before the camera, his mouth locked wide in this silent grimace of anguish until, after what seems an eternity, the scream emerges – a kind of primal roar, like the death throes of some operatic hero. The scene resounds with a fearful irony, making a mockery of those words spoken off-screen by Michael at the very outset of the film: 'The only wealth in this world is children, more than all the money and power on earth.' In this gruesome finale, the film blends life and art, the director's own profound despair at the loss of his elder son, Gio, only three years earlier, underpinning that of Michael, the indi-

vidual with whom Coppola has identified most closely throughout the trilogy.

True to the traditions of grand opera, the closing sequence of *Part III* reprises musical moments from all three parts of the *Godfather* story – Michael dancing with Apollonia in Sicily (*Part I*), with Kay at Lake Tahoe (*Part II*) and with Mary in New York (*Part III*). These reminiscences are dovetailed both rhythmically and sentimentally and become a fusion of bliss in the mind of the dying Michael – a forlorn alternative to the redemption that has eluded him. There is a close-up of his withered face and white hair, as he dons a diabetic's dark glasses to shut out the memories and the horror of life alike; then a long shot of him alone in the garden. His dog approaches and as he reaches idly to fondle it, Michael Corleone slips to the ground in silence as an orange – that fruit so closely associated with imminent death throughout the trilogy – rolls from his hand.

The closing moments of the trilogy . . .

2 The Misuses of Power

'All empire is no more than power in trust' – John Dryden (1631–1700)

Brando in the opening scene of *The Godfather*.

Power governs every move made by Don Vito Corleone and his son during the five decades that the Family lives in America – and Michael ends his days, as his father began his, in Sicily. Power rhymes with protection in Sicilian parlance, and young Vito imports this philosophy to the New York of 1917 which, like the Wild West, is terrorized by ruffians and blackmailers. He acquires his power in ways that are unpretentious yet lethal. First he earns the trust of his friends and neighbours such as Clemenza, Tessio and Genco. Then he uses sweet reason to change the minds of those who cause trouble in the neighbourhood. 'I'll make him an offer he can't refuse' becomes a mantra in Corleone circles. Only if reason fails does Don Vito resort to violence (murdering Fanucci, for example, or – with the formidable Luca Brasi at his side – obliging an agent to release Johnny Fontane from his singing contract).

From the start of *The Godfather*, Coppola restrains us from classifying Don Corleone as a comic-book villain. The Don fixes Bonasera with an imperious stare, as though by merely listening he were bestowing a gift on this unfortunate supplicant. The camera's computer-timed lens retreats with scarcely perceptible stealth back past the head of Brando's Don while he listens to Bonasera's muttered lament about his daughter's degradation at the hands of some youths in Little Italy. The Don sits in monolithic silence, stroking a cat in a telling visual metaphor for the hooded claws of his domain. All these elements, and the conspiratorial shadows of Gordon Willis's photography, evoke the intimacy of some pagan confessional: Bonasera is a subject pleading not with God but with Mammon. 'The thing that's good about this story, why I put it first,' says Coppola, 'is that it's personal. Everyone in the audience understood how he felt. Slowly you see the other people.'

Irritable because Bonasera does not accord him friendship and appears only when he requires help, the Don growls to his adviser, Tom Hagen, 'We're not murderers, in spite of what this undertaker says.' Sniffing fastidiously at the rose in his buttonhole, he tells Hagen that he wants the matter handled by 'reliable people, people that aren't going to be carried away'. The words, so mundane and unexceptional, mask the vicious street violence of the Mafia, and recall the arrogant apologia by the *mafioso* Antonio Calderone: 'We are men of power. And not so much because we have taken an oath, but because we are the "élite" of the underworld. We are far superior to common criminals. We are the worst.' During the Dons' conclave after the death of Sonny, Barzini tosses off a similar comment: 'We don't have to give assurances as if we were lawyers.' The Mafia, quite simply, rides beyond the law.

The Don can flourish only because society has abrogated its duty to protect the citizen. The origins of the Mafia coincide with the end of Habsburg rule in Italy, when *la fede pubblica* (the public trust) collapsed and had to be replaced with *la fede privata*, 'that private realm populated only by kin and close friends in which people take refuge from high levels of social unpredictability, aggression, and injustice'.

The opening scene of *The Godfather* finds its counterpart in *Part II*, when a widow with her dog comes to see Vito in his shop and asks for his aid in retaining her apartment. Power at this stage – 1917 – is like a new toy for the young Corleone. Peter Maas, author of *The Valachi Papers*, has pointed out that the Italians were not the first to attempt to organize crime in the United States. 'But what a small number of these Italian newcomers – mostly from Naples, Calabria and Sicily – did bring was a traditional clannishness, contempt for lawful authority, and a talent for organization that would eventually enable them to dominate racketeering in the US.'

Puzo's novel charts the rise of Don Vito throughout the 1920s and 1930s, but the need for compression obliged Coppola to foreshorten this phase, so that even in *Part II* there is no reference to Prohibition, the source of Mafia strength in New York during the Depression era. Now a new, more deadly brand of Italian-American gangster surged to the top of the pile – men such as Lucky Luciano, Al Capone, Vito Genovese and Francesco Castiglio. Most of the Sicilians grouped together according to the region, or even village, in Sicily from which they had emigrated in the first place. Salvatore Maranzano headed 'a contingent of men from in and around the Sicilian town of Castellammare del Golfo'. Maranzano spoke seven languages and had a library full of books on Julius Caesar, whose exploits inspired him to set up the structure of the modern Cosa Nostra in the United States – five families. Luciano, who murdered Maranzano in 1931, established the system of *consiglieri*, entering into joint ventures with such non-Italian criminals as Meyer Lansky

(Hyman Roth in *The Godfather Part II*) and Dutch Schultz (who figures largely in *The Cotton Club*). For Luciano, it has been said, 'peaceful coexistence was merely a step toward total domination of organized crime.'

Vito Corleone recognizes that to reinforce his power base, he must supply the needs of the community, and the olive oil business becomes the perfect cover for the Family's illicit revenues. Even as late as 1946, the Don's empire thrives on protection money, with every merchant, wholesaler and manufacturer beholden to the Family. With that cash, the Don can purchase influence: judges, accountants, politicians, union leaders . . . Members of the Family are set in place throughout the empire. Carlo dabbles in the numbers racket, while Fredo enjoys the life of a playboy at one of the hotels in Las Vegas.

The Don retains certain ethical standards. When Sollozzo approaches him to fund his drug-running operation, the Don listens courteously to his proposal. The potential profits sound gigantic, but the Don declines. As fastidious in regard to drugs as his son will be abstemious towards liquor, the Don prefers to let the other Families profit from the 'white powder' so readily exported from Sicily. 'I believe this drugs business is going to destroy us in the years to come,' he tells his fellow *mafioso*. He may yet prove to be right. Fourteen years after the release of *The Godfather*, Salvatore Catalano, Gaetano Badalamenti and some twenty others were arraigned in New York and charged with importing $1.6 billion worth of heroin. The authorities nailed their quarry thanks to evidence from Tommaso Buscetta, a supergrass

worthy to rank alongside Pentangeli in *Part II*.

Michael regards gambling as an inexhaustible source of money to the Family but, like his father, refuses to traffic in drugs. As late as 1978 he accuses Joey Zasa, in front of other Mafia leaders, of permitting drugs in his neighbourhood. Mario Puzo's romantic attitude to his characters may explain this blind spot, for in practice *mafiosi* were involved in the drugs trade as early as 1935, when Serafino Mancuso was sentenced by a US court to forty years in jail for dealing in narcotics. Mancuso was deported to Italy in 1947, and such fellow gangsters as Lucky Luciano, Frank Coppola and Angelo Di Carlo were also sent back to their homeland – along with their expertise in trafficking.

Somewhere along the line, the original Don's acquisition of power translates into abuse and corruption. Clearly, Coppola approves of the Don's grandiose despotism more than he does of Michael's post-war savvy. Perhaps he sees in the father something of the spirit of pioneering America, an ample vision that has been displaced by a kind of colourless, industrial barony. 'My father's no different to any other man,' Michael tells Kay, 'any man who's responsible for other people, like a senator or president.' Even the devious Barzini pays tribute to Don Vito: 'We all know him as a man of his word, a modest man. He'll always listen to reason.'

Don Vito's humility is discarded by Michael and the new generation. Only the inner ruthlessness endures – diamond-hard and unforgiving, more devious, less personable – to mesh with the real-life gangland of contemporary New York. Typical of this pragmatic new approach is Sollozzo's comment to Hagen after the attempt on the Don's life: 'I don't like violence, Tom. I'm a businessman. Blood is a big expense.'

Michael allows himself to be stung by insults and cannot accept opinions contrary to his own. In the moment that he learns that Moe Greene has 'straightened out' Fredo 'for banging cocktail waitresses two at a time', Michael condemns the man. When Senator Geary tries to intimidate him into paying over the odds for a gaming licence in Nevada, Michael responds in kind, using his network of informants to trap the careless Senator when he gets involved in the death of a prostitute in Carson City (the brothel conveniently managed by Fredo).

His father spent a lifetime acquiring friends and dependants. Michael acquires none but enemies, and believes that only by eliminating those foes can his power survive. Unlike his father, Michael never soils his own hands with blood after his 'baptism' in the restaurant with Sollozzo. Neri, and in *Part III* Vincent, must execute his wishes. The bell tolls for a succession of traitors, gangsters and opponents – Philip Tattaglia, Cuneo, Stracci, Barzini, Moe Greene, Tessio, Carlo, Cicci, Johnny Ola, Frank Pentangeli (suicide 'suggested' by Tom Hagen), Roth, Fredo, Keinszig, the Archbishop and finally Lucchesi.

The notion of the Family as a paradigm for American capitalism – survival of the fittest, the ruthless annihilation of rivals and the amassing of money which in turn purchases power – emerges more and more forcefully as the films proceed. From the moment when Don Corleone and his sons, the *consigliere* and the *caporegimes*, assemble like a corporate board to discuss drug trafficking with Sollozzo, to the electric moment in *Part II* when the ailing Hyman Roth confides to Michael that the pair of them are 'bigger than US Steel', there are frequent reminders that all violence is a means to a single end – Big Business.

Vito Andolini came to the New World and built his fortune in New York. Once his father has passed away, Michael contemplates richer pickings, in Las Vegas and Nevada, and also in Latin America. If that means dealing with Hyman Roth, a Jew, then so be it – although Frank Pentangeli leaves Michael in no doubt as to his mistake in straying outside the Italian-American community for a partner. 'Your father did business with Hyman Roth, your father respected Hyman Roth – but your father never *trusted* Hyman Roth!' exclaims the old *mafioso*. Roth had run molasses out of Cuba during the Prohibition era ('the trucks owned by your father,' he reminds Michael).

Roth furnishes the Corleone empire with a link to the Third World, and flourishes from his profits on gambling in Cuba. It was estimated that some 2,000 people earned their keep as card dealers, croupiers, cashiers, musicians, barmen, waiters and entertainers under Fulgéncio Batista, President of Cuba from 1940 onwards and arbiter of power on the island since the mid-1930s. After seizing power, Fidel Castro felt obliged to restore legal gambling to its former splendour.

'Your father never trusted *Hyman Roth!' Michael with Pentangeli in* Part II.

The episode in Cuba emphasizes the American predisposition to support dictators in Latin America and the developing world. At the meeting with Batista, eerily reminiscent of the five Families' summit in *The Godfather*, Coppola once again uses the boardroom table as a symbol of Big Business. Around it are seated the chief executive officers of the top communications, mining, food and sugar corporations, along with Hyman Roth and Michael Corleone (the latter welcomed with a nice touch of euphemism as 'representing our associates in tourism and leisure activities'). One of them has given Batista a solid-gold telephone for Christmas. As it passes from hand to hand, Michael barely glances at it. Fastidious to a fault, he remains untempted by vulgarity.

Roth and Michael flee Havana during the New Year celebrations, just as Meyer Lansky did in real life. Research conducted by the Zoetrope team indicated that on 1 January 1959 Castro's forces entered Havana, occupying the streets and the Hotel Nacional. A general strike gripped the capital. Would the Mafia still be doing business with Batista at the time, with the end so imminent? The party shown in the film could not have taken place at the Presidential Palace, because Batista had moved into special quarters at the Army garrison (Campamento Columbia) several months before, following an assault on the Palace. The President's hasty abdication speech is presented plausibly by Coppola,

The boardroom table as a symbol of Big Business. Batista addresses his guests in *Part II.*

and the atmosphere of the festivities and the confusion in the streets appear convincing on screen. Batista did in fact flee by private plane that night. Even his Vice-president did not know he was about to leave, until he encountered a maid carrying a suitcase. But he was refused permission to land in Miami, and so went to the Dominican Republic – where, thanks to Gulf + Western's connections, the Cuban sequences of *The Godfather Part II* were actually shot.

Michael does not deliver the $2 million cash gift he and Roth have earmarked for Batista. He waits, and has his bodyguard murder Johnny Ola and almost kill Hyman Roth, who has fallen gravely ill. Knowing that Fredo has betrayed him, he jumps into a limousine bound for the airport. Like his father,

Michael survives such situations by virtue of a street-smart pragmatism. Like the United States during the past twenty-five years – and like Nixon in particular – his fear of being unseated degenerates into paranoia and isolationism. During the Senate hearings, as one of the Corleone killers refers to the 'buffers' that stood between him and the upper echelons of the Family, associations with Watergate appear inescapable. When Hyman Roth, surrounded by lawmen at Miami airport, is shot by a stranger wearing a hat, the incident looks like a reconstruction of Jack Ruby's assassination of Lee Harvey Oswald. Paranoia and xenophobia tainted the Reagan era also, supplanting – and perverting – the ideals of the 1960s.

Twenty years later, when *Part III* opens,

The murder of Hyman Roth at Miami airport in *Part II*.

the Corleone businesses have been assimilated into American society. Coppola's views
of Mulberry Street in Don Vito's youth have
been replaced by aerial views of Wall Street as
Michael and his investment counsellor, B. J.
Harrison, meet with stockholders and merchant bankers. Harrison, with his elegant
suits and designer hair-do, appears at a far
remove from Tom Hagen. They talk of hundreds of millions of dollars, and of controlling
multinational corporations. At the party to
celebrate Michael's being awarded a Papal
honour, a cheque for $100 million dollars is
donated by the Vito Corleone Foundation to

Massacre in Atlantic City, from *Part III.*

the Vatican for distribution to 'the poor of Sicily'. The Italian-born swindler Michele Sindona's links with the highest levels of Italian business and officialdom inspired Puzo and Coppola to develop this theme in their screenplay for *Part III.*

Michael delights in pouncing when his opponents are under pressure from circumstances beyond their control. In *Part II*, he outwits Hyman Roth when the Cuban revolution comes tumbling about their ears, and in *Part III* he offers to save the Vatican Bank just when it is most in need of cash, by purchasing a controlling interest in Immobiliare. The situation affords him the chance to launder his ill-gotten gains, rather than having to relinquish them. The corrupt Archbishop (whose character seems based partly on Bishop Marcinkus in the Vatican and partly on Michele Sindona in the United States) puffs on his cigarette and squeezes the Corleone offer $100 million higher. 'In today's world,' he sighs, 'it seems the power to absolve debt is greater than the power of forgiveness.'

Yet Michael craves forgiveness above all else. He tries to renounce his supremacy, only to find that his hot-headed young nephew, Vincent Mancini, wants, in his own phrase, 'the power to preserve the Family'. Michael will fall victim to a force more potent than his

'Power wears out those who do not have it!' The murder of Lucchesi in *Part III*.

own, a force more sophisticated, more subtle, more lethal. At its heart stands a suave villain named Lucchesi, who double-crosses the Corleone Family over their offer to take a controlling interest in Immobiliare. 'Politics is knowing when to pull the trigger,' smiles Lucchesi. His aphorisms recall those of the Italian Christian Democrat former Prime Minister, Giulio Andreotti, now still under investigation for his links with the Sicilian Mafia. When Carlo murders Lucchesi towards the end of the film, he hisses into his ear, 'Power wears out those who do not have it!' – words that are famous for having been uttered by Andreotti. A more intriguing model for Lucchesi might be Licio Gelli, who built up the tentacular influence of P2, a masonic lodge with members holding key positions in Italian politics, industry and finance. Gelli's reputation as 'Il Burattinaio' ('the Puppeteer') stemmed from the control he exercised over such unfortunate swindlers as Michele Sindona and Roberto Calvi (whose equivalent in the film, Keinszig, defers to Lucchesi's gaze in a key scene). In another bizarre twist of fact and fiction, the real-life hit-man Francesco Di Carlo, who has allegedly confessed to the murder of Calvi in London in 1982, belongs to the powerful Corleone clan!

3 Characters

'The only wealth in this world is children, more than all the money and power on earth' – Michael Corleone in The Godfather Part III

The young Vito arriving in the New World in *Part II.*

For audiences in 1972, Marlon Brando's Don Vito Corleone had no youth. He would always be the dignified if undeniably menacing patriarch whose ascent to power in New York had been achieved in a vanished, pre-Second World War era. For a new generation seeing the *Godfather* films for the first time today, Don Vito progresses from childhood through youth and seems to miss out on middle age only. Robert De Niro studied Brando's performance over and over again before committing himself to camera on *Part II*, and the characteristics the two men share are those that reveal the true personality of Don Vito.

Vito Andolini sails for the United States an orphan, his parents killed by the local Mafia chieftain, Don Ciccio. Like countless other immigrants, he gazes in reverent expectation at the Statue of Liberty as the ship reaches Ellis Island. The camera travels along those grave faces, seeing in them no guile or predisposition to violence, merely a candour and a resolution to survive in a mysterious new land. After a bewildering series of examinations Vito, who even in Sicily has been reluctant to speak, is quarantined on Ellis Island. Coppola (whose aunt Caroline passed through the same procedure at about the same time) views him alone in his spartan room, as he stares out of a brightly lit window. 'Vito Corleone, Ellis Island, 1901', states a caption on the screen.

Brando's Don radiates an irresistible charm and nobility, and in the 'prequel' De Niro's Vito adroitly reflects these qualities. As a consequence, the audience allows itself to be duped, lulled into accepting the legitimacy of

'Vito Corleone. Ellis Island. 1901.'

Vito turns his modesty and innate gravitas to his advantage in the hectic world of Hell's Kitchen. When he establishes an olive oil importing business, he names it not after himself but after his boyhood chum, Genco Abbandando. He observes, and speaks only when required to do so. While Clemenza and Tessio react to the menace of Don Fanucci with ill-disguised trepidation, their friend from Corleone calculates and bides his time before fixing on a plan to rid the neighbourhood of the Black Hand.

Few other people in the story can live with their power so calmly, with the possible exception of Sollozzo. Don Ciccio's hands tremble and have a restless life of their own while he sits outside his Sicilian villa, listening to Vito's mother as she pleads for mercy on her son. Fanucci, all chic and no substance, becomes a pathetic old man when ambushed by two youths (in *The Complete Novel for Television*). Hyman Roth suffers from a nervous cough that interrupts each sentence like a tic. Joey Zasa, a tailor's insecure dummy, straightens his suit at every opportunity.

Only Don Vito and his son remain at ease with their role and their sovereignty.

In domestic life, Vito is so different from his son Michael. He treats his wife with deference. She will of course say little, and she will serve the meal when friends come to the apartment. But Vito appreciates her loyalty. In one delightful scene, having refused from pride a box full of fruit from the store owner forced by Fanucci to let him go, Vito brings home a single pear. He unwraps it and places it on the bare table with a graceful gesture, and his wife reacts accordingly. 'Oh, what a

the budding Don's crimes. Clemenza initiates Vito into the glib, opportunistic life of the streets, asking him to hide some arms during a shake-down and then cajoling him into stealing a carpet for his apartment. Coppola presents these incidents with a mischievous humour. Vito appears as the innocent bystander, startled by the revelation of such streetwise pranks. When he unwraps Clemenza's bundle, for example, he discovers the guns. He contemplates them for a long pause, glancing around the bathroom as though he had never seen a weapon in his life and only now could suspect that such objects contain significant power.

'Glancing around the bathroom as though he had never seen a weapon in his life.' Robert De Niro as Vito in *Part II.*

nice pear!' she smiles, as though Vito brought her a fine jewel. And when their children arrive, Vito, arms folded over his sweatshirt, watches in respect while Mama Corleone tends to their suffering.

His voice already radiates that hoarse, melancholy whisper associated with Brando's Don in *The Godfather.* This young Italian is perceived as a victim, a decent youth who minds his own business and then turns Robin Hood to free the community from the Mafia's grasp. Instinctively, he learns from Clemenza the time-honoured Mafia habit of returning favours. He observes the cruelty and the

effectiveness of Fanucci's strong-arm tactics as he extorts money from a trembling theatre owner by holding a blade to the throat of his daughter. So when he sallies forth to do battle with Don Fanucci on Ninth Avenue, he can mutter the now famous phrase, 'I'll make him an offer he can't refuse', with a nonchalance and a brio that rob the words of their sinister ring. Even after shooting his enemy, he can return to sit in innocent pleasure with his family on the stoop, wife and three children joining him in a tableau that seems to encapsulate the immigrant folk memory. 'Michael, your father loves you very much,' he says as he dandles the infant on his knees and caresses his tiny hand.

Vito Corleone is always relaxed with his power. He leans back amiably in his office chair as a grovelling landlord apologizes for exploiting a tenant, just as in old age Brando's Don listens to a stream of supplicants at his daughter's wedding. In Brando's performance, this trait is even more pronounced. Italianate gestures of assent with his hands, a faint shrug of the head or a tilt of the eyebrows imply an acceptance of the way of the world. Nowhere is the Don more commanding than when addressing a small meeting of Family and colleagues, reducing their frustrations to a silent compliance as he claims their sympathy with such remarks as, 'I'm a reasonable man . . .' and 'When did I refuse anyone an accommodation?'

At certain junctures he strikes one as being almost ashamed of the violence that sustains his empire. He likes his wine, and he laughs a lot. He persists in doing the little things that powerful men cannot usually do – feeding the

Relaxed with his power. The young Don Vito in *Part II*.

fish in his aquarium, tending his garden, shopping for fruit (something that exposes him to Sollozzo's hit-men).

Brando resists any temptation to camp it up. Rather, he distills his distress to a point at which it becomes overwhelmingly poignant – as he listens to Tom Hagen's news about the death of Sonny, letting out a gasp of pain like the air from a deflating tyre ('I want no inquiries made. I want no acts of vengeance.'). Or when he arrives at the funeral parlour and, with a helpless gesture of his arm, exclaims through his tears, 'Look how they massacred my boy!' Few other actors could have taken such a risk and preserved their dignity.

Respectability forms an essential virtue in

the world of Don Corleone. Coppola has said that the character was a synthesis of two Mafia chieftains, Vito Genovese and Joseph Profaci. Genovese, like Vito, ordered his soldiers never to deal in drugs, even if he himself did exactly that on the side. Genovese once threatened Joseph Valachi in words that could have been spoken by Brando's Don: 'You know, we take a barrel of apples, and in this barrel of apples there might be a bad apple. Well, this apple has to be removed, and if it ain't removed, it would hurt the rest of the apples.'

If his father stands tantalizingly beyond censure in the eyes of many, Michael confronts

Marlon Brando in *The Godfather*, still dictating the rules of the game.

the contradictions of his life without compunction. 'We're both part of the same hypocrisy,' he tells Senator Geary in *Part II*.

In the last conversation with his father in *The Godfather*, he comforts the old man. The Don refers wistfully to a career that might have been his – Senator Corleone (shades of the Kennedy clan), Governor Corleone – hoping that Michael would hold all the strings.

'There just wasn't enough time,' he concludes.

'We'll get there, Pop, we'll get there,' replies a gentle Michael. In the midst of this scene, the mantle passes almost imperceptibly to Michael. Robert Towne may have created

this exchange for the screen, but Mario Puzo already voices the sentiments in his original novel. Michael reflects on his father's death and on his last words, 'Life is beautiful.' Then he resolves to follow his father's path. 'He would care for his children, his family, his world. But his children would grow in a different world. They would be doctors, artists, scientists, governors, presidents. Anything at all. He would see to it that they joined the general family of humanity, but he as a powerful and prudent parent would most certainly keep a wary eye on that general family.'

Don Vito enjoys a serene finale, playing with his grandchild in the vegetable garden of his home, stuffing his mouth with orange

'There just wasn't enough time.' Al Pacino and Marlon Brando in the garden scene written by Robert Towne.

peel, and *pretending* to be a monster. And so even his death takes on a grace that surpasses the agony of his heart seizure. As the little grandson fusses over the stricken Don, Coppola cuts to a long shot of the tomato grove, with its white muslin billowing over the scene like a protective shroud. Decades later, Michael wears similarly rumpled clothes and a battered hat, as he too dies of old age.

Deluded by power, Michael exerts a control over his Family that Don Vito would never have countenanced, even if, as Al Pacino contends, he 'has a kind of disdain for gangsterism'. Plunged into the Family 'business' by the attempt on his father's life, Michael comes through his first test well. At the hospital he has the gumption to move his father's bed to another room, and then stands watch on the steps of the hospital with the shy young baker, Enzo, as an unexpected ally. Michael feigns strength and menace as some hit-men gaze up at him from the dark recesses of a cruising sedan.

The single blow from Captain McCluskey's fist changes Michael for ever. He immediately proposes to the Family that he murder Sollozzo, and severs his ties with Kay in a brief, matter-of-fact phone call. In Sicily he taps into the roots of his ancestry, falls truly in love for the first and only time in his life and witnesses the death of Apollonia in a car bomb attack. The next time Michael appears on

'Is it true?' asks Kay. Al Pacino and Diane Keaton in the closing scene of *The Godfather*.

screen he has changed to an unnerving degree. He wears a black coat and a black fedora. His eyes are devoid of humour or sentiment. He no longer walks, he trudges, the burden of his loss translated into bleak, implacable anger. At one point in the novel, Mario Puzo describes 'the surge of wintry cold hatred that pervaded [Michael's] body'. Al Pacino has remarked that, 'No doubt there's sort of a thug in Michael, something he doesn't really cater to, or admit to, and even if he does, it's not something he's comfortable with.'

He woos Kay for a second time as a criminal commands his victim – and his urging Kay to leave her schoolchildren and climb into his hearselike, chauffeur-driven car may be com-

pared to Sollozzo's abduction of Tom Hagen outside the store on Fifth Avenue. Kay has no alternative but to obey, and that becomes the basis of her marriage with Michael. At the close of *The Godfather*, she asks Michael anxiously to confirm that he has had nothing to do with the murder of Carlo Rizzi, her brother-in-law.

'Michael, is it true?' she says.

'Don't ask me about my business, Kay.'

'Is it *true*?'

'Don't ask me about my business.'

'No –'

'Enough!' shouts Michael, slamming his hand on his desk in frustration. He moves restlessly around the room. Then he seems to relent. 'All right. This one time,' he says, waving a finger at her. 'This one time I'll let you ask me about my affairs.'

'Is it true?'

Michael hesitates before replying, 'No,' with a shake of his head. Kay starts to weep and they embrace. In his novel Puzo describes the crucial moment thus: 'He had never been more convincing. He looked directly into her eyes. He was using all the mutual trust they had built up in their married life to make her believe him. And she could not doubt any longer.' In the film Kay returns to the kitchen, while in the background Clemenza, accompanied by Rocco and Al Neri, kisses the hand of 'Don' Corleone. As she turns to look, Neri comes forward and gently but inexorably closes the door, its blackness obliterating the image and ending the film. Michael's last tie with the reasoned, sensitive world is excluded from his inner sanctum.

In *Part II* Kay can move freely within the Family compound at Lake Tahoe, but guards turn her back at the gate when she tries to leave on an unscheduled trip. Even during Anthony's First Communion celebrations, Michael's possession of Kay is manifest. As they dance together, he clutches her in a bear-like embrace, seeming to rob her of independent movement. When, disillusioned, she tells Michael during the Washington hearings that she intends to leave him, the reply is chilling: 'Do you expect me to let you take my children away from me? Don't you know me? Don't you know that that's an impossibility – that I'd use all my power to keep something like that from happening?'

Kay then tells him that she deliberately killed her third child. 'It was an *abortion*,

Michael, an abortion just like our marriage, something that's unholy and evil ... I wouldn't bring another son of yours into the world, not as long as this Sicilian *thing* that's been going for two thousand –' Michael cuts her off in mid-sentence, striking her down in the hotel room with a vicious slap to the head.

From this point onwards in *Part II*, Michael commits the most heinous of all emotional crimes in Italian-American society: he separates a mother from her young children. Kay's son Anthony no longer embraces her on the brief visits she is permitted to make. In one of the trilogy's most terrifying moments, Michael appears as Kay is leaving the house, fixes her with a deathly stare and shuts the door in her face with a definitive click. This Manichaean individual, who sips nothing but club soda and who strikes his wife with deliberate brutality, seems more than a generation removed from the gentility of Don Vito.

For Pacino, *Part II* becomes 'a descent, trying to hold on to everything, and losing it'. Coppola believes that Michael's life follows a path to an inevitable conclusion: 'After winning all the battles and overcoming all of his enemies, thanks to his intelligence and superiority, I did not want to see him die. Nor did I want him to go to jail. Or be assassinated by his rivals. But, in a larger sense, I wanted him to be a broken man.'

Throughout the final part of the *Godfather* story, Michael tries to reconcile himself with these sins. He cannot grasp that for individuals such as Kay his contrition has come too late. If the character of Michael Corleone in *Part III* strikes many viewers as less persuasive than it was in the first two films, it may be because crime makes more compelling cinema than virtue does.

The other members of the Family do not have the chance to develop along such powerful lines. Sonny seems likely to do so, for the first hour or so of *The Godfather*, as he charges out among the press photographers at Connie's wedding reception, smashing a camera and tossing some dollars down on the ground in a derisory gesture of compensation. We cannot see him in his priapic glory, as we can when reading Puzo's novel, but there is no mistaking his reckless nature as he dashes upstairs with Lucy Mancini and screws her in a convenient bedroom while his father sends Hagen looking for him and his own wife is chatting with guests in the garden. Sonny, so called 'because of his devotion to his father', attends all the Family's key meetings, and dominates his brothers through physical charisma alone. But he tends to speak before considering his options, and the Don rebukes him on at least two occasions. When he interrupts his father during the confrontation with Sollozzo, he gives the Turk a hint of hope, and probably the courage to hit the Don in the belief that Sonny will make the peace and accept the drugs deal he and the Tattaglias propose.

Sonny's finest moment comes in the imme-

The flashback at the end of *Part II*.

diate wake of the assault on his father. His natural authority and quick wits serve the Family well as it goes into defence mode, and Sonny picks up each and every phone call, dialling out himself from the Don's study, munching on a piece of bread dipped in his mother's sauce and hesitating the while to occupy his father's leather chair.

Before his rashness and aggression destroy him, Sonny has had the sense to concur with Michael's plan for eliminating Sollozzo and McCluskey. He cannot help treating his brother with affectionate condescension, but he accepts that the murder will keep them apart for a year or more, and presses on with his duties. Nobody could be more loyal to the Family than Sonny.

The first time he learns that Carlo has beaten up Connie, he flies into a rage and almost kills Carlo in the street where he works, leaving him unconscious in the gutter. But he can contain his instinct to kill the man. The second time proves fatal, and Sonny hurtles off in his Buick towards the causeway and the tollbooths where his foes have laid their ambush. His father, recuperating from his wounds, will always regard Sonny as 'a bad Don – rest in peace', because his headstrong nature is so far removed from his own circumspect way of approaching life. James Caan's ebullient performance singes the first part of the film with its energy, and audiences recall the character of Sonny with almost as much enjoyment as they do that of the Don or Michael. At least he could be raised from the dead for the finale of *The Godfather Part II*, when Michael in his solitude remembers his father's surprise birthday party in 1942,

and Sonny sits at the head of the table once again, arguing, cajoling, ruling with an infectious joy.

Puzo describes Fredo as 'a child every Italian prayed to the saints for. Dutiful, loyal, always at the service of his father, living with his parents at age thirty.' Like many middle sons, Fredo acquires an inferiority complex in the shadow of Sonny's bull-like arrogance and Michael's watchful intelligence. Drunk for much of the time, he can be engaging (in his introductory scene with Kay and Michael at the wedding), irritable (with his bimbo wife, understandably) and irresolute. His worst moment comes as he watches the gunmen pump their bullets into his father in the street. Fumbling with his gun, dropping it and then cracking up completely, covering his head with his hands instead of rushing to his father's aid, Fredo gives way to a self-loathing that will forever prevent him from taking charge of the Family. As Puzo wrote: 'Everyone knew that the Don had given up on this middle son ever being important to the business. He wasn't quite smart enough, and failing that, not quite ruthless enough. He was too retiring a person, did not have enough force.'

Usually he controls his resentment, deferring to Michael with a drooping gaze, but deferring anyway – as when he clears the hotel suite of hostesses and musicians on the night Michael arrives in Las Vegas. Hyman Roth, hearing of Fredo's weakness, exerts his cunning to nobble him and expose Michael. Yet Fredo's betrayal of the Family is so transparent (and John Cazale's acting so sympathetic) that we feel sorry for him in the scenes in Havana when Michael manœuvres him into showing his true colours. As Fredo orders another banana daiquiri and laments that he has not chosen a wife like Kay and had children of his own ('for once in my life be more like Pop'), his brother sips a club soda and appals us with his ruthless, vigilant gaze. 'Why didn't we spend more time like this before!' exclaims Fredo, in that instant acknowledging his guilt for working with Roth and Johnny Ola.

Fredo enjoys a final night of drinking in Havana, escorting the Corleones' assortment of corrupt politicians and industrialists around the nightclub circuit. As midnight sounds on New Year's Eve, Michael embraces his brother, breaks away and then, with a physical violence he rarely shows elsewhere, seizes Fredo's head with both hands, plants a vicious kiss on his lips and growls, 'I know it was you, Fredo. You broke my heart!' Then repeats, almost softly, 'You broke my heart.' Fredo can find no response, retreating into the crowds and fleeing from Michael in the confusion of Batista's fall that night in Cuba. 'You're still my brother!' cries Michael as Fredo lurches away into the darkness.

Although he returns to the Family compound, Fredo behaves like a man condemned. When Michael asks him, a tad naively, why he has betrayed him, Fredo's response climaxes in an explosion of impotent fury: 'I was your older brother, Mikey, and I was stepped over!' But when Michael pronounces his verdict ('You're nothing to me now . . .'), Fredo lies supine on a reclining chair, as immobile and defenceless as a corpse.

Susceptible to the last, Fredo goes to his

Brothers together in Havana: John Cazale and Al Pacino in *Part II*.

death without a whimper. Before entering the boat with Neri, he tells little Anthony a story about catching a fish every time one says a Hail Mary. 'That was me!' said Coppola. 'I once caught twenty-two fish because I said twenty-two Hail Marys. And then all of a sudden, you say the Hail Mary and it doesn't work, in the most profound sense you could imagine.' Far out over the grey waters of the lake, Fredo remains for ever a hunched figure reciting his Hail Marys, and when Neri's single shot rings out, it does so with an emotional resonance that will haunt both Michael's conscience and much of *The*

'You're nothing to me now . . .' Michael condemns Fredo in *Part II.*

Godfather Part III. A seagull wheels above the boat, letting out a shriek as though of pain at the enormity of Michael's crime.

As he sits in the garden reflecting on his life, Michael thinks of Fredo at the table with the Family in 1942 – Fredo who dares congratulate him for enlisting in the Marines, only to have his handshake roughly broken by an enraged Sonny, who believes that blood is more important than country.

The most exasperating member of the Family is Tom Hagen, characterized in the book as tall and crew-cut. Robert Duvall, a Coppola stalwart of the 1960s, is short of stature and has thinning blond hair combed discreetly over his head. But the casting

works, for Duvall projects the intelligence and distaste for violence so essential to the personality of Hagen. Cool under pressure, Hagen often seems too diffident for his own good, too sentimental about life and its losses. Brought into the Family as a German-Irish orphan, he has been treated always as a son by the Don and as a brother by Sonny, Fredo and Michael. A lawyer by inclination and then by training, he serves as the Don's *consigliere* or adviser – 'the most vital subordinate position in the family business', writes Puzo.

Hagen's finest hour comes when he visits Jack Woltz, the Hollywood producer who must be persuaded to give Johnny Fontane the lead in a new war movie. While Woltz

'A hunched figure reciting his Hail Marys.' John Cazale and Richard Bright in *Part II*.

tries to unnerve him and impress him with his wealth, Hagen clings to his briefcase, listens politely and munches his dinner. Only when Woltz's temper makes it plain that he will never give Johnny the role of his dreams does Tom wipe his lips with his napkin and ask for a car to take him to the airport. 'My client is a man who insists on hearing bad news quickly,' he says, without a hint of ostensible menace. But Woltz is impressed.

At other junctures, Hagen's weakness and unwillingness to bear responsibility seem exasperating. Kidnapped by Sollozzo, he maintains a fearful silence, holding back a spurt of tears as the Turk tells him the Don has been killed. Yet he refuses to crack, listen-

ing instead to Sollozzo's persuasive patter and accepting his role as the peacemaker between Sonny and the Tattaglia Family.

When Michael returns from Sicily to take control of the Family's affairs, he dismisses Tom for no cogent reason. In the novel, Puzo lets it be known that Michael is jealous of Hagen's closeness to Sonny, and this provides the motivation for his downgrading of the *consigliere*. In Las Vegas, Fredo turns to his foster-brother for help to smooth the tension of Michael's arrival, but Hagen cuts him short, reminding him that Michael makes the decisions now. Yet not long afterwards, Tom is seen next to Michael at the Don's funeral, daring to damn both Tessio and Clemenza to his boss, suggesting that he remains every inch the relaxed confidant he was at the outset of the movie.

During the climax of the film, Tessio suddenly realizes that his treachery has been discovered, and that he is doomed. He looks at the impassive Hagen and asks him with a hint of a smile, 'Tom, can you get me off the hook – for old times' sake?' Hagen averts his eyes. 'Can't do it, Solly,' he replies curtly. Tessio is driven away and Tom Hagen stares in regret after the departing saloon.

Tom must mind the Family when Michael travels to Cuba to do his business with Hyman Roth. This renewed trust between the two brothers gives Hagen the strength to carry on within the Family. He brings Senator Geary into line by having Neri drug him and then kill the prostitute with whom he's been playing bondage games. He restrains Kay, politely but firmly, from leaving the compound. And when Michael returns, weary and irritable after his escape from Havana, Tom has to break some tough news just as in *The Godfather* he summoned the courage to tell the Don about Sonny's slaughter. Kay has suffered a miscarriage, and the child is dead.

'Was it a boy?' asks Michael.

'Mikey, after three and a half months –'

'Now can't you give me a straight answer for once,' barks Michael. *'Was it a boy?'*

'I really don't know,' replies Tom, his

'Now can't you give me a straight answer for once? *Was it a boy?'* Al Pacino and Robert Duvall in *Part II.*

lawyer's facility saving him from further wrath.

Another impressive scene for Tom Hagen shows him persuading Pentangeli to take his own life rather than testify against the Family. He visits the old Family soldier in his restricted quarters on a US Army base, where Pentangeli is held as the FBI's star witness against Michael Corleone. Puffing on cigars, they stroll inside the perimeter fence, reminiscing about the old days, and little by little Tom draws a parallel between the great era of the Corleone Family and the ideals of ancient Rome. Those who had betrayed the emperor, says Tom, always had a chance of redemption. Pentangeli agrees, saying the plotters knew that if they did the right thing their families would be cared for and their reputation would remain intact. Pentangeli, an amateur historian, gets the message. Not long afterwards, his guards find him in a bath full of blood. Frank Pentangeli has 'opened his veins' in the best Roman tradition.

Robert Duvall's obduracy in refusing the highest fee Paramount could offer him for *Part III* destroyed the opportunity for Hagen's character to enjoy a crowning moment – his seventieth birthday party and, perhaps, a mortal battle of wits with the ageing Michael. On the evidence of his appearances in the first two films, he almost matches Pacino in economy of gesture, while endow-

Robert Duvall and Michael V. Gazzo discussing the ideals of the Roman Empire in *Part II*.

ing his part with a rare warmth and a palpable sense of loyalty. It has been said that Hagen bears some resemblance to Joseph Gallo, who was adviser to the Gambino Family and was sentenced to ten years in jail in 1988.

Mature, important female characters do not figure much in Coppola's landscape, save Mina in *Bram Stoker's Dracula*, and of course Peggy Sue Kelcher. In part this is explained by the subject matter of his films – the Mafia, the Vietnam War – but Coppola's own Italian-American background accounts for the dominance of masculine roles. Women are either elderly, *mama mia* matrons who cook the spaghetti and know how to withdraw from a room when the men start discussing 'business', or youthful and essentially decorative, bowing meekly to their husband's whims (or at best teasing them, as Apollonia does Michael in Sicily). In the first two films of the trilogy, Kay Adams seems fulfilled only by her children. Her 'failure' to retain her third pregnancy wounds Michael to such a degree that he does not even speak to her after hearing the news. Puzo writes that she did not impress the Family. 'She was too thin, she was too fair, her face was too sharply intelligent for a woman, her manner too free for a maiden.'

Kay does not belong to the Italian-American world. Her maiden name, Adams, points to an entirely different tradition of American life. In the novel, Puzo describes, in an eloquent scene, how her WASP parents cope with a visit from the police in the aftermath of the murder of Sollozzo and Michael's flight to Sicily. Her father, a pastor in the

Tom Hagen refuses to accept Kay's letter to Michael in *The Godfather*.

Baptist Church as well as a reputed scholar, refuses to contemplate the thought of Kay's being caught up with gangsters. 'What I find incredible,' he tells the detectives, 'is that my daughter could be in serious trouble. Unless you're suggesting that she is a "moll", I believe it's called.' Kay's college education allows her to acquiesce in some of the Corleone formalities, but at certain moments, in all three films, she articulates her resentment to a degree that startles Michael. Like Emilia, who denounces Iago at the end of *Othello*, she pays dearly for this refusal to charm her tongue. And when Michael, in front of their children, shuts the door in her face, it seems as terminal a gesture as the fall of an executioner's blade.

Her renaissance in *The Godfather Part III* gives her an altogether more dignified opportunity of crossing swords with Michael. With the security of a prosperous second marriage, and more influence over her children than she could ever have dared hope in the dark days of *Part II*, Kay defies her former husband from the first moments of their meeting at the party in Manhattan. She supports young Anthony's determination to become an opera singer, and then argues with Michael about his past as a monster, a murderer. For all Michael's protestations about devoting his life to the protection of his Family (in a precise echo of Don Vito's words in his final conversation in *The Godfather*), Kay remains unconvinced. 'I'm telling you how I feel,' she says. 'That you hate me,' replies Michael with an affectionate smile.

'No,' comes the unexpected riposte from Kay, 'I *dread* you.'

When Anthony Corleone makes his début at the opera house in Palermo, Kay flies over for the occasion and Michael (disguised as a chauffeur) takes her on a surprise tour of the region. This sentimental journey marks Kay's first visit to Sicily and also a reconciliation between her and Michael. In a small village square, they watch a puppet show (the *Baronessa di Carini*, in which a father kills his daughter because of her love for her cousin, and thus an oblique comment on Michael's concern over Mary's affair with Vincent). Michael shows her the house where his father was born, and then the room where he first

Kay's arrival in Sicily in *Part III*. Diane Keaton and Al Pacino.

lived with Apollonia. As late as 27 November 1989, the screenplay included a love scene between Kay and Michael, 'more in remembrance of the tragedies they shared than anything else'. But by that juncture, the off-screen relationship between Al Pacino and Diane Keaton had ended, and so the scene segues, more convincingly, into another room where the couple eat some cold food. Besides, Michael's contrition and affection are evident, and his line, 'I never forgot you; I still dream about you,' speaks volumes. Kay's poise deserts her at last, and she tells him that, if it's any consolation, she still loves him – and always will. In a trilogy not known for its soft-heartedness, this sequence more than any other brims with sentiment.

In retaliation for the unrelenting *machismo* of their menfolk, women such as Fredo's wife and Michael's sister, Connie, draw satisfaction from humiliating the men around them. During the festivities at Lake Tahoe, Fredo's wife, drunk, must be dragged off the dance-floor by a bodyguard because Fredo himself cannot cope with her. Connie arrives at the party towing an insipid partner named Merle (played by 1960s heart-throb Troy Donahue), who absorbs a series of stinging insults from Michael without uttering a word of protest.

Connie's evolution throughout the films has three phases. In *The Godfather* she is a bright young thing, reduced quickly to an abused and paranoid wife, hiding her bruises from her family and rebelling against Carlo in one of the best orgies of domestic destruction since *Citizen Kane*. On the day her fiancé, Carlo, is introduced to the Family (in 1942, but

Connie (Talia Shire) and Merle (Troy Donahue) at Lake Tahoe in *Part II*.

actually the final sequence of *Part II*), Connie is silenced by her oldest brother, Sonny, after daring to interfere in 'men's talk' about the war. 'You talk to Carlo!' sneers Sonny dismissively.

In *Part II* the Family already regards her with ill-disguised exasperation. Even her mother cannot stomach her playgirl lifestyle – seeing her children on weekends, drifting from one divorce to another lover and, as Michael discovers, in constant need of cash. She reappears during the film's long coda, trying in vain to protect Fredo and Kay from Michael's wrath, even if she serves as accomplice to the murder of Fredo, calling little

Anthony in from the fishing boat so that Neri can be alone with his victim.

In *Part III*, however, Connie becomes a mature, even dangerous personality in her own right. Dressed habitually in black, her hair drawn back in a severe bun, she protects Michael at every turn. Connie recognizes the virility in Vincent's character, and knows that Michael's late-flowering fear of confrontation may prove the undoing of the Family. She it is who gives Vincent the go-ahead to kill Joey Zasa, she the one who prepares the poisoned *cannoli* (sweet pasta dish, a Sicilian specialty) for Don Altobello, she the nurse who administers the vital insulin to the diabetic Michael. Connie also urges her brother to anoint Vincent as his successor, and brings the two men together for the scene in which Vinnie is given the name 'Corleone'.

The need to introduce fresh blood into the Corleone Family perplexed a succession of screenwriters. When *The Godfather Part III* at last materialized, Vincent, Anthony and Mary all had to come to terms with their Family past. Anthony, despite his sympathetic stand against his father, remains an underwritten role. This winsome son of Michael is happiest when commanding the stage in *Cavalleria Rusticana* (and Franc D'Ambrosio does his own singing). Mary, leaving aside the quality of Sofia Coppola's performance, means much more both to the plot and to the director. When she becomes infatuated with her cousin Vincent, she puts her father in a quandary. Should he condemn the relationship and alienate the affections of his daughter, who only now is returning to his

orbit? Or should he allow her to marry Vincent, who is very much the son of his headstrong father, Santino, and who can lead his cherished Mary into jeopardy? Mary rejects her father with an outright 'No!' when he asks her to stop seeing Vincent, just as Anthony refused to obey Michael about pursuing his law degree.

Mary does work with Anthony, though, to bring her parents together again. When Kay arrives at the station in Sicily, and Michael stands awkwardly to one side, Mary takes his arm and her mother's, and leads them down the platform so they can all relax. She is chosen by fate to suffer the death intended for Michael, and her last word, as she steps bloodied towards him on the steps of the Teatro Massimo, is a simple, almost banal 'Dad . . .?' as though she were vouchsafing to him her soul.

If the chemistry between Vincent and Mary seems never quite to work, it has more to do with the young man's hunger for power than with any shortcomings in the acting of Sofia Coppola. Vincent believes in violence, revenge and the inviolability of the Family. He was conceived as a combination of all the brothers – Michael, Sonny and Fredo – and his grandfather, and Andy Garcia plays him at just the right pitch, flaunting his manhood in front of all and sundry. When he enters Michael's study with an awkward swagger, he instinctively touches his balls in a passing gesture as he looks mockingly at his enemy Joey Zasa. His hands hang loose at his sides, ready to fight. His leather jacket proclaims his generation as well as his ability to earn money. His true Corleone pedigree explodes in the

Vincent (Andy Garcia) and Mary (Sofia Coppola) realize that they are falling in love.

scene at his apartment, when he takes on two masked intruders and kills them both. He keeps the second at his mercy until he has forced him to disclose the identity of his pay-master, Zasa – and then abruptly and without compunction shoots him. This ruthless streak echoes that of his uncle in *The Godfather*, who reassures Carlo that he will be spared provided he confesses to his guilt – and then watches while Clemenza garrottes him in the car outside the house. As Vincent pursues Zasa on horseback through the streets of

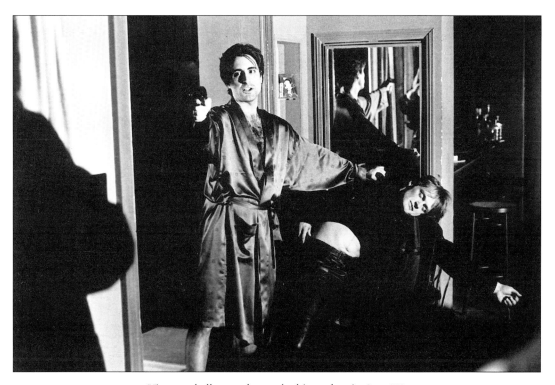

Vincent challenges the masked intruders in *Part III*.

Little Italy, he does so with the relentless stare of Vito and Michael before him.

Although tact will never be his strong suit, Vincent does mature throughout the film. He listens more and more intently to his uncle's advice ('Never hate your enemies – it affects your judgement,' Michael tells him), and by the time he agrees to ditch Mary in exchange for becoming Don in his own right, he intimidates those around him with his gravity and commanding behaviour. As the film ends, Vincent stands on the cusp of greatness, a 'Prince of the City' like his long-gone father, Sonny.

4 Religion and Redemption

'If anything in this life is certain, if history has taught us anything, it's that everyone can be killed' – Michael Corleone in The Godfather Part II

The mighty wedding in Long Beach seems like an exclusively lay celebration. No priest officiates, and none appears in any capacity until two-thirds of the way through *The Godfather*, when Michael and Apollonia kneel outside the little church in Sicily and a priest pronounces the blessing on their marriage. The religious element in the film prevails only in the bloody finale, when the baptism of Connie's baby is intercut with the murders ordered by Michael. As the priest catechizing Michael (now a Godfather in more than one sense) demands, 'Do you renounce Satan?', so the slaughter begins. The editing supplies a heavy, inexorable rhythm, like the tolling of bells. The massacre both chimes with, and defiles, the lofty aspirations and minute details of the religious service. All the Don's foes are eliminated in an adroitly engineered plot that approximates to blasphemy, for Michael has deployed the gravity and ceremonial of the Church to legitimize his actions.

A whole thesis could be written on mendacity in the *Godfather* trilogy. People lie without any apparent awareness of the ethical implications. Michael may be the worst offender, but he is not the only liar. Some characters prevaricate with cunning (Fanucci, Roth, Altobello), others from cowardice – Clemenza spinning Paulie a tale about looking for apartments on the West Side when he knows perfectly well he is about to execute him; Fredo pretending not to know Johnny Ola for fear of his brother's reprisal; Senator Geary extolling the virtues of Italian-Americans before a Senate committee because he is being blackmailed by the Family; or

'That's my Family, Kay, that's not me.' Diane Keaton and Al Pacino in *The Godfather.*

Frank Pentangeli, suddenly forswearing his evidence on being confronted by his brother, brought from Sicily by the Corleones to ensure his silence.

The young Vito lies only to gain time. He tells Fanucci that he does not have enough money to give him yet, even though we all know that he has no intention of paying anything to this *pezzo'novanta*. His son, however, lies so directly that people believe him. He lies to Kay in the opening wedding sequence – 'That's my Family, Kay, that's not me' – and he deceives her again during their first conversation after his return from Sicily. He lies to Carlo just before sending him to his death. He lies to Kay about that murder. In *Part II* he can lie, under oath before the Senate committee, dismissing evidence against him as 'a complete falsehood' without so much as a catch in his voice. Only in *Part III* does he abandon lying in his efforts to achieve redemption. Of course that does not prevent his consorting courteously with enemies such as Altobello – a knack he acquired from his father, whose most famous threat, 'I'll make him an offer he can't refuse', sounds like some divine favour.

The contemporary part of *Part II* also contains little deference to Catholic tradition, although Anthony Corleone takes his First Communion inside a church near Lake

Tahoe. Michael celebrates the occasion with a vast party on the Family estate and a munificent endowment for the local university. It all smacks of Hyannisport and the Kennedy compound – another conjunction of Catholics and dynasts. In the pre-title shot of *Part II*, members of the Family kiss Michael's hand in a gesture of fealty, something rendered usually to a bishop or a chalice. Only in the flashbacks to Don Vito's childhood in Sicily and his youth in Manhattan does the influence of Catholic ritual take centre stage. Priests in white robes lead the ill-fated funeral procession across the rocks in the opening scene of *Part II* and in the elaborate Festa in Little Italy, the image of Christ is borne aloft through the streets, dollar bills attached to the hem as they would be to a belly-dancer in Turkey. Don Fanucci adds his own high-denomination offering, with an ostentatious flourish, earning the applause of the crowd. Otherwise, the only indication that Christ has penetrated the lives of the Corleone Family comes when Fredo embarks on his last fishing trip, and recites Hail Marys in the hope of attracting a bite, just before Neri shoots him in the head.

Not until *Part III* does the secular strength of the Family begin to bow to the sovereignty of Catholicism. Once again, the film starts with a church ceremony – Michael receiving the Order of Saint Sebastian in St Patrick's Cathedral – and an endowment on behalf of the Vito Corleone Foundation. But now the Archbishop himself consorts with the Mafia and, on the Corleone side, one of Michael's godsons, Andrew Hagen, heads for the Vatican to pursue his career as a priest. The central thrust of the film involves the collision between business and idealism, the venal and the spiritual. From the outset, a sense of inner torment is discernible: as the Archbishop intones the Hail Mary in St Patrick's, Michael harks back to the murder of Fredo at Lake Tahoe, with the same prayer echoing over the grey surface of the water.

Michael steadily assumes the role of a penitent, while his violent traits are adopted by young Vinnie Mancini. The dream of respectability is also the dream of exoneration ('Never underestimate the power of forgiveness,' smiles Michael at the Archbishop during their negotiations). If the Corleone Family can channel its ill-gotten billions through the respectable portals of the Vatican, then true power will become equated with true redemption.

But just as his grandfather violated the solemnity of the Festa, by shooting Fanucci at the very moment the fireworks are released by the joyous faithful, so Vincent cocks a snook at the hypocrisy of the church. His henchmen pose as bearers of the Madonna, thrusting their *lupara* (sawn-off shotguns) through their white robes to destroy Zasa's bodyguards, enabling Vincent himself, disguised as a cop on horseback, to pursue and execute his foe. This plot has been hatched between Connie, Vincent and Neri in the hushed privacy of a chapel in the hospital where Michael lies recuperating from a diabetic attack. In a moment of chilling profanity, Connie hisses to Vincent, 'Do it!', and then drops to her knees before the altar.

The Godfather Part III approaches real history to a much more tangible degree than the preceding two films. The brief, controversial reign of Pope John Paul I and the scandals involving the Banco Ambrosiano and the Vatican in the early 1980s occupy a crucial place in the destiny of Michael Corleone. Cardinal Lamberto serves as the screen version of Albino Luciani, who became Supreme Pontiff after the death of Paul VI in 1978. Like Luciani, Cardinal Lamberto believes that the Church should be poor, not rich, and initiates an investigation into the alleged abuses at the Vatican Bank after learning of the Immobiliare swindle from Michael. He stands at the opposite pole to the Archbishop, whose venality and unreliability provoke Michael to tell his entourage, 'We're back to the Borgias!', a line so resonant for Coppola that he fastened it to the bulletin board in his office at Cinecittà.

In the most intelligently written scene in the film, Lamberto meets with Michael in a cloister garden. 'If what you say is true, there will be a great scandal,' remarks the Cardinal. He sighs and reaches his hand into a shallow pool of water. He picks up a pebble. 'Look at this stone,' he tells Michael. 'It has been lying in the water for a very long time, but the water has not penetrated it.' He cracks the pebble in half and shows it to his guest. 'The same thing has happened to men in Europe. For centuries they have been surrounded by Christianity, but Christ has not penetrated.'

Michael suddenly feels unwell and asks the Cardinal for some orange juice and candies.

Preparing to confess. Al Pacino and Raf Vallone as Cardinal Lamberto in *Part III*.

'I killed my father's son.' Al Pacino in *Part III*.

Gulping down the juice and gnawing at a candy bar, he tells Lamberto about his diabetes. 'The mind suffers, the body cries out,' comes the benign response. Little by little, Lamberto persuades Michael to make his confession. They move to another part of the garden, and sit divided by a shield of azaleas. Michael starts to confess, screened from his confessor by the shrubs in an unsettling approximation of the confessional box in church. Michael, for the first time in his life, talks to someone other than himself about his crimes. The words tumble out in a desperate flow: 'I betrayed my wife, I betrayed myself, I killed men and I ordered men to be killed.'

'Go on, my son,' says Lamberto between each admission. 'Go on, my son.' A church bell tolls once, and again, and once more.

At last Michael, weeping, whispers the thing he dreads most: 'I ordered the death of my brother. He injured me. I killed my mother's son. I killed my father's son.'

Lamberto tells him that his sins are terrible and that his suffering is just, but as he absolves Michael there is an awareness of the Church gathering its son into the fold once again, bringing him comfort in a religious sense just as Connie will reassure him in a secular fashion when she says later that, 'Sometimes I think of poor Fredo, drowned. Fredo's accident was God's will, Michael.' (In the original draft screenplay, she continued with the bizarre comment: 'And Lake Tahoe is very cold. They say if a person drowns in it, that the body will remain mid-suspended – perfectly preserved. Some say it will remain for ever.') As Mario Puzo has commented, 'There's a point when you get a virtuous man and he commits an unvirtuous act. He's so horrified that he's committed that unvirtuous act that it becomes even more terrible.'

Michael makes a second 'confession', beside the bier of Don Tommasino. His words are delivered like a prayer, with the tantalizing rhythm of blank verse and to the accompaniment of muffled timpani and a high-pitched, tinkling piano melody:

Goodbye, my old friend.
    You could have lived a little longer. I could be closer to my dream.
    You were so loved, Don Tommasino. Why was I so feared, and you so loved?
    What betrayed me – my mind, my heart? Why do I condemn myself so?
    I swear on the lives of my children – give me a chance to redeem myself, and I will sin no more.

Between takes, Coppola whispered to Pacino: 'From the time you've committed that first sin, you've never had the weight off you.' Wistful in approaching age, he wants to purge himself of the past. As the plot against the new Pope hastens to its climax, Michael attempts to settle his scores in the time-honoured Corleone manner. Neri sneaks into the Vatican and shoots the treacherous Archbishop; Keinszig is smothered to death and left dangling from a bridge in Rome, his ill-gotten currency notes fluttering from his corpse in a wry variation on Roberto Calvi's real-life death by

hanging from Blackfriars Bridge in London; and Calo, Michael's loyal bodyguard from the old days, sacrifices his life in killing Lucchesi. Since his confession, Michael feels bound to the newly elected Pope. He may not save him, but through his efforts he believes he can purge the Vatican of its corruption.

Michael Corleone admits to self-doubt only once in *Part II*, and in true Italian-American fashion, he turns to his mother for counsel. Plodding wearily over to her house on the Lake Tahoe estate, he sits and muses before the fire:

    'Tell me something, Ma,' he says in Sicilian. 'What did Papa think deep in his heart? He was being strong, strong for his Family. But by being strong for his Family, could he lose it?'

    His mother replies that he must be fretting about Kay's miscarriage. 'You can always have another baby,' she reassures him, 'but you can never lose your Family.' Face half-obliterated by shadow, Michael stares down into some private abyss and mutters, 'Times are changing' – an utterance that provides simultaneously a bridge to the next flashback to Vito's youth and also a hint that Michael has lost his faith in the concept of Family.

    The moral dichotomy in Michael's character involves on the one hand his obsession with Family, and on the other the insecurity that obliges him to punish anyone who crosses his path, whether it be his wife, a senator or even his own brother.

The magnanimity of Don Vito acquires an increasingly nostalgic tinge, his treatment of petty abuse in his neighbourhood almost quaint by comparison with the practices of his son.

Although violence provides the ominous bass-line underscoring *The Godfather* trilogy, there is no mistaking the note of melancholy that accompanies so many sequences, lingering even longer than Rota's music. Michael and those around him believe more and more that Don Vito lived in a state of lost innocence – preceding not only the Second World War but also the abandonment of dignified standards by the other Families and by newcomers trying to muscle in on the rackets. When glasses are raised at the dinner table on the night of Anthony's First Communion in Lake Tahoe, someone shouts '*Cent'anni!*' and Fredo's dumb-blonde, WASP wife asks what that means. 'It means we should all live happily ever after for a hundred years – the Family,' says Connie with more than a hint of bitterness. 'It'd be true if my father were alive.' When Pentangeli in his FBI detention centre says that the Corleone Family used to be like the Roman Empire, Tom Hagen responds wistfully, 'It was – once,' and the comparison with modern US history is plain.

Like all dreams of innocence, the notion dissolves into reality. But Coppola treasures the dream, constructing word and image and sound to suit it. In 1901 Vito Corleone sits before a sunstruck window in Ellis Island and sings a haunting melody, evoking purity and a sense of home. Michael, in one of his few emotional lapses in *Part II*, sits close to Tom Hagen after the attempt on his life in Lake Tahoe. He tells him that he loves him and confers absolute power on him in his absence: 'I'm trusting you with the lives of my wife, my children – the future of this Family.' Just for a moment the guard slips and the vulnerable soul beneath appears.

The forlorn quest for legitimacy, a legitimacy that will somehow expunge the crimes committed in the name not of the Father but of the Family, occupies Michael for year after year. He tells Kay that in five years such a legitimacy will be achieved. 'That was seven years ago,' says Kay wryly as she dances with Michael after Anthony's Communion party. In *Part III*, she reminds him again of that failed promise. Only with time does Michael acknowledge to himself that in protecting the Family's integrity he has destroyed his own moral standards. Relatives such as Carlo and Fredo, old allies such as Tessio, do indeed betray the Family – but they *are* the Family.

5 The Classical Style

'Evil reverberates over a period of generations' – Francis Coppola

As the centenary of cinema was being celebrated in 1995, a number of polls demonstrated the abiding appeal of *The Godfather* and its sequel. In a *Time Out* survey, the films if counted as a single achievement edged out *Citizen Kane*, and in the same magazine's poll among international directors *The Godfather* came second to *Kane* by only a few votes. When the original film went out on rerelease in the UK in 1996, the critics hailed its stature. Geoff Brown in *The Times* expressed the widely felt enthusiasm: 'Many crime movies since have splattered the screens with violence. A few, like Scorsese's, have gone behind the bloodshed to probe American society. But none has the organic strength, or visual power, of *The Godfather.*'

Coppola and Puzo lay the vigour and brashness of American society like some palimpsest over a ground of European tradition and culture. Their films endure because of the classical simplicity of Coppola's shooting and editing; because of the conviction that underpins almost every performance; and because they deal with the rituals of birth and death, youth and old age. Charles Foster Kane, that other monster in modern American cinema, acquires objects with the same impassioned zeal as Michael possesses people.

The camera remains immobile for much of the time. When it does move, it glides inexorably to illustrate a point or a character. Nobody films a table better than Coppola, perhaps because he loves the notion of people sitting together to eat and laugh and argue. In *The Godfather* he tracks discreetly along each side of the table when the heads of the

Families foregather at Don Vito's request, each name, as it's announced by Brando, disclosing an unfamiliar face. In *Part II*, he applies the same technique to the meeting chaired by Batista in Havana. This time the camera makes two circuits – once when the guests are introduced, and once as a grotesque gold telephone is passed from hand to hand.

Although Coppola admires Bernardo Bertolucci's *The Conformist* as one of the greatest films ever made, and assimilated its brilliance via Vittorio Storaro's cinematography on *Apocalypse Now*, he has not in *The Godfather* trilogy embraced the flamboyance of the Italian's camerawork. The spirit of Bertolucci marks one sequence, and that is the opening of *Part III*, as the camera tracks and seems almost to tiptoe through the deserted rooms and lakeside of the Family compound. Dead leaves scurry across the ground as they do in *The Conformist*, detritus floats in the marina and a wind of despondency seems to blow through the imagery.

At other times the camera pans or dollies unobtrusively, responding to the audience's curiosity. So, after Sonny has been killed, there is a long shot of Tom Hagen seated alone at a table, drinking. The camera advances and, as it does so, Brando emerges from the shadows to the right and precedes us into the room, ready to hear the bad news. When Kay asks her husband if he is involved in the killing of Carlo, Michael paces his study restlessly, avoiding her eyes. Willis's camera goes with him, and when there is a cut back to Kay, the stillness of the shot on her face carries even more weight than usual.

In *Part II*, Coppola could concentrate on perfecting both construction and detail. He creates a memorable symbiosis between past and present, using lighting, decor, editing and sound to do so. Gordon Willis applies a soft, overhead lighting to the early sequences in Little Italy. De Niro's Vito relaxes in interiors that are flooded with sunshine, so strong that the windows cast a halo around the figure of the young Don. Even his return to Sicily, with the assassination of Don Ciccio as its main purpose, is bathed in a warm amber light. But in the second film Michael seems associated with murk and shadow, matching the malice he reserves for his enemies. His rooms in the Lake Tahoe compound are soberly furnished and lit only by reading lamps and sconces. His own face is obscured more often than not, save for one memorable long shot at the end when his features are caught in a spectral glare inside the boat-house, as he waits for the murder of Fredo to occur far out over the lake. The windows are invariably criss-crossed with steel ribs, lending such scenes a feeling of incarceration. Low ceilings accentuate the claustrophobic mood.

Reference to the different seasons underlines this distinction between characters and eras. In *The Godfather*, the snow in Manhattan takes on a comforting Christmas tinge, but in *Part II* the snow at Lake Tahoe seems to be freezing the soul of Michael Corleone as his car swings through the gates of the estate and he trudges to his mother's house. Autumn leaves are falling when Michael comes to claim Kay in her quiet New England suburb, matching the grim look of his suit and hat. Towards the end of *The Godfather*, as Michael's plot swings into

The sunlit return to Sicily in *Part II.*

action, the heat makes the stout Clemenza, and even the restrained Neri, mop his face to deal with the perspiration.

Dean Tavoularis demonstrates the idealism of the Italian immigrants by using recurring signs and visual idioms such as the Statue of Liberty (which is viewed in reality as the ship enters Manhattan Harbour, then emblazoned on the stage curtain in the theatre Vito attends in New York and finally in the form of a bronze souvenir brought by the Don to Sicily for some aged relative). No comparable talisman of hope exists in the post-war episodes.

Barry Malkin (along with Peter Zinner and Richard Marks) deserves special praise for the editing of *The Godfather Part II.* The film gives the illusion of an almost equal split of time between the early days of the Corleone saga and the post-war changes wrought by Michael. In fact, only just over one-quarter of the running time is allotted to the story of Vito, and almost two and a quarter hours focus on Michael's world. The film consists of ten parallel stretches of narrative, five for Vito and five for Michael. Reassembled, they would form two independent stories, two films. But Coppola and his editors bridge the episodes so imaginatively that the roving back and forth in time is justified.

Six of the transitions take the form of a dissolve from one image to another. Two are sharp cuts. One is a more profound interval – a fade-out to black from the ironically idyllic shot of Vito and his wife and three children after he has shot Fanucci. No fewer than six of the time links involve babies and children, as though Coppola were eager to plant in the minds of his audience a subliminal acceptance of the Family continuum. Vito, as a boy of nine, in Ellis Island. Anthony Corleone, his grandson, in church for his first communion, and then again in bed being embraced by his father. Santino, Vito's firstborn, in his cot and then again, bawling on the new carpet that his father and Clemenza have stolen. Michael himself, first as a baby and then being cuddled by his father on the stoop in Hell's Kitchen, and at last as a boy waving goodbye to his relatives as the train draws out of a station in Sicily.

One of these dissolves has a marvellous intensity thanks to the editing of sound and image. Michael, hand on face in close-up, ponders the news of Kay's miscarriage and we hear the sound of a baby crying. Slowly the image dissolves to an equally pensive Vito, standing in mid-shot, also pondering with hand on chin, as he listens to that crying, from little Fredo in his struggle with pneumonia. The resemblance between the two men, father and son, goes beyond mere physical likeness. They seem in this dissolve to share the same thoughts and the same inbuilt sensibility to life's anguish.

The crescendo that concludes *Part II*, with Roth, Pentangeli and Fredo each meeting his doom, impresses us not just by virtue of its editing, but also with its ethical flavour. All three men contrive to transcend the grubby reality of their lives and to meet death with

dignity. Roth proclaims with pride and defiance that he is a Jew and wants to spend his twilight years in the state of Israel. Pentangeli believes that his family will be cared for if he follows the honourable example of plotters against the Roman emperor and commits suicide. And, on the verge of being gunned down by Neri, Fredo recites his Hail Mary with the devotion of a child.

Coppola has compared *Part II* to *The Oresteia* by Aeschylus, showing how 'evil reverberates over a period of generations'. Scene after scene recalls a shot or a line from *The Godfather*. 'It's something in the direction, or in the dialogue, or in the mood of each scene,' explained Coppola. 'It's like harmony where one note echoes another. As a whole, the first film ought to haunt the second like a spectre.' Other bridges in time are more subtle. Anthony sings for his father the same 'authentic Sicilian' song in *Part III* as a neighbour sings while sitting behind Vito and his family on the stoop after the assassination of Fanucci.

The effect of Nino Rota's music can never be measured in box-office terms, although without it the mythic, romantic colour of the films would not be the same. The lilting melody that Rota composed in waltz time assaults us in so many airport lounges and elevators all over the world. It has become as familiar and as cherished as Steiner's theme for *Gone With the Wind* or Maurice Jarre's scores for *Lawrence of Arabia* and *Doctor Zhivago*. So too has 'Michael's Theme', a sombre, melancholy leitmotif reminding us of Michael's destiny. As the trilogy progressed, so Carmine Coppola added his own agreeable variations on the original score, using mandolins, percussion and timpani to enhance a transition or a flashback. He has also contributed some Sicilian tunes that underline the genuine ethnic tone of the films, notably the *Marcia religiosa* played raucously during the Festa scenes in *Part II*, and the *tarantella* that enlivens the wedding sequence in *The Godfather*. He even dares to mock himself when a tipsy Pentangeli asks the band to play that same favourite *tarantella* at the Lake Tahoe party – and the musicians launch instead into 'Pop Goes the Weasel!'

Coppola's inventiveness saved him during the filming of the assassination of Sollozzo. Michael has been instructed to go to the john, find the gun that Clemenza's people have taped to the cistern and then 'come out firing'. Instead, he decides to linger for a moment. He returns to the table, and the camera closes in on his nervous, flushed face and roving eyes, while off-screen the blend of a subway train's rumbling and screeching below the restaurant and Sollozzo's urgent patter of Sicilian serve to fuel the charge of fury and resolve in Michael. So when suddenly he does rise to his feet, shooting first Sollozzo and then McCluskey, we are as startled by the timing as he himself must be.

Coppola underlines the perception of Michael as a condemned man in a number of subtle ways. The use of cars affords us a visual reminder of death throughout the trilogy. When bodyguards are in attendance and several cars move one after another, they give the impression of a cortège – and indeed they constitute precisely that when arriving for the funeral of Don Vito, each chauffeur alighting and opening the doors simultaneously with military precision. In *The Godfather*, the hapless Paulie drives himself at a deliberate pace to his own execution, accompanied by Clemenza and Rocco. Michael's car – whether it be the black saloon that accompanies him to the reunion with Kay or the one he drives himself through the streets of Miami en route to Hyman Roth's home – creeps forward at a funereal pace, rather like Isak Borg's in *Wild Strawberries*, as though bearing its occupant to a burial. When he accompanies Kay through the Sicilian countryside in *Part III*, Michael takes the wheel himself, and at one point Coppola cuts to a high, remote shot from hundreds of metres away, watching the car crawl towards ancestral hills.

Michael's make-up becomes more and more pallid as *Part II* proceeds. His lips acquire a livid tinge. Gordon Willis does not allow the light to strike Michael's eyes, so that they appear macabre, even lifeless.

Two of Michael's mortal enemies, Hyman Roth and Don Altobello, declare with sinister emphasis that health is more important than money or power, and throughout *Parts II* and *III* Michael's health comes into question. At first taking tablets with his water while others get drunk on wine and champagne cocktails, he later succumbs to diabetes. Ill-health seems to signal weakness for Puzo and Coppola. Hyman Roth is dying on his feet, and even the sardonic Senator Geary must take a tablet as he confronts Michael in the house at Lake Tahoe.

The *Godfather* films may not be grounded in a documentary tradition, but with each passing

Michael's eyes appear macabre, even lifeless. Al Pacino in *Part II*.

year more parallels can be found between real life and the events on screen. Mario Puzo enjoyed full access to the Valachi documents, which his friend Peter Maas was researching for his own successful book about the Mafia. Many of the traits that enliven the characters in *The Godfather* and its sequels were inspired by real-life characters. Joseph Valachi, a super-grass to rank with Buscetta before him, had perfected a recipe for meatballs, and Clemenza explains to Michael how to cook the dish. His favourite cream pastry was *cannoli*, which Connie uses to entice Don Altobello to his death in *Part III*. Like Pentangeli, Valachi was held in custody by the FBI, and brought his food by two FBI agents. When he had to be

smuggled past the press to appear before an investigating subcommittee chaired by Senator John McClellan of Arkansas, Valachi and his guards left the stockade disguised as military police – again like Pentangeli in the film. The Senate hearings described by Coppola in *Part II* are also quite authentic, even to the 'family tree' board erected for all to see and charting the structure of power among the Corleones.

Ironically, Coppola and Puzo incorpo-rated into the dialogue of the Senate hearings the grandiose hyperbole that the Italian-American newspaper *Il Progresso* had used to protest against Valachi's evidence. They railed against 'an image which millions of law-abiding Americans of Italian descent have consistently proven false through their outstanding achievements in the arts, in the sciences, in industry, in labour, in the professions, in government and in the religious orders.' Valachi tried to commit suicide by hanging himself with a cord taken from his radio and attached to the shower head. The attempt failed. Frank Pentangeli also tries to take his own life – and succeeds.

The insight into Lucky Luciano's methods exerted some influence on Puzo and Coppola. Luciano had thought of the idea of having *consiglieri* (advisers or counsellors) and embarked on joint ventures with such non-Italian gangsters as Dutch Schultz and Meyer Lansky. During the 1940s, he sought to establish a power base from his residence in Cuba, something Michael seems eager to do in *Part II* – until the fall of Batista. Valachi's evidence also indicated that by the 1960s the Cosa Nostra was seeking to become a legitimate concern, by gaining control of accredited businesses such as banks, Wall Street securities houses or garment manufacturers.

The blasphemous image of Mosca, the assassin, disguised as a priest in *Part III* may not be so fanciful as it first appears. During the late nineteenth century, certain priests doubled as leaders of Mafia groups in Sicily, and a young gunman from the Gambino Family once adopted the guise of a Catholic priest while carrying out a murder.

Indeed, the evidence of subsequent years demonstrates the degree to which the Mafia embraced the concept of *The Godfather*. During the late 1970s a Mafia boss used the villa of a well-known aristocratic Sicilian family for his daughter's wedding reception. Five hundred guests relaxed to the strains of the music from – *The Godfather*.

In May 1991 three building contractors from near Palermo found the severed head of a horse in their company car. In another incident, the Sicilian *capo* Totò Di Cristina devoured Puzo's novel and decided to copy its style of assassination. His men donned doctors' uniforms and killed their victim in his bed.

There are further examples of the admiration for the 'ideals' behind *The Godfather*. In 1986 Father Louis Gigante, a popular Brooklyn priest and brother of the alleged Mafia boss, Vincent ('The Chin') Gigante, declared: 'I really loved *The Godfather* . . . I like Don Corleone's character. As he was about to be ruined by a blackmailer, he killed him to save his wife and family. By showing his power, he began to become somebody. I am not suggesting that this is the proper way to treat other people, but sometimes justice cannot be administered only by a tribunal. I have seen many people die in the electric chair, and I always wondered whether society had the right to make that decision.' One of John Gotti's fellow *mafiosi* would boast of 'my Luca Brasi', meaning the hit-man Joseph Paruta whose stealth and ferocity were much feared. And Peter Maas listened to an undercover FBI tape of a sombre gathering of *mafiosi*. 'The subject under prolonged discussion was the casting of *The Godfather*. Everyone's favourite (to play himself, naturally) appeared to be Paul Newman.'

In Japan, the *yakuza* expressed serious admiration for *The Godfather*, and in the years that followed began to finance films about themselves in order to reinforce and propagate their own slick underworld image.

The late Charlie Bluhdorn, whose explosive temper had illuminated so many arguments in the early days of *The Godfather* project, paid more than mere lip-service to the Italian-American criminal connection. In July 1971, on being decorated as a Grand Officer in the Order of Civil Merit of the Italian Government at a glittering ceremony in Rome, the Gulf + Western magnate declared in his inimitable style: 'When you bring the Società Immobiliare and cinema together, it's like seating Democrats and Republicans at the same table [. . .] Paramount is proud to make films in Italy and proud to make films for Italy by Italians.' Bluhdorn had sold the Paramount back-lot to Michele Sindona, the notorious swindler who had friends in high places in the Italian criminal community.

There was a host of more banal imitations – pizza parlours named after *The Godfather*, a rash of forgettable B movies, comedy record albums and even novelettes. Mario Puzo remains proud of the fact that '"The Godfather" was never, never used as a term for a gangster until I made it up. I thought of it in the same sense as we use "uncle" and "aunt" as a courtesy in the States. Now the Mafia uses it itself!'

Audiences, more than directors, have come under the influence of *The Godfather*. The film embodies a celebration of classical film-making, rather than blazing a new trail in the way that Welles's *Citizen Kane* or Godard's *Breathless* did in their time. Coppola, for per-haps the first time in the history of the cinema, lent violence a true patina of respectability. Since the appearance of *The Godfather*, audiences – and censors – have become steadily more inured to screen bloodshed. The work of Martin Scorsese, another Italian-American, comes first to mind, but Scorsese developed his own distinct style of film-making. The savagery of *The Godfather*, however, must have reassured him that he could present similar violence in such productions as *Taxi Driver*, *Raging Bull* and *Goodfellas*.

The watermark of Coppola's film may be detected in the work of directors as disparate as Jane Campion (*Portrait of a Lady*), Michael Mann (*Heat*), Michael Cimino (*The Deer Hunter*), Clint Eastwood (*Unforgiven*), Quentin Tarantino (*Pulp Fiction*) and most of all in a single, near-masterpiece by the late Sergio Leone, *Once Upon a Time in America*. In all these films, the very *look* of *The Godfather* is plain for all to see. So is the regal, menacing rhythm. So too is the sense of characters mingling one with another on a profound level. Like Coppola's, the gangsters of Mann's or Tarantino's world are redeemed not by God but by sheer flair.

Coppola has shared the pressures and emotions of his characters more than most American directors. His subjects tend to reflect the pattern of his own life: Tucker, the inventor who was ostracized by the Establishment as Coppola himself was cold-shouldered by Hollywood; and *Gardens of Stone*, which trembles with the anguish felt by the director when his son Gio died in an accident during the shooting of the film. *Apocalypse Now* was a prolonged quest for his own inner self, located in that 'heart of darkness' at the head of the river. But *The Godfather* and its sequels run closest to Coppola's life and concerns. 'To some extent I have become Michael,' he admitted to Italian journalists while filming the Ellis Island sequence in Trieste, 'in that I'm a powerful man in charge of an entire production [. . .] You see, there are personal things that emerge in this film more, perhaps, than I myself am aware of.' During the christening sequence at the close of *The Godfather*, the priest addresses Michael Corleone as though he were answering for Carlo's and Connie's baby: 'Do you, Michael *Francis* Rizzi, renounce Satan . . .' As Michael responds, 'I do renounce him . . .', his foes are being eliminated one after another. In *Part II*, Kay sits up in bed talking to Michael, and on the sheets is the stitched monogram, 'MFC' (Michael Francis Corleone).

In *Part II*, Michael listens to the attack on his Family by Senator Geary, pauses and then replies: 'Senator – we're both part of the same hypocrisy . . .' One can almost hear Coppola himself saying the words, referring to his relationship with the Hollywood studios, making big-budget films with which he has no sympathy, and yet maintaining the superficial enthusiasm so necessary to survival in the entertainment jungle.

In the heat of production, Coppola can behave like Michael – not, of course, killing people – but dealing with situations in a certain way. For example, Michael moves Tom Hagen out of the inner circle and tells him gently, 'You're not a wartime *consigliere*, Tom. Things are going to get rough around

here.' In the wake of all the controversy over the casting of Sofia as Mary in *Part III*, Coppola sent his long-time associate Gray Frederickson home to New York with virtually the same words: 'You're still producer of the picture, but things are going to get nasty around here.'

Coppola inspires fealty in the same way as the Don, without ostensible effort. His family inspires his finest moments, and if he and Michael share a need to possess others who are close to them, this implies that they too yearn to give of themselves. The line ascribed to both Vito and Michael – 'I worked my whole life, I don't apologize, to take care of my Family' – might well apply to Coppola himself. He loves nothing so much as a family reunion, and when on location he likes to discuss issues over a meal. Some of his best ideas materialize from such occasions. Forced to down tools for an Italian public holiday in late 1989, he and his colleagues ate lunch alfresco on the Via Veneto, and conceived the image of tables trembling as the helicopter attacked the Dons in Atlantic City.

Bob Evans, who a decade later would turn to Coppola in an attempt to save *The Cotton Club*, believes that 'Of all that generation of new talent, he *was* the Godfather, and in a way he was the most talented – but incomplete, incomplete in structuring a finished product. He went off on tangents.'

The most agonizing link between the films and private life comes at the very conclusion of the Corleone story. Michael loses his daughter, Mary, in an unexpected moment, and Coppola shares his anguish because he too lost a son, brutally and suddenly. The fact

'Coppola inspires fealty in the same way as the Don . . .'

that his real-life daughter Sofia plays the role of Mary only intensifies the feeling of distress.

In Bergman's *Smiles of a Summer Night*, Egerman refers to Desirée's beauty as 'having the imperfection which perfection itself lacks'.

So in *The Godfather* trilogy the imperfections possess a certain distinction of their own. The acting across all three films is so persuasive that an exaggerated characterization, such as Eli Wallach's Don Altobello, jars like a clarinet out of tune in an orchestra. Some roles, such as

Planning at the meal table. Francis Coppola with Fred Roos and Gordon Willis (at left) and Dean Tavoularis (at right).

those of Mary Corleone, Mama Corleone and Don Barzini, are not so much ill-played as underwritten. These parts amount to little except on a symbolic level. Still others remain silent throughout the story, Michael's bodyguard Al Neri the most conspicuously silent of all. Poor Richard Bright, who plays Neri, longed for his role to be expanded, and during the shooting of *Part III* sent Coppola letters every few days with suggestions as to how Neri might move centre stage in the drama. The 'Twins' in *Part III* are also virtually silent bodyguards. It's clear from early drafts of the screenplay that Coppola and Puzo would have liked to flesh them out, as they would have

liked to highlight the Rosato Brothers in *Part II*, but the constraints of time and budget put paid to that.

The revised and extended versions of the trilogy created for television and video justify a debate over the internal construction of the films, and especially *Part II*. The original novel contained flashbacks to the Don's youth in Sicily and Hell's Kitchen in 1917, but these were more than either the studio or Puzo and Coppola themselves could contemplate, given the budget ceiling of $2 to $3 million that the studio had imposed. Even so, under pressure to bring the film in at a reasonable length, some transitions were lost in the shuffle. For example, Tom Hagen is shown leaving the Woltz mansion after dinner, and the next scene shows the estate at dawn and the movie mogul awaking to find his horse's head in his bedclothes. How did Hagen achieve this? Did he lurk somewhere in the grounds? Did he involve Corleone associates based in Los Angeles? Only when the 'Complete Novel' appeared on television five years later did audiences realize that Hagen returns to New York, reports to the Don and that the Don instructs the dreaded Luca Brasi to take care of the matter.

When Coppola, flushed with the success of *The Godfather*, embarked on *Part II*, he decided to deepen and enrich the story of the Corleone Family, and constructed an intricate web of flashbacks. But he also introduced several new characters (Frank Pentangeli, Senator Geary, Johnny Ola, Hyman Roth) and this can combine with the structure of the film to create confusion in the viewer's mind. The scenes involving Pentangeli work well only if we have fathomed his role as successor to Clemenza within the Family, although Michael seems to have abandoned the *caporegime* concept altogether.

Some of the flashbacks seem gratuitous. Michael returns home one day to his estate after learning that Kay has suffered a miscarriage. He enters the main house silently, observes Kay at her sewing machine, and turns away, unable to (or not wanting to) speak to her. As he puts his hand to his head in gloom, there is a cut to the Senate hearings room, where one of the Corleone 'soldiers', Willi Cicci, is under interrogation. The court scene lasts only ninety seconds, but then

Coppola returns unexpectedly to Michael, crossing the snow to his mother's bungalow. As the film rejoins the Senate hearings right after the next scene (the chat between Michael and Mama Corleone), we may reasonably ask why Coppola found it necessary to fragment the order of things and interrupt the flow of emotion expressed by Michael at this point.

Having held the first two films in awe for a generation, several critics – and indeed audiences – took a masochistic delight in blasting *The Godfather Part III*. The presence of Sofia Coppola in the cast served only as a trigger for their scorn. At a deeper level, the dissatisfaction with the concluding story of Michael's career seems to stem from a dislike of the context – investment banking, Vatican politics, etc. With the Corleone mobsters now uncomfortably close to our own era, perhaps we expect them to behave in a less mannered fashion. Joey Zasa and his henchman appear like comic-book villains; George Hamilton's financial adviser moves like a well-groomed dummy through most scenes and, most damaging of all, Al Pacino plays Michael with a wry, tongue-in-cheek acknowledgement of his own fallibility, even irrelevance. The audience yearns for the Don to be a threatening figure, or wishes that, as Coppola wrote in his original notes on the first film, 'with the Godfather there is always the possibility of immediate and sudden violence'.

In real life, Michael would probably have become more like John Gotti, who continued to run his Gambino Family from the confines of a cell until ousted by the leaders of the other Families in favour of 'Little Nick' Corozzo in November 1996. In short, the spiritual side of Michael Corleone gains too much ground, becomes too implausible, for a mass audience to accept. Besides, the final scene of Michael's death in Sicily is so abrupt in its beauty that it leaves people curious about his fate – does he die of natural causes? What happens to the Family?

The irony is that Coppola, having weathered so much censure because of the violence in the first two films, tries in *Part III* to show Michael's contrition. But in the public perception, the words *mafiosi* and contrition are, alas, contradictory.

Fame and riches awaited many who had participated in *The Godfather*. Al Ruddy, Francis Coppola and Mario Puzo certainly, but also such stars as Al Pacino and James Caan, who twenty-five years later were still to have their names above the title of studio productions. Diane Keaton made her reputation as a comedienne through Woody Allen's cinema, although her star status on *The Godfather* helped lend her credibility in the eyes of Hollywood. Because of her exposure in the first film, Talia Shire was selected to play Stallone's girlfriend in *Rocky* and its sequels. John Cazale, so effective as Fredo, starred in *Dog Day Afternoon* (again with Pacino) and *The Deer Hunter*, and then died in 1978 from cancer, far too young. Robert Duvall quietly accumulated prestige as a thinking man's star, with a rousing appearance as the surf-obsessed Colonel Kilgore in *Apocalypse Now*, and claimed his own Academy Award in 1983 for *Tender Mercies*. By the time Coppola came to assemble the usual suspects for *Part III*, Duvall alone felt himself above the fray,

asking a huge fee commensurate with his place in the Hollywood firmament.

Marlon Brando, of course, never quite left the headlines, even if he could not again find a role so perfectly attuned to his talents – or, rather, if he himself would never again take a part so seriously. He knows that he will forever be associated with Don Corleone: 'Even today I can't pay a check in Little Italy,' writes Brando in his autobiography. 'If I go to a restaurant for a plate of spaghetti, the manager always says, "Come on in, Marlo, your money's no good here . . . Look, everybody, here's the Godfather, the Godfather's here."' A lover of high jinks and camp, Brando leapt at the opportunity of lampooning himself and the gangster genre in Andrew Bergman's *The Freshman* (1990).

Al Ruddy, who produced *The Godfather* with a commitment that by the later stages of shooting resembled gallantry, made a serious fortune from his points in the picture, and also from his next film, *The Longest Yard*. Since then he has followed the career of a typical Hollywood producer, with several projects on the hob at any one time. 'Why do I go on working?' he mused in 1996. 'Well, your next movie is like your next love affair . . .'

Some of the technicians have passed away. Others, like Peter Zinner, Bill Reynolds and Dick Smith, live in semi-retirement (although Reynolds cut the Bette Midler TV movie, *Gypsy*, as late as the mid-1990s). Fred Roos has produced numerous films for Coppola and cast even more for others. A passionate sports enthusiast, he co-produced Carroll Ballard's *Wind* and almost won the rights to make the Atlanta Olympic Games documentary. Gray Frederickson, a partner in Ruddy's operations in 1972, has come back to the Ruddy-Morgan company today after a career devoted principally to seeking locations for Coppola's movies.

Robert Evans was able to revel in the praise showered on his 1974 production, *Chinatown*, which more than compensated for being frozen out by Coppola on *The Godfather Part II*. Then, in the mid-1980s, Evans became embroiled in his independent production, *The Cotton Club*, and lost most of his fortune (and his career momentum) after hiring Coppola one more time to return to his side and assume direction of the musical about the famous Harlem club of the 1920s. Today he is back at Paramount with his own slate of pictures, a respected if eccentric figure with films like *The Phantom* and *The Saint* to his credit. 'Seduction has nothing to do with sex, because of the seven people [profiled in his new book] I have been fucked by one, but royally, and that's Francis Coppola,' writes Evans. 'He is Elmer Gantry. His looks work for him, his manners work for him. He stays in the kitchen and makes pasta, and he's *brilliant*.' Peter Bart, whose intuition led to the choice of Coppola as director for *The Godfather*, produced films at MGM-UA and Lorimar as well as under his own banner (*Islands in the Stream*, for example). In 1989 he became editor of *Variety*, and has spent the years since turning that venerable publication into a mandatory morning read for the industry in Hollywood and around the world.

As for Francis Ford Coppola, he has forged a career unique in American cinema. From moments of sublime invention

(*Rumble Fish*, *Bram Stoker's Dracula*) to childish fantasy (*Jack*); from epic brilliance (*Apocalypse Now*) to intimate intuition (*The Conversation*); from personal indulgence (*One from the Heart, Tucker*) to a misbegotten musical (*The Cotton Club*), he has never shrunk from a challenge, never embraced the orthodox. 'Dear Mommy,' he had once written home as a boy, 'I want to be rich and famous. I'm so discouraged. I don't think it will come true.' Years later, as he, George Lucas and Steven Spielberg found themselves on the same plane, just after *Star Wars* had opened, he could exclaim with them, 'We're the billion-dollar boys!' And as James Monaco has reflected in his book *American Film Now*, 'If Francis Coppola never made another film save *The Godfather*, his place in the history of American film would be assured.' In 1997, Coppola told the *New Yorker* that in some ways the film 'did ruin me. It just made my whole career go this way instead of the way I really wanted it to go, which was into doing original work as writer-director.'

After the comparative failure of *The Godfather Part III* at the box office, the quest for a *Part IV* has not become a corporate obsession. But what still tantalizes both Puzo and Coppola is the missing link between Don Vito as a young, successful *mafioso* and the post-war opening of *The Godfather*. A significant period in the destiny of the Corleone Family remains to be tackled on screen. It concerns the Don's acquisition of power in the 1930s, when 'Corleone was one of the biggest Mafia men in the country with more political connections than [Al] Capone ever had.' Perhaps De Niro could still be the right age for such a role or, failing that, perhaps Andy Garcia could star as the successor to Don Michael in the final part of a tetralogy.

Sitting on the verandah of his home in Napa, gazing out across the vines in the valley, Coppola agrees that there should be a *Part IV.* 'But I don't think that Viacom [the parent company of Paramount Pictures] is interested in that kind of thing. I suggested to Jonathan Dolgen that Paramount should commission Puzo to do a draft screenplay. But I would not direct it.' Twenty-five years after embarking on an adventure that changed his life and forged both critical and box-office history, Coppola recalls the story of the king with three sons, which lit his path through the chaos of shooting the first film in the trilogy. He himself has now become a king among independents, but his three sons may always remain the *Godfather* movies.

Notes

Note: AZRL refers to documents inspected at American Zoetrope Research Library, Napa.

PROLOGUE
p. xii 'owing $20,000 to friends . . .' *The God-father Papers and Other Confessions* by Mario Puzo, G. P. Putnam's Sons, New York, 1972.

ACQUISITION
p. 4 'He was vulgar to his core . . .', author's interview with Peter Bart, 18 June 1996.
p. 4 'Robert Evans is an outrage . . .', *Life* magazine, 7 March 1969.
p. 4 'There's never been a better partnership . . .', author's interview with Robert Evans, 18 June 1996.

Coppola talking through the wedding sequence with Robert Duvall and Marlon Brando on *The Godfather.*

p. 4 'Charlie Bluhdorn believed in Bob Evans . . .', interview on BBC-TV quoting Peter Bart.

p. 5 'Natives of the south . . .', *The Fortunate Pilgrim* by Mario Puzo, Heinemann, London, 1965.

p. 5 'Then I met a guy . . .', author's phone interview with Mario Puzo, 1 July 1996.

p. 5 'I was downtown in New York . . .', the *Observer*, London, 1 December 1996.

p. 6 'Maybe Wieser had just heard about it,' author's interview with Peter Bart, 3 October 1996.

p. 6 'Nowadays, there are fifteen or twenty Vice Presidents . . .', author's interview with Gray Frederickson, 12 July 1996.

p. 6 'one day away from Burt Lancaster . . .', author's interview with Robert Evans, *op. cit.*

p. 6 'I had just changed agents . . .', author's interview with Mario Puzo, 1 July 1996.

p. 6 'Charlie Bluhdorn came charging into my office . . .', author's interview with Peter Bart, 18 June 1996.

p. 6 'It wasn't great writing . . .', *ibid.*

p. 7 'Thinkin' of writin' an inside story . . .', *The Kid Stays in the Picture* by Robert Evans, Hyperion, New York, 1994.

p. 7 'I never saw or heard of Evans or Bart . . .', letter from Mario Puzo to the author.

p. 8 'a good, bright young producer . . .', author's interview with Peter Bart, 18 June 1996.

p. 8 'Make an ice-blue, terrifying movie . . .', author's phone interview with Al Ruddy, 1990.

p. 8 'I explained that it would be difficult . . .', author's phone interview with Al Ruddy, 12 July 1996.

p. 8 'produced from her handbag . . .', *The Godfather Papers and Other Confessions*, *op. cit.*

p. 8 '[Bob] Evans was unpretentious . . .', *ibid.*

p. 9 'some unfortunate mutual acquaintance . . .', *Ladies Home Journal*, New York, June 1972.

p. 9 'Francis, I'd play the Godfather for you . . .', *The Godfather Papers and Other Confessions*, *op. cit.*

p. 9 'The studio was on shaky ground . . .', author's phone interview with Al Ruddy, 12 July, 1996.

p. 9 'It costs more to film in New York . . .', *Daily Variety*, 2 September 1970.

p. 9 'a $3,000,000 film . . .', *ibid.*

p. 9 'Ruddy really wanted him . . .', 'Dynasty Italian Style' by Stephen Farber and Marc Green in *California* magazine, San Francisco, April 1984.

p. 9 'Sam Peckinpah wanted to do it . . .', author's interview with Peter Bart, 18 June 1996.

p. 10 'I had met Francis . . .', *ibid.*

p. 10 'I did not immediately see myself . . .', author's interview with Francis Coppola, 14 June 1996.

p. 10 'I was at Paramount all day yesterday . . .', 'Dynasty Italian Style', *op. cit.*

p. 10 'You should meet this guy . . .', author's phone interview with Al Ruddy, 12 July 1996.

p. 10 'Then I had to bring him back . . .', *ibid.*

p. 10 'There hadn't been one successful Mafia picture . . .', author's interview with Robert Evans, *op. cit.*

p. 10 '[Coppola] knew the way these men . . .', 'Dynasty Italian Style', *op. cit.*

p. 11 'Paramount cheated me out of a point . . .',

author's interview with Francis Coppola, 14 June 1996.

p. 11 'We took the *Michelangelo* or one of those Italian boats . . .', author's interview with Eleanor Coppola, 15 June 1996.

p. 11 'Wait until the studio . . .', author's phone interview with Mario Puzo, 1 July 1996.

p. 11 'You couldn't even get $50,000 . . .', *Larry King Live*, CNN, 5 October 1996.

p. 11 'It's odd, but one day in early 1970 . . .', author's interview with Francis Coppola, 14 June 1996.

p. 11 'If Brando plays the Don . . .', *The Kid Stays in the Picture, op. cit.*

p. 12 'I looked too young to play Don Corleone . . .', *Songs My Mother Taught Me* by Marlon Brando with Robert Lindsay, Random House, New York, 1994.

p. 12 'He voted against Brando . . .', author's interview with Ian Scorer, 22 August 1996.

p. 12 'So long as I am President . . .', author's interview with Fred Roos, 19 June 1996.

p. 12 'On the plane Francis said to me . . .', author's interview with Dean Tavoularis, 3 October 1996.

p. 12 'I took a talented Japanese . . .', author's interview with Francis Coppola, 14 June 1996.

p. 13 'Coppola had described his old Italian uncle's thin moustache . . .', *Brando, The Biography* by Peter Manso, Hyperion, New York, 1994.

p. 13 'We just watched for fifteen to twenty minutes . . .', author's phone interview with Hiro Narita, 22 October 1996.

p. 13 'That's incredible! Who's dat man? Who's dat man?' author's interview with Dean Tavoularis, *op. cit.*

p. 13 'fired his lawyer, his agent . . .', *The Kid Stays in the Picture, op. cit.*

p. 14 'So I went on a diet . . .', *Songs My Mother Taught Me, op. cit.*

CASTING AND WRITING

p. 15 'What depressed me . . .', *Variety*, 15 March 1972.

p. 15 'as that of a king, almost Greek . . .', author's interview with Francis Coppola, 14 June 1996.

p. 16 'People love to read about an organization . . .', 'Dynasty Italian Style', *op. cit.*

p. 17 'the characters in fiction . . .', author's phone interview with Mario Puzo, 1 July 1996.

p. 17 'It has been pointed out . . .', *The Sicilian Mafia* by Diego Gambetta, Harvard University Press, 1993.

p. 18 'market brokers, barbers, shepherds . . .', *ibid.*

p. 18 'Puzo asserts that he selected . . .', Mario Puzo's letter to author dated 10 July 1996.

p. 18 'Our life is hell . . .', *La Repubblica*, Rome, 23 June 1996.

p. 18 'This was the period when an Italian producer . . .', author's phone interview with Gray Frederickson, 12 July 1996.

p. 18 'Gray called me in New York . . .', author's interview with Dean Tavoularis, *op. cit.*

p. 19 'During the late 1960s Francis used to call me up . . .', author's interview with Fred Roos, *op. cit.*

p. 19 'I introduced him to Francis . . .', author's phone interview with Al Ruddy, 12 July 1996.

p. 20 'Kept banging her in the face . . .', *The Godfather Companion* by Peter Biskind,

HarperCollins, New York, 1990.

p. 20 'Ryan was so stunning . . .', *The Godfather Papers and Other Confessions, op. cit.*

p. 20 'which was lucky . . .', author's interview with Fred Roos, *op. cit.*

p. 21 'Richard Dreyfuss was a friend of mine . . .', *ibid.*

p. 22 'Tally's too pretty for the part . . .', 'Dynasty Italian Style', *op. cit.*

p. 23 'When I read the novel I saw his face . . .', author's interview with Francis Coppola, 14 June 1996.

p. 23 'The studio didn't want him . . .', author's interview with Fred Roos, *op. cit.*

p. 24 'It was his tenacity that got me in there . . .', *The Godfather Family: A Look Inside* (documentary released with laser disc boxed set of *The Godfather Trilogy*, 1991).

p. 24 'You guys really wanta know?' *The Godfather Papers and Other Confessions, op. cit.*

p. 24 'I was with Bluhdorn one night . . .', author's phone interview with Al Ruddy, 12 July 1996.

p. 24 'I'm not even Italian . . .', *Ladies Home Journal, op. cit.*

p. 24 'Hey, ma, pass the fucking salt . . .', transcript of interview for *The Godfather Family: A Look Inside*, lodged in AZRL, Napa.

p. 26 'He rewrote one half . . .', *The Godfather Papers and Other Confessions, op. cit.*

p. 26 'It was done long after the rest of the picture had wrapped . . .', author's interview with Francis Coppola, 14 June 1996.

p. 26 'I think that everyone has worked so hard . . .', memo to Coppola from Peter Bart, 19 January 1971.

p. 27 'Feel that the character of Sonny . . .', memo to Coppola from Robert Evans, 5 March 1971.

COPPOLA'S BIBLE

p. 28 'He showed me a huge spiral notebook . . .', author's interview with Gray Frederickson, *op. cit.*

p. 30 'But since then, my son and my nephew . . .', Mario Puzo's letter to author, 10 July 1996.

p. 31 'I hope to have very stunning and original effects . . .', memo dated 22 January 1971, in AZRL, Napa.

COMING TO TERMS WITH THE MAFIA

p. 36 'Brando wrote a reply by hand . . .', letter in AZRL, Napa.

p. 36 'We had given Marlon tapes . . .', author's interview with Fred Roos, *op. cit.*

p. 37 'for yet another of those horrendous meetings . . .', author's interview with Peter Bart, 18 June 1996.

p. 37 'He demanded at least five . . .', *The Godfather Companion, op. cit.*

p. 37 'I was seven months' pregnant . . .', author's interview with Eleanor Coppola, *op. cit.*

p. 37 'Exasperated, and furious . . .', *The Kid Stays in the Picture, op. cit.*

p. 38 'because in a way they're fans too . . .', author's interview with Fred Roos, *op. cit.*

p. 39 'Bob Evans's son was born that spring . . .', author's interview with Robert Evans, *op. cit.*

p. 39 'At the request of the Grand Council . . .', in AZRL, Napa.

p. 39 'The gathering raised some $600,000 . . .',

Ladies Home Journal, op. cit.

p. 39 'I didn't know whether the calls were coming from the Mafia or not . . .', *ibid.*

p. 40 'I couldn't care less if [the studio] gave us . . .', the *New York Times/San Francisco Examiner*, 22 August 1971.

p. 40 'I explained to Joe Colombo . . .', *Ladies Home Journal, op. cit.*

p. 40 'Yet even after I made the deal . . .', *Ladies Home Journal, op. cit.*

p. 41 'I'm not in the business of protecting the price of your stock . . .', author's phone interview with Al Ruddy, 12 July 1996.

p. 41 'But one more line in the press . . .', *ibid.*

p. 41 'Apparently you are a ready market . . .', *Daily Variety*, 24 March 1971.

p. 42 'This was due, the League felt, because . . .', *Variety*, 28 June 1972.

p. 42 'There would have been pickets . . .', *Ladies Home Journal, op. cit.*

p. 44 'It was a very seedy area . . .', author's interview with Dean Tavoularis, *op. cit.*

p. 44 'Here was this place . . .', *ibid.*

p. 44 'The main idea . . .', *The Godfather Family: A Look Inside, op. cit.*

p. 44 'Brando sat at the head of the table . . .', author's interview with Francis Coppola, 14 June 1996.

p. 44 'I remember the first time Brando . . .', author's phone interview with Al Ruddy, 12 July 1996.

FILMING IN NEW YORK

p. 45 'The front-of-house neon . . .', *The Godfather Companion, op. cit.*

p. 45 'Ballard, then an executive production manager . . .', *Daily Variety*, 11 August 1971.

p. 45 'a Yul Brynner-headed guy . . .', *The*

Godfather Papers and Other Confessions, op. cit.

p. 45 'From day one . . .', author's interview with Francis Coppola, 14 June 1996.

p. 46 'Avakian and Steve Keston tried . . .', author's interview with Robert Evans, *op. cit.*

p. 46 'Francis at that time was impoverished . . .', author's interview with Peter Bart, 18 June 1996.

p. 46 'could get great performances from his actors . . .', *The Kid Stays in the Picture, op. cit.*

p. 46 '[Avakian] wanted to present himself . . .', author's interview with Dean Tavoularis, *op. cit.*

p. 46 'I wasn't the most beloved person on this movie . . .', author's phone interview with Gordon Willis, 7 August 1996.

p. 46 'in deep trouble, because the studio . . .', author's interview with Francis Coppola, 14 June 1996.

p. 46 'Right from the beginning the studio was unhappy . . .', author's interview with Eleanor Coppola, *op. cit.*

p. 46 'Francis told me how . . .', author's interview with Tom Luddy, 6 October 1996.

p. 46 'I never felt that Jack Ballard . . .', author's interview with Peter Bart, 3 October 1996.

p. 48 'On the first day we spent hours . . .', author's phone interview with Dick Smith, 24 October 1996.

p. 48 'What the fuck's going on? . . .', author's phone interview with Al Ruddy, 12 July 1996.

p. 48 'It is the general opinion of the crew . . .', *The Godfather Journal* by Ira Zuckerman, Manor Books, New York, 1972.

p. 48 'For Coppola, the only person . . .',

author's interview with Francis Coppola, 14 June 1996.

p. 48 'Bob Evans confirms . . .', *The Kid Stays in the Picture, op. cit.*

p. 48 'was not just good, but brilliant . . .', *ibid.*

p. 48 'I kept dreaming that Kazan would arrive on the set . . .', author's interview with Francis Coppola, 17 November 1987.

p. 48 'At one point Charles Bluhdorn threatened . . .', *Songs My Mother Taught Me, op. cit.*

p. 48 'Bob, ever-tanned, looked a little pale . . .', author's interview with Peter Bart, 3 October 1996.

p. 48 'At the end of the day . . .', author's interview with Fred Roos, *op. cit.*

p. 49 'I'll tell you my ideas . . .', author's interview with Dean Tavoularis, *op. cit.*

p. 49 'Mario Puzo remained blithely unaware . . .', *Variety*, 24 March 1971.

p. 49 'So we ordered [a real] one that would be slaughtered . . .', author's interview with Dick Smith, *op. cit.*

p. 49 'For the knife that pins Brasi's hand to the bar . . .', *ibid.*

p. 50 'We riddled [it] with bullet holes . . .', *Ladies Home Journal, op. cit.*

p. 50 'More than a hundred brass casings . . .', *The Godfather Companion, op. cit.*

p. 50 'When those guys started firing the tommy-guns . . .', *Ladies Home Journal, op. cit.*

p. 50 'I put one on his forehead . . .', author's interview with Dick Smith, *op. cit.*

p. 50 'At the 118th Street and Pleasant Avenue location . . .', *The Godfather Companion, op. cit.*

p. 50 'Such crowds needed superintendence . . .', *Variety*, 8 March 1972.

p. 51 'the two characters who are throwing . . .', *The Godfather Family: A Look Inside, op. cit.*

p. 52 'My family started carrying me up the stairs . . .', *Songs My Mother Taught Me, op. cit.*

p. 52 'When he fell to the street . . .', *Ladies Home Journal, op. cit.*

p. 52 'I saw the dailies of the scene . . .', author's interview with Gray Frederickson, *op. cit.*

p. 53 'He struck the director as such an arresting actor . . .', author's interview with Francis Coppola, 14 June 1996.

p. 53 'You could programme it to run . . .', author's interview with Gordon Willis, *op. cit.*

p. 53 'It should look like a newspaper photograph . . .', *Daily Variety*, 17 February 1995.

p. 53 'wanted a retrospective, 1940s kind of feel to it . . .', author's interview with Gordon Willis, *op. cit.*

p. 53 'I'd already met Bob on my first film . . .', author's interview with Francis Coppola, 14 June 1996.

p. 53 'The resulting scene shows . . .', *Projections 6*, Faber and Faber, London, 1996.

p. 55 'We were sitting at the table . . .', author's interview with Eleanor Coppola, *op. cit.*

p. 55 'But a squall had struck Staten Island . . .', author's interview with Al Ruddy, 12 July 1996.

p. 55 'He makes the best spaghetti in the world . . .', *The Godfather Companion, op. cit.*

SICILY AND THE TRAUMA OF POST-PRODUCTION

p. 57 'So I got to know Catania . . .', author's interview with Gray Frederickson, *op. cit.*

p. 57 'because someone who shot a judge . . .', author's interview with Dean Tavoularis, *op. cit.*

p. 58 'Taormina is not like Palermo . . .', author's interview with Francis Coppola, 17 November 1987.

p. 58 'I cast her because . . .', note to author from Francis Coppola, June 1997.

p. 58 'One director who had made numerous films in Sicily . . .', *The Sicilian Mafia, op. cit.*

p. 59 'I maintained that all the scenes in Sicily . . .', author's interview with Gordon Willis, *op. cit.*

p. 59 'Softer, more romantic . . .', *ibid.*

p. 60 'didn't go to Sicily until . . .', author's phone interview with Mario Puzo, 1 July 1996.

p. 60 *The Godfather* will not be available . . .', *Variety,* 21 July 1971.

p. 60 'the rushes have such a fantastic look . . .', *Variety,* 7 July 1971.

p. 60 'Our below-the-line [labour] costs . . .', *Variety,* 8 September 1971.

p. 60 'The decision [after the original editor had departed] . . .', author's phone interview with Walter Murch, 30 October 1996.

p. 60 'There was so much film to deal with . . .', author's phone interview with Peter Zinner, 8 October 1996.

p. 61 'Francis had been adlibbing the wedding sequence . . .', author's phone interview with Bill Reynolds, 10 December 1996.

p. 61 'Since the second week of shooting . . .', author's interview with Gray Frederickson, *op. cit.*

p. 61 'It was desperation time . . .', author's interview with Peter Zinner, *op. cit.*

p. 61 'he already had eight original screen-plays . . .', *Variety,* 29 September 1971.

p. 61 'We were told by Bob Evans . . .', author's interview with Francis Coppola, 14 June 1996.

p. 62 'Cut! Cut!' *The Hollywood Reporter,* 17 April 1972.

p. 62 'Francis was cutting the film . . .', author's interview with Al Ruddy, 12 July 1996.

p. 62 'the first screening took place . . .', *The Kid Stays in the Picture, op. cit.*

p. 62 'In New York, Yablans intended to screen . . .', *Variety,* 17 November 1971.

p. 62 'Francis and I had a perfect record . . .', *The Kid Stays in the Picture, op. cit.*

p. 62 'had as much authority to cut the picture . . .', author's interview with Robert Evans, *op. cit.*

p. 62 *The Godfather* existed in a two hours fifty minutes version . . .', author's interview with Walter Murch, 30 October 1996.

p. 62 'We made eliminations all the way through . . .', author's interview with Bill Reynolds, *op. cit.*

p. 62 'This movie is longer at two hours fifteen . . .', author's interview with Al Ruddy, 12 July 1996.

p. 62 'I remember lots of wonderful things . . .', author's interview with Bill Reynolds, *op. cit.*

p. 62 'I told him, we can't release this film . . .', author's interview with Robert Evans, *op. cit.*

p. 63 'Bob did have a tactile instinct . . .', author's interview with Peter Bart, 18 June 1996.

p. 63 '[Bob] is never arbitrary about cuts . . .', *Variety,* 8 March 1972.

p. 63 'We rigged up two hospital beds . . .',

author's interview with Peter Zinner, *op. cit.*

p. 63 'The non-narrative, family ambience . . .', Francis Coppola's e-mail to author, 21 November 1996.

p. 63 'Bob, don't cut a frame.' *The Hollywood Reporter*, 16 April 1972.

p. 63 'Quite honestly . . .', author's interview with Al Ruddy, 12 July 1996.

p. 63 'When Francis first mentioned Nino Rota . . .', author's interview with Peter Zinner, *op. cit.*

p. 64 'We wanted more source music in it . . .', author's interview with Robert Evans, *op. cit.*

p. 64 'Bob Evans and I had a big fight . . .', author's interview with Francis Coppola, 14 June 1996.

p. 65 'And I thought, "Shall I bring up the [Rota] refrain?"' author's interview with Al Ruddy, 12 July 1996.

p. 65 'I was opposed to the ending . . .', *The Godfather Papers and Other Confessions, op. cit.*

p. 65 'So much for being head of a studio . . .', *ibid.*

p. 65 'I love the line . . .', note to author from Francis Coppola, June 1997.

p. 65 'Brando said [the line] was too preachy . . .', *The Godfather Journal, op. cit.*

p. 65 'Why do you get tears in your eyes . . .', author's interview with Robert Evans, *op. cit.*

p. 65 'The screen went dark . . .', author's interview with Al Ruddy, 12 July 1996.

OPENING CAMPAIGN

p. 66 'Frank Yablans claimed that Paramount . . .', *Variety*, 2 February 1972.

p. 66 'On television, and in full-page ads . . .', *The Godfather Companion, op. cit.*

p. 66 'It played a little slow . . .', author's interview with Robert Evans, *op. cit.*

p. 66 'One guy came out and I asked him . . .', author's interview with Francis Coppola, 14 June 1996.

p. 67 'Peter Bart remembers a screening . . .', author's interview with Peter Bart, 3 October 1996.

p. 67 'The Boys' Club bash included supper . . .', *Variety*, 22 March 1972.

p. 68 'He had even persuaded Henry Kissinger . . .', *The Kid Stays in the Picture, op. cit.*

p. 68 'Francis Coppola, the director whom I'd hired . . .', *ibid.*

p. 68 'I felt the picture made a useful commentary . . .', *Life* magazine, 10 March 1972.

p. 68 'Francis Ford Coppola [. . .] has stayed very closer . . .', *New Yorker*, 18 March 1972.

p. 69 'haunting conclusion exemplifies . . .', *Sight and Sound*, London, Autumn 1972.

p. 69 'The success of *The Godfather* is deplorable . . .', *The Nation*, 3 April 1972.

p. 69 'As the picture winds on and on . . .', the *New Republic*, 1 April 1972.

p. 69 'When I saw *The Godfather* the first time . . .', *Songs My Mother Taught Me, op. cit.*

p. 69 'Some youngsters queued up for hours on end . . .', *Variety*, 5 April 1972.

p. 70 'He could see the lines around the block . . .', author's interview with Peter Bart, 3 October 1996.

p. 70 'Francis thought *The Godfather* . . .', author's interview with Eleanor Coppola, *op. cit.*

p. 70 'In his heart, Coppola may have felt . . .', *City Magazine*, San Francisco, Vol. 7, No. 54, 11–24 December 1974.

p. 70 'The estimated gross of $454,000 . . .', *Variety*, 22 March 1972.

p. 70 'At 3 a.m. on the opening Saturday . . .', *ibid.*

p. 70 'The Governor of New York . . .', *The Godfather Companion*, *op. cit.*

p. 70 'Do not live in the way . . .', *Variety*, 22 March 1972.

p. 70 'Don't Judge us All by the Godfathers . . .', *Variety*, 29 March 1972.

p. 71 'That Paramount's *The Godfather* is an historic smash . . .' *Variety*, 5 April 1972.

p. 71 'On 17 May Frank Yablans sent cheques . . .', *Variety*, 10 May 1972.

p. 71 'I just wanted to let you know . . .', letter from Peter Bart to Francis Coppola, dated 21 April 1972.

p. 71 'It's the best film I've seen in the last ten years . . .', letter in AZRL, Napa.

p. 71 'Glancing back from the vantage point . . .', author's phone interview with Mario Puzo, 1 July 1996.

p. 71 'I'd like to have [Coppola direct the sequel] . . .', *Hollywood Reporter*, 16 April 1972.

p. 72 'Bob Evans was the embodiment of success . . .', author's interview with Ian Scorer, *op. cit.*

p. 72 'The dialogue was adapted by Eric Kahane . . .', *Variety*, 11 October 1972.

p. 72 'This was before the autoroutes . . .', author's interview with Ian Scorer, *op. cit.*

p. 73 'This was in response to an outcry . . .', *Variety*, 1 November 1972.

p. 73 'But in each successive city . . .', letter to Francis Coppola from Luigi Luraschi, 25 September 1972.

p. 73 'Roberto Ciuni, the young and hand-some editor . . .', *Los Angeles Times*, 13 October 1972.

p. 73 'The Italian-dubbed version . . .', *Variety*, 11 October 1972.

p. 73 'Behind the popularity of the movie . . .', *Variety*, 20 September 1972.

p. 73 'The only disappointment . . .', *Variety*, 22 November 1972.

p. 74 'Everyone owning a piece of *The Godfather* . . .', *Variety*, 6 September 1972.

p. 74 'It now lies a sorry thirty-fourth . . .', *Variety*, 28 October 1996.

p. 74 '*The Godfather* launched Francis into a world-class director . . .', author's interview with Eleanor Coppola, *op. cit.*

THE MOTHER OF ALL SEQUELS

p. 75 'I said to Francis . . .', author's interview with Peter Bart, 18 June 1996.

p. 75 'He persuaded me to do the sequel . . .', author's interview with Francis Coppola, 14 June 1996.

p. 76 'We have engaged Harry Korshak . . .', memo dated 9 June 1972, in AZRL, Napa.

p. 77 'none of the photography or soundtrack . . .', memo dated 12 June 1996, in AZRL, Napa.

p. 77 'Focusing his thoughts, he sat at the portable typewriter . . .', document lodged in AZRL, Napa.

p. 79 'I had other beautiful scenes in mind . . .', *Francis Ford Coppola* by Jean-Paul Chaillet and Elizabeth Vincent, St. Martin's Press, New York, 1984.

p. 79 'Francis gave me a cassette of music . . .', author's interview with Walter Murch, 12 December 1985.

p. 80 'The Valachi revelations . . .', refers to

The Valachi Papers by Peter Maas, G. P. Putnam's Sons, New York, 1968.

p. 80 'a heavy-set, fierce-looking Italian . . .', *The Godfather* by Mario Puzo, G. P. Putnam's Sons, New York, 1969.

p. 81 'Michael should destroy Lansky's power . . .', letter to Francis Coppola from Mario Puzo, 23 July 1973, in AZRL, Napa.

p. 81 'I think now that Fredo . . .', letter to Mario Puzo from Francis Coppola, 1 August 1973, in AZRL, Napa.

p. 82 'Al Ruddy was out of the picture . . .', *Variety*, 8 March 1972.

p. 82 'Always remember three things . . .', *The Godfather Journal*, op. cit.

p. 83 'When we made *Part II* . . .', author's interview with Gordon Willis, op. cit.

p. 83 'The one major dispute . . .', author's interview with Francis Coppola, 14 June 1996.

p. 84 'Francis had seen his performance . . .', *Scorsese on Scorsese*, edited by Ian Christie, Faber & Faber, London, 1996.

p. 84 'I remember we were not sure about it . . .', *ibid*.

p. 85 'Dignified amid the heckling and confusion . . .', *Variety*, 4 April 1973.

p. 86 'one of those Horatio Alger speeches . . .', *ibid*.

SHOOTING PART *II*

p. 87 'But Francis said that art-direction-wise . . .', author's interview with Dean Tavoularis, *op. cit*.

p. 88 'I went out there one Saturday . . .', author's phone interview with Carroll Ballard, 11 December 1996.

p. 89 'He and Pacino flew to San Francisco . . .', author's interview with Eleanor Coppola, *op. cit*.

p. 89 'As the opening shots were filmed . . .', *The Godfather Companion*, op. cit.

p. 89 'They would be shooting right outside the door . . .', author's interview with Eleanor Coppola, *op. cit*.

p. 90 'A touching private note was injected . . .', author's interview with Francis Coppola, 17 November 1987.

p. 90 'working from midnight to noon each day . . .', *The Godfather Companion*, op. cit.

p. 90 'Marlon was mad at Paramount . . .', author's interview with Fred Roos, *op. cit*.

p. 90 'I'd been calling Brando from phone booths . . .' author's interview with Francis Coppola, 14 June 1996.

p. 90 'When we made *The Rain People* . . .', author's interview with Francis Coppola, 17 November 1987.

p. 90 'We filmed in so many different places . . .', *The Godfather Family: A Look Inside*, op. cit.

p. 91 'the food was appalling . . .', author's interview with Dick Smith, *op. cit*.

p. 91 'One of my profound moments of parenthood . . .', author's interview with Eleanor Coppola, *op. cit*.

p. 91 'He had been caught in a downpour . . .', *The Godfather Companion*, op. cit.

p. 91 '[Pacino's] condition became worse . . .', Paramount inter-office memo signed Mike Glick and dated 16 May 1974, in AZRL, Napa.

p. 91 'He's the same man from beginning to end . . .', author's interview with Francis Coppola, 17 November 1987.

p. 91 'His performance is on the thin edge . . .', author's interview with Fred Roos, *op. cit*.

p. 92 'which is hard as hell . . .', letter to Francis Coppola from Elia Kazan, in AZRL, Napa.

p. 92 'I had problems with my words . . .', audio tape in AZRL, Napa.

p. 94 'cover all the windows on one side . . .', author's interview with Gordon Willis, *op. cit.*

p. 94 'We'd go down into basements . . .', author's interview with Dean Tavoularis, *op. cit.*

p. 94 'I moulded a duplicate gun . . .', author's interview with Dick Smith, *op. cit.*

p. 95 'I put a tube of blood under his throat . . .', *ibid.*

p. 95 'due to the rising cost of living . . .', memo in AZRL, Napa.

p. 95 'Due to the horrendous cost of living . . .', memo in AZRL, Napa.

p. 95 'Then the crew had to take out all the stalls . . .', *The Godfather Family: A Look Inside, op. cit.*

p. 95 'We wanted the people in those scenes . . .', author's phone interview with Gray Frederickson, *op. cit.*

p. 95 'Coppola and companions put their spare time . . .', author's interview with Lorenzo Codelli, 14 August 1996.

p. 96 'In the Sicilian sequences . . .', author's interview with Gordon Willis, *op. cit.*

p. 96 'It was raining every day . . .', transcript of interview for *The Godfather Family: A Look Inside, op. cit.*

p. 98 'At any rate, it certainly looks spectacular . . .', memo in AZRL, Napa.

p. 98 'I had complete power on *Part II* . . .', author's interview with Francis Coppola, 14 June 1996.

p. 98 'Although the responsibility for editing . . .', *In the Blink of an Eye, A Perspective in*

Film Editing by Walter Murch, Silman-James Press, Los Angeles, 1995.

p. 98 'Peter Biskind, who wrote a book on the subject . . .', *The Godfather Companion, op. cit.*

p. 98 'By the time we finished *Part II* . . .', author's interview with Gordon Willis, *op. cit.*

p. 98 'The first cut of the film was five hours long . . .', letter to Julie Gregg from Francis Coppola, dated 6 November 1974, in AZRL, Napa.

p. 98 'When we previewed *Part II* . . .', author's interview with Robert Evans, *op. cit.*

p. 99 'In its opening five days . . .', *Variety*, 18 December 1974.

p. 99 'Some kind of record in the pornography of violence . . .', quoted in *Variety*, 25 December 1974.

p. 99 'Fred Roos remembers how he, Francis and others . . .', author's interview with Fred Roos, *op. cit.*

p. 100 'The final argument in favour of *Part II* . . .', *Esquire*, March 1975.

p. 101 'When we won Best Picture I was speechless . . .', telegram in AZRL, Napa.

p. 101 'It was a more demanding story . . .', author's interview with Eleanor Coppola, *op. cit.*

p. 101 'And when the entire Havana sequence . . .', *The Godfather Companion, op. cit.*

THE FAMILY ON TELEVISION

p. 102 'Robert Howard, President of NBC-TV . . .', *Daily Variety*, 10 July 1975.

p. 102 'All I could find to show off . . .', author's interview with Francis Coppola, 18 November 1987.

p. 103 'I had begun *Apocalypse Now* and left . . .', author's phone interview with Barry

Malkin, 25 October 1996.

p. 103 'So for the omnibus . . .', *ibid.*

THE QUEST FOR *PART III*

p. 106 'I'm not at all interested in *Godfather III* . . .', author's interview with Francis Coppola, 18 November 1987.

p. 107 'Here I was the boss, and Charlie Bluhdorn took orders . . .', author's phone interview with Mario Puzo, 11 November 1996.

p. 108 'He alleged that the script written by Wright and himself . . .', *Variety*, 17 December 1990.

p. 109 'little more emphasis on the present . . .', in AZRL, Napa (as are all descriptions of treatments and outlines for *The Godfather Part III*).

p. 110 'Gathering interest over the years . . .', *Variety*, 3 January 1990.

p. 111 'because that's where the tragedy lies . . .', *ibid.*

p. 111 'In Sicily what you're always looking for . . .', in AZRL, Napa.

p. 112 'I kept telling Mario . . .', *Sunday Correspondent*, London, 7 October 1990.

p. 115 'I like *Part III* because it's almost the story . . .', author's interview with Francis Coppola, 14 June 1996.

p. 116 'It was the largest bank failure in US history . . .', *In God's Name* by David Yallop, Jonathan Cape, London, 1984.

p. 116 'unctuously intimidating man . . .', *God's Banker* by Rupert Cornwell, Victor Gollancz, London, 1983.

p. 116 'When Gelli's protective network finally collapsed . . .', *ibid.*

p. 116 'Today he remains under investigation

. . .', *Observer*, London, 13 October 1996.

p. 117 'The Vatican's declared budget deficit . . .', *God's Banker*, *op. cit.*

p. 117 'mixing promises of help . . .', *ibid.*

p. 117 'had strayed from the ideals of its founders . . .', *ibid.*

p. 117 'was the point where Sindona's Mafia legacy . . .', *ibid.*

p. 117 'The bank was de facto ruled by . . .', *The Vatican Connection* by Richard Hammer, Holt Rinehart and Winston, New York, 1982.

p. 117 'rather like a priest with his Bible,' *In God's Name*, *op. cit.*

p. 117 'who felt it would be neither fitting nor proper . . .', The *Vatican Connection*, *op. cit.*

p. 117 'Convicted, and sentenced to twenty-five years in jail . . .', In *God's Name*, *op. cit.*

p. 118 'spent much of his time immersed in the pages of Nietzsche . . .', *God's Banker*, *op. cit.*

p. 118 'this Pope has different ideas from the last one . . .', *In God's Name*, *op. cit.*

p. 118 'Davis was so completely different to Charlie Bluhdorn . . .', transcript of meeting in Reno, March 1989.

p. 118 'Francis insisted; he knew Italy . . .', author's interview with Gray Frederickson, *op. cit.*

p. 119 'A million dollar offer for this project . . .', in AZRL, Napa.

p. 121 'He's been an unused resource . . .', author's interview with Francis Coppola, 9 December 1989.

p. 121 'We are at work, and I feel pulling the elements together.' In AZRL, Napa.

p. 122 'We are going to do a full cast READING AND REHEARSAL . . .', *ibid.*

p. 122 'If there is one image that I think I have of Francis . . .', transcript of interviews for The *Godfather Family: A Look Inside*, *op. cit.*

p. 122 'If we could be allowed to have ample time . . .', letter in AZRL, Napa.

p. 122 'was fascinated to be plunged once again . . .', letter in AZRL, Napa.

SHOOTING FOR THE MOON

p. 124 'Fred Roos, the casting director, was waiting on the front porch . . .', *Projections 6, op. cit.*

p. 124 'When they finally landed . . .', *ibid.*

p. 124 'In its early script stages . . .', author's phone interview with Walter Murch, 30 October 1996.

p. 125 'The script's like a newspaper!' *The Godfather Family: A Look Inside*, *op. cit.*

p. 126 'Key technicians were instructed to read their scripts . . .', *Variety*, 3 January 1990.

p. 126 'One day this driver comes up to me . . .', author's interview with Dean Tavoularis, *op. cit.*

p. 126 'We asked Francis if it's true . . .', *Daily Variety*, 7 November 1989.

p. 127 'Our feeling on the casting . . .', memo dated 31 October 1989, in AZRL, Napa.

p. 127 'Sometimes I have been impressed with these guys in their fifties . . .', *Premiere* magazine, New York, September 1996.

p. 128 'Michael, in effect, will look toward Europe . . .', author's interview with Francis Coppola, 9 December 1989.

p. 128 'Smith complied, but . . .', author's interview with Dick Smith, *op. cit.*

p. 129 'We'd time each shot . . .', author's interview with Dean Tavoularis, *op. cit.*

p. 129 'When you are dealing on this scale of movie-making . . .', author's interview with

Francis Coppola, 9 December 1989.

p. 129 'I had the pleasure yesterday . . .', memo in AZRL, Napa.

p. 129 'This is the cathedral of the *Godfather* movies . . .', *Variety*, 3 January 1990.

p. 129 'This is the least "oft-delayed" of movies . . .', author's interview with Francis Coppola, 9 December 1989.

p. 132 'made her traditional seafood sauce . . .', *Projections 6, op. cit.*

p. 132 'We were twenty people spending the day together . . .', *ibid.*

p. 132 'Francis has decided to cast Sofia . . .', *ibid.*

p. 132 'But on reflection, Coppola plumped for Sofia . . .', author's interview with Sofia Coppola, 15 June 1996.

p. 133 'The main thing is I feel well . . .', memo dated 29 December 1989, in AZRL, Napa.

p. 135 'In the spirit of our personal and collaborative relationship . . .', memo in AZRL, Napa.

p. 136 'It may be that my requests are unusual . . .', memo in AZRL, Napa.

p. 136 '[She's] got to be Diane Keaton's daughter . . .', interview in *Rolling Stone* magazine, New York, 7 February 1991.

p. 136 'Coppola alerted his attorney . . .', *Vanity Fair*, New York, June 1990.

p. 136 'Basically, what they said [to me] . . .', *ibid.*

p. 136 'I remember he quoted Brando's line . . .', author's interview with Sofia Coppola, *op. cit.*

p. 137 'Each artist has his own way of working . . .', memo in AZRL, Napa.

p. 137 'I was in every scene of [*Mermaids*] . . .', *The Godfather Companion, op. cit.*

p. 138 'I asked Francis if I'd done anything

wrong . . .', author's interview with Gray Frederickson, *op. cit.*

p. 138 'So, I guess it's back to the drawing board . . .', memo to Anahid Nazarian in AZRL, Napa.

p. 138 'went to sleep in a cold sweat . . .', *Projections 6, op. cit.*

p. 138 'Well-meaning people tell me . . .', *ibid.*

p. 138 'Fred Roos arranged for a voice coach . . .', *Vanity Fair, op. cit.*

p. 138 'thought hard about it for about forty-five seconds . . .', *The Godfather Companion, op. cit.*

p. 138 'wise and impartial . . .', memo dated 24 January 1990, in AZRL, Napa.

p. 140 'Everyone was looking forward to having a piece of the cake . . .', *Projections 6, op. cit.*

p. 140 'He was a young guy, energetic . . .', author's interview with Dean Tavoularis, *op. cit.*

p. 141 'On the first day of shooting in Palermo . . .', *Projections 6, op. cit.*

p. 141 'There was a gigantic hole at the back of the proscenium . . .', author's interview with Dean Tavoularis, *op. cit.*

p. 143 'Many people think the film should end . . .', *Projections 6, op. cit.*

p. 143 'Just got finished looking . . .', memo dated 18 May 1990, in AZRL, Napa.

p. 144 'James Bishop, former secretary and treasurer . . .', *Guardian*, London, 14 May 1990.

p. 144 'Francis responded strongly . . .', *Projections 6, op. cit.*

p. 144 'There were structural problems . . .', author's phone interview with Walter Murch, 30 October 1996.

p. 144 'it just didn't seem practical . . .', *In the Blink of an Eye, A Perspective in Film Editing, op. cit.*

p. 145 'He felt those criticisms were meant for him . . .', *Projections 6, op. cit.*

p. 145 'Sofia was encouraged . . .', author's interview with Sofia Coppola, *op. cit.*

p. 146 'I'd kept pleading for another few months . . .', author's interview with Francis Coppola, 14 June 1996.

THE FAMILY CONNECTION

p. 151 'on rocky, hilly farms in the countryside . . .', *The Godfather Papers and Other Confessions, op. cit.*

p. 151 'We travel together like a circus family . . .', quoted in 'Some Figures on a Fantasy' by Lillian Ross in *New Yorker*, 8 November 1982.

p. 151 'In our family life, there was great passion . . .', author's interview with August Coppola, 10 December 1985.

p. 153 'vow of fealty requiring them always to obey the boss . . .', *Gotti, Rise and Fall* by Jerry Capeci and Gene Mustain, Onyx/Dutton Signet, New York, 1996.

p. 155 'According to Sicilian tradition . . .', *The Sicilian Mafia, op. cit.*

p. 156 '*The Godfather* was textured, or perfumed in a way . . .', *The Godfather Family: A Look Inside, op. cit.*

p. 157 'Much impressed by this sequence, Mafia chieftain John Gotti . . .', *Gotti, Rise and Fall, op. cit.*

THE MISUSES OF POWER

p. 172 'The thing that's good about this story . . .', transcript of discussion in Reno, March 1989, lodged in AZRL, Napa.

p. 172 'We are men of power . . .', *The Sicilian Mafia*, *op. cit.*

p. 172 'that private realm populated only by kin and close friends,' *ibid.*

p. 172 'But what a small number of these Italian newcomers . . .', *The Valachi Papers*, *op. cit.*

p. 172 'Salvatore Maranzano headed . . .', *ibid.*

p. 173 'For Luciano, it has been said . . .', *ibid.*

p. 173 'Mancuso was deported to Italy in 1947 . . .', *The Sicilian Mafia*, *op. cit.*

CHARACTERS

p. 184 'Coppola has said that the character was a synthesis . . .', interview in *Playboy* magazine, 1975.

p. 184 'You know, we take a barrel of apples . . .', *The Valachi Papers*, *op. cit.*

p. 185 'He would care for his children . . .', *The Godfather*, *op. cit.*

p. 186 'has a kind of disdain for gangsterism . . .', *The Godfather Family: A Look Inside*, *op. cit.*

p. 187 'No doubt there's sort of a thug in . . .', *ibid.*

p. 188 'a descent, trying to hold on to everything . . .', *The Godfather Family: A Look Inside*, *op. cit.*

p. 188 'After winning all the battles . . .', *Francis Ford Coppola*, *op. cit.*

p. 189 'because of his devotion to his father . . .', *The Godfather*, *op. cit.*

p. 190 'A child every Italian prayed to the saints for . . .' *ibid.*

p. 190 'Everyone knew that the Don had given up on this middle son . . .', *ibid.*

p. 191 '"That was me!" said Coppola . . .', interview in *Rolling Stone*, *op. cit.*

p. 196 'She was too thin, she was too fair . . .', *The Godfather*, *op. cit.*

p. 197 'In a small village square . . .', *The Godfather Companion*, *op. cit.*

RELIGION AND REDEMPTION

p. 206 'In the original draft screenplay . . .', draft screenplay in AZRL, Napa.

p. 207 'There's a point when you get a virtuous man . . .', *The Godfather Family: A Look Inside*, *op. cit.*

THE CLASSICAL STYLE

p. 209 'Many crime movies since have splattered the screens . . .', *The Times*, London, 4 July 1996.

p. 212 'It's something in the direction . . .', interview in *Positif*, Paris, #161.

p. 214 'an image which millions of law-abiding Americans . . .', *The Valachi Papers*, *op. cit.*

p. 215 'Valachi's evidence also indicated . . .', *ibid.*

p. 215 'During the late nineteenth century . . .', *Gotti, Rise and Fall*, *op. cit.*

p. 215 'Five hundred guests relaxed to the strains of the music . . .', The *Sicilian Mafia*, *op. cit.*

p. 215 'His men donned doctors' uniforms . . .', *ibid.*

p. 215 'I really loved *The Godfather* . . .', *ibid.*

p. 215 'One of John Gotti's fellow *mafiosi* . . .', *Gotti, Rise and Fall*, *op. cit.*

p. 215 'The subject under prolonged discussion . . .', *The Sicilian Mafia*, *op. cit.*

p. 215 'In Japan, the *yakuza* expressed serious admiration . . .', *Independent*, London, 3 February 1990.

p. 216 'When you bring the Società Immobiliare and cinema together . . .', *Variety*, 7 July 1971.

p. 216 'Mario Puzo remains proud of the fact . . .', author's phone interview with Mario Puzo, 1 July 1996.

p. 217 'To some extent I have become Michael . . .', interview in *Positif*, Paris, #161.

p. 217 'You're still producer of the picture . . .', author's interview with Gray Frederickson, *op. cit.*

p. 217 'Of all that generation of new talent . . .', author's interview with Robert Evans, *op. cit.*

p. 221 'Even today I can't pay a check in Little Italy . . .', *Songs My Mother Taught Me, op. cit.*

p. 221 'Why do I go on working?' author's phone interview with Al Ruddy, 12 July 1996.

p. 222 'Seduction has nothing to do with sex . . .', author's interview with Robert Evans, *op. cit.*

p. 222 'We're the billion-dollar boys!' author's interview with Eleanor Coppola, *op. cit.*

p. 222 'If Francis Coppola never made another film . . .', *American Film Now* by James Monaco, New American Library, New York, 1979.

p. 222 'did ruin me . . .' 'Godfatherhood' by Michael Sragow, *New Yorker*, New York, 24 March 1997.

Credits

The Godfather

Screenplay: Mario Puzo and Francis Ford Coppola, from the novel by Mario Puzo. *Director*: Francis Ford Coppola. *Photography* (Technicolor): Gordon Willis. *Editing*: William Reynolds, Peter Zinner. *Production Designer*: Dean Tavoularis. *Art Director*: Warren Clymer. *Set Decorator*: Philip Smith. *Music*: Nino Rota, conducted by Carlo Savina. *Additional Music*: Mall Wedding Sequence, Carmine Coppola. *Songs*: 'I Have But One Heart', Johnny Farrow, Marty Symes; 'Luna mezz'o mare', Paolo Citarella; 'Manhattan Serenade', Louis Alter; 'Have Yourself a Merry Little Christmas', Hugh Martin, Ralph Blane; 'Santa Claus is Coming to Town', Haven Gillespie, J. Fred Coots; 'The Bells of St Mary's', A. E. Adams, Douglas Furber; 'All of My Life', Irving Berlin; 'Mona Lisa', Jay Livingston, Ray Evans; baptism sequence: J. S. Bach. *Costumes*: Anna Hill Johnstone. *Sound Recording*: Christopher Newman. *Casting*: Fred Roos, Andrea Eastman, Louis Digiaimo. *Post-production Consultant*: Walter Murch. *Make-up*: Dick Smith, Philip Rhodes. *Hair Stylist*: Phil Leto. *Wardrobe Supervisor*: George Newman. *Women's Wardrobe*: Marilyn Putnam. *Camera Operator*: Michael Chapman. *Script Continuity*: Nancy Tonery. *Production Recording*: Christopher Newman. *Re-recording*: Bud Grenzbach, Richard Portman. *Assistant to Producer*: Gary Chazan. *Executive Assistant*: Robert S. Mendelsohn. *Location Co-ordinators*: Michael Briggs, Tony Bowers. *Foreign Post-production*: Peter Zinner. *Unit Production Manager*: Fred Caruso. *Assistant Director*: Fred Gallo. *Unit Co-ordinator*: Robert Barth. *Special Effects*: A. D. Flowers, Joe Lombardi, Sass Bedig. *Location Service*: Cinemobile Systems Inc. SICILIAN UNIT – *Production manager*: Valerio de Paolis. *Assistant Director*: Tony Brandt. *Assistant Art Director*: Samuel Verts. *Associate Producer*: Gray Frederickson. *Producer*: Albert S. Ruddy. *Production Company*: Alfran Productions for Paramount Pictures. Released March 1972. 175 mins.

Cast: Marlon Brando (Don Vito Corleone), Al Pacino (Michael Corleone), James Caan (Sonny Corleone), Richard Castellano (Clemenza), Robert Duvall (Tom Hagen), Sterling Hayden (Capt. McCluskey), John Marley (Jack Woltz), Richard Conte (Barzini), Al Lettieri (Sollozzo), Diane Keaton (Kay Adams), Abe Vigoda (Tessio), Talia Shire (Connie), Gianni Russo (Carlo Rizzi), John Cazale (Fredo Corleone), Rudy Bond (Cuneo), Al Martino (Johnny Fontane), Morgana King (Mama Corleone), Lenny Montana (Luca Brasi), John Martino (Paulie Gatto), Salvatore Corsitto (Bonasera), Richard Bright (Neri), Alex Rocco (Moe Greene), Tony Giorgio (Bruno Tattaglia), Vito Scotti (Nazorine), Tere Livrano (Theresa Hagen), Victor Rendina (Philip Tattaglia), Jeannie Linero (Lucy Mancini), Julie Gregg (Sandra Corleone), Ardell Sheridan (Mrs Clemenza), Simonetta Stefanelli (Apollonia), Angelo Infanti (Fabrizio), Corrado Gaipa (Don Tommasino), Franco Citti (Calo), Saro Urzì (Vitellì), Anthony Gounaris (Anthony as a child).

The Godfather Part II

Screenplay: Francis Ford Coppola and Mario Puzo, based in part on the novel by Puzo. *Director*: Francis Ford Coppola. *Director of Photography*: Gordon Willis (Technicolor). *Editors*: Peter Zinner, Barry Malkin, Richard Marks. *Production Designer*: Dean Tavoularis. *Art Director*: Angelo Graham. *Set Decorator*: George R. Nelson. *Make-up*: Dick Smith, Charles Schram. *Hair Stylist*: Naomi Cavin. *Research*: Deborah Fine. *Music*: Nino Rota, conducted by Carmine Coppola. *Additional Music*: Carmine Coppola. *Songs*: 'Senza Mamma', Francesco Pennino; 'Napule ve salute', Francesco Pennino; 'Mr. Wonderful', Jerry Bock, Larry Holofcener, George Weiss; 'Heart and Soul', Frank Loesser and Hoagy Carmichael. *Music Editor*: George Brand. *Script Supervisors*: John Franco, B. J. Bachman. *Costumes*: Theadora van Runkle. *Sound Montage and Re-recording*: Walter Murch. *Casting*: Michael Fenton Jane Feinberg, Vic Ramos. *Production Manager*: Michael S. Glick.

First Assistant Director: Newton Arnold. *Second Assistant Directors*: Henry J. Lange, Jr, Chuck Myers, Mike Kusley, Alan Hopkins, Burt Bluestein. *New York Location Supervisor*: Ron Colby. *Production Secretary*: Nanette Siegert. *Location Auditor*: Carl Skelton. *Location Coordinator*: Jack English. *Unit Publicist*: Eileen Peterson. *Title Design*: Wayne Fitzgerald. *Assistant Editors*: George Bernot, Bobbe Kurtz, Lisa Fruchtman. *Sound Effects Editors*: Howard Beals, Jim Fritch, Jim Klinger. *Sound Montage Associates*: Pat Jackson, Mark Berger. *Special Effects*: A. D. Flowers, Joe Lombardi. *Location Assistants*: Randy Carter, Mona Houghton, Melissa Mathison. *Subtitling*: Sonya Friedman. *Sicilian Translation*: Romano Pianti. *Foreign Post-production*: Peter Zinner. *Camera Operator*: Ralph Gerling. *Camera Assistant*: Bill Gereghty. *Key Grip*: Bob Rose. *Gaffer*: George Holmes. *Production Recording*: Chuck Wilborn, Nathan Boxer. *Script Supervisors*: John Franco, B. J. Bachman. *Props*: V. Bud Shelton, Doug Madison. SICILIAN UNIT – *Production Supervisor*: Valerio De Paolis. *Unit Manager*: Mario Cotone. *Assistant Director*: Tony Brandt. *Assistant Set Decorator*: Joe Chevalier. *Casting*: Emy DeSica, Maurizio Lucci. *Script Supervisor*: Serea Canevari. *Production Assistant*: Bruno Perria. *Miami Coordinator*: Tammy Newell. *Senate Hearings Adviser*: Ed Guthman. *Associate Producer*: Mona Skager. *Co-producers*: Gray Frederickson, Fred Roos. *Producer*: Francis Ford Coppola. *Production Company*: The Coppola Company for Paramount Pictures. Released December 1974. 200 mins (190 on video).

Cast: Al Pacino (Michael Corleone), Robert Duvall (Tom Hagen), Diane Keaton (Kay Adams), Robert De Niro (Vito Corleone), John Cazale (Fredo Corleone), Talia Shire (Connie Corleone), Lee Strasberg (Hyman Roth), Michael V. Gazzo (Frankie Pentangeli), G. D. Spradlin (Senator Pat Geary), Richard Bright (Al Neri), Gaston Moschin (Fanucci), Tom Rosqui (Rocco Lampone), B. Kirby Jr (Young Clemenza), Frank Sivero (Genco), Francesca De Sapio (Young Mama

Corleone), Morgana King (Mama Corleone), Mariana Hill (Deanna Corleone), Leopoldo Trieste (Signor Roberto), Dominic Chianese (Johnny Ola), Amerigo Tot (Michael's bodyguard), Troy Donahue (Merle Johnson), John Aprea (Young Tessio), Joe Spinell (Willi Cicci), Abe Vigoda (Tessio), Tere Livrano (Theresa Hagen), Gianni Russo (Carlo), Maria Carta (Vito's Mother), Oreste Baldini (Vito Andolini as a boy), Giuseppe Sillato (Don Ciccio), Mario Cotone (Don Tommasino), James Gounaris (Anthony Corleone), Fay Spain (Mrs Marcia Roth), Harry Dean Stanton (FBI Man #1), David Baker (FBI Man #2), Carmine Caridi (Carmine Rosato), Danny Aiello (Tony Rosato), Carmine Foresta (Policeman), Nick Discenza (Bartender), Father Joseph Medeglia (Father Carmeto), William Bowers (Senate Committee Chairman), Joe Della Sorte (Michael's Buttonman #1), Carmen Argenziano (Buttonman #2), Joe Lo Grippo (Buttonman #3), Ezio Flagello (Impresario), Livio Giorgi (Tenor in 'Senza Mamma'), Kathy Beller (Girl in 'Senza Mamma'), Saveria Mazzola (Signora Colombo), Tito Alba (Cuban President), Johnny Naranjo (Cuban Translator), Elda Maida (Pentangeli's wife), Salvatore Po (Pentangeli's brother), Ignazio Pappalardo (Mosca), Andrea Maugeri (Strollo), Peter Lacorte (Signor Abbandando), Vincent Coppola (Street Vendor), Peter Donat (Questadi), Tom Dahlgren (Fred Corngold), Paul B. Brown (Senator Ream), Phil Feldman (Senator #1), Roger Corman (Senator #2), Yvonne Coll (Yolanda), J. D. Nicols (Attendant at Brothel), Edward Van Sickle (Ellis Island Doctor), Gabria Belloni (Ellis Island Nurse), Richard Watson (Customs Official), Venancia Grangerard (Cuban Nurse), Erica Yohn (Governess), Theresa Tirelli (Midwife), James Caan (Sonny Corleone).

The Godfather Part III

Screenplay: Mario Puzo and Francis Ford Coppola. *Director*: Francis Ford Coppola. *Director of Photography*: Gordon Willis (Technicolor). *Editors*: Barry Malkin, Lisa Fruchtman, Walter Murch. *Production Designer*: Dean Tavoularis. *Supervising Art Director*: Alex Tavoularis. *Set Decorator*: Gary Fettis. *Make-up*: Fabrizio Sforza. *Hair Stylist*: Giuseppina Bovino, Grazia De Rossi. *Research*: Anahid Nazarian. *Music*: Carmine Coppola, conducted by Carmine Coppola. *Additional Music and Themes*: Nino Rota. *Music Editor*: Mark Adler. *Songs*: 'To Each His Own', Jay Livingston, Ray Evans; 'Vitti 'Na Crozza', Francesco Li Causi; 'Eh Cumpari', Julius La Rosa, Archie Bleyer; 'Beyond the Blue Horizon', Leo Robin, Richard Whiting, W. Franke Harling; 'Lover', Lorenz Hart, Richard Rodgers; 'Senza Perdono', Francesco Pennino; 'Miracle Man', Elvis Costello; 'Dimmi, Dimmi, Dimmi', Carmine Coppola, arranged by Celso Valli; 'Gregorian Chant'; 'Brucia La Terra', Nino Rota; 'Santa Rosalia', from 'La Baronessa Di Carini'; 'Promise Me You'll Remember', Carmine Coppola, lyric by John Bettis; excerpts from *Cavalleria Rusticana*, Pietro Mascagni, lyrics by G. Targioni-Tozzetti and G. Menasci. *Script Supervisor*: Wilma Garscadden-Gahret. *Costumes*: Milena Canonero. *Sound Designer*: Richard Beggs. *Casting*: Janet Hirshenson, Jane Jenkins, Roger Mussenden. *Production Manager*: Bruce Pustin. *First Assistant Director*: H. Gordon Boos. *Second Assistant Director*: K. C. Hodenfield. *Second Second Assistant Director*: Michael DeCasper. *Extras' Casting*: Navarro/Bertoni. *Still Photographer*: John Seakwood. *Additional Film Editing*: Louise Rubacky, Glen Scantlebury. *Stunt Coordinator*: Buddy Joe Hooker. *Assistant to Francis Coppola*: Loolee DeLeon. *Music Supervisor*: Stephan R. Goldman. *Casting in Italy*: Aleta Chappelle. *Opera Adviser*: Anton Coppola. *Camera Operator*: Craig Dibona. *Chief Lighting Technician*: James Fitzpatrick. *First Company Grip*: George Patsos. *Sound Mixer*: Clive Winter. *Boom Operator*: Allan Brereton. *Additional Make-up Artist*: Antonio Maltempo. *Make-up Artist for Ms Keaton*: Tom Lucas. *Hairstylists*: Giuseppina Bovino, Grazia De Rossio. *Assistant Costume Designers*: Richard Shissler, Elisabetta Beraloo.

Production Illustrator: Mauro Borelli. *Properties*: Douglas Madison. *Special Effects Coordinator*: Lawrence James Cavanaugh. *Special Effects Supervisor*: R. Bruce Steinheimer. *Assistant Art Director*: Franckie Diago. *Wardrobe Supervisor*: William R. Campbell. *Supervising Sound Editor*: Gloria S. Borders. *Dialogue Editors*: Stacey Foiles, Ronald Jacobs, Paige Sartorius, Teresa Eckton, Barbara McBane. *Music Editor*: Mark Adler. *Title Design*: Wayne Fitzgerald. *Additional Visual Effects*: Industrial Light & Magic. ITALIAN UNIT – *Unit Manager*: Lynn Kamern. *First Assistant Director*: Gianni Arouini-Plaisant. *Production Manager*: Franco Ballati. *Production Coordinator*: Daniela Vecchi. *Set Decorator*: Franco Fumagalli. *Storyboard Artist*: Paolo Morales. NEW YORK UNIT – *Unit Production Manager*: Bruce S. Pustin. *Second Assistant Director*: Michael De Casper. *Production Coordinator*: Jane Raab. *Location Manager*: Barbara Heller. *Special Effects*: Ronald Ottesen, Bob Wilson. *Production Supervisor*: Alessandro von Normann. *Associate Producer*: Marina Gefter. *Executive Producers*: Fred Fuchs, Nicholas Gage. *Co-producers*: Fred Roos, Gray Frederickson, Charles Mulvehill. *Producer*: Francis Ford Coppola. *Production Company*: Paramount Pictures. 'Dedicated to Charlie Bluhdorn, who inspired it.' Released December 1990. 161 mins.

Cast: Al Pacino (Michael Corleone), Diane Keaton (Kay Adams), Andy Garcia (Vincent Mancini), Talia Shire (Connie Corleone Rizzi), Sofia Coppola (Mary Corleone), Joe Mantegna (Joey Zasa), Franc d'Ambrosio (Anthony Corleone), Eli Wallach (Altobello), Donal Donnelly (Archbishop Gilday), Bridget Fonda (Grace Hamilton), John Savage (Andrew Hagen), Richard Bright (Al Neri), Al Martino (Johnny Fontane), George Hamilton (B. J. Harrison), Raf Vallone (Cardinal Lamberto), Mario Donatone (Mosca), Franco Citti (Calo), Vittorio Duse (Don Tommasino), Rogerio and Carlos Miranda (Armand and Francesco, twin bodyguards), Enzo Robutti (Lucchesi), Jeannie Linero (Lucy Mancini), Helmut Berger (Keinszig), Tere Baker (Theresa Hagen), Robert Cicchini (Lou Pennino), Janet Savarino Smith (Kathryn Corleone), Carmine Caridi (Albert Volpi), Don Castello (Frank Romano), Al Ruscio (Leo Cuneo), Vito Antuofermo ('The Ant'), Rick Aviles (Masked Man #1), Michael Bowen (Masked Man #2), Mickey Knox (Matty Parisi), Julie Gregg (Sandra), Don Novello (Dom), Brian Freilino, Gregory Corso (Stockholders), Robert Vento (Father John), Michele Russo (Spera), Willie Brown (Party Politician), Remo Remotti (Cardinal in the Sistine), Jeanne Savarino Pesch (Francesca Corleone), Douglas Michelson (Brett Halsey), Gabriele Torrei (Enzo the Baker), John Abineri (Hamilton banker), Marino Mase (Lupo), Dado Ruspoli (Vanni), Valeria Sabel (Sister Vincenza), Luigi Laezza, Beppe Pianviti (Keinszig's killers), Santo Indelicato (Bodyguard), Simonetta Stefanelli (Apollonia, in closing sequence), Paco Reconti (Gesu), Mimmo Cuticchio (Puppet Narrator), Richard Honigman (Party Reporter), Nicky Blair (Nicky the casino host), Anthony Guidera (Anthony the bodyguard), Frank Taasia (Frankie the bodyguard), Diane Agostini (Woman with child at street fair), Jessica Di Cicco (Child), Catherine Scorsese, Ida Bernardini (Women at café), Joseph Drago (Party security), David Hume Kennerly (Party photographer), James D. Damiano (Son playing soccer), Michael Boccio (Father of soccer player), Pat Romano, Steve Davison, Chad Randall (stunt performers).

Acknowledgements

My primary research for this book was accomplished in the rustic tranquillity of the American Zoetrope Research Library in Rutherford, California. Here Anahid Nazarian, like some keeper of the flame, presides over the archives of all three *Godfather* films – memoranda, script revisions, and thousands of documents covering the most minute of disbursements as well as the most intimate of e-mails. I cannot thank Anahid enough for her kindness and patience in making available these resources.

Paramount Pictures (William Bernstein, Jeffrey Baskin, Paula Block, Melissa Duke) also extended me every courtesy, including access to the studio's impressive collection of stills taken during the making of the trilogy. At the American Zoetrope office in San Francisco, the enthusiasm and effective diplomacy of Julie Costanzo and Finley Glaize helped me achieve my goals throughout the year of the book's gestation.

Many individuals took valuable time to speak with me about their memories of the *Godfather* films. Some talked for hours, some for a few minutes. The following list is in alphabetical order: Carroll Ballard, Peter Bart, Lorenzo Codelli, Eleanor Coppola, Francis Coppola, Sofia Coppola, Robert Evans, Gray Frederickson, Susan Ingleby, Tom Luddy, Barry Malkin, Walter Murch, Hiroshi Narita, Mario Puzo, Bill Reynolds, Fred Roos, Al Ruddy, Ian Scorer, Dick Smith, Dean Tavoularis, Gordon Willis and Peter Zinner.

I acknowledge the specialist advice of both my old friends, Bob Hawkins and Allen Eyles, and at Faber and Faber the ever-calm Walter Donohue could not have been a more comforting and encouraging editor. As always my gratitude extends to Laura Morris, my friend and agent at Abner Stein.

Index

Figures in italics refer to captions.
G., *G.II* and *G.III* refer to *The Godfather*, *The Godfather Part II* and *The Godfather Part III* respectively; 'C' indicates Francis Ford Coppola.